GERA

DATE DUE

GERARD MANLEY HOPKINS

Selected Prose

EDITED BY GERALD ROBERTS

Oxford New York Toronto Melbourne

OXFORD UNIVERSITY PRESS

1980

Oxford University Press, Walton Street, Oxford OX2 6DP

London Glasgow New York Toronto
Delhi Bombay Calcutta Madras Karachi
Kuala Lumpur Singapore Hong Kong Tokyo
Nairobi Dar es Salaam Cape Town
Melbourne Wellington

and associate companies in
Beirut Berlin Ibadan Mexico City

This selection is compiled from a series of five volumes comprising the collected correspondence and writings of Gerard Manley Hopkins, published by the Oxford University Press 1935–59

The letter to Everard Hopkins of which an extract appears on pp. 136–8 of this volume was first published in the Hopkins Research Bulletin No. 4 (1973), pp. 7–13, and is reprinted here by permission of Humanities Research Center, The University of Texas at Austin, as owners of the original manuscript, and the Society of Jesus as owners of the copyright

Published by leave of and with the approval of the Trustees for Roman Catholic Purposes Registered

British Library Cataloguing in Publication Data
Hopkins, Gerard Manley
Selected prose.
I. Roberts, Gerald
828'.8'08   PR4803.H44   80–40067
ISBN 0–19–254173–0
ISBN 0–19–281272–6 Pbk

Printed in Great Britain by
Cox & Wyman Limited,
Reading, Berks

CONTENTS

Contents

Contents

1884–1889

Contents

ABBREVIATIONS

Journal	*The Journals and Papers of Gerard Manley Hopkins*, ed. Humphrey House and Graham Storey, OUP, 1966.
LB	*The Letters of Gerard Manley Hopkins to Robert Bridges*, ed. C. C. Abbott, OUP, 1970.
LD	*The Correspondence of Gerard Manley Hopkins and Richard Watson Dixon*, ed. C. C. Abbott, OUP, 1970.
FL	*Further Letters of Gerard Manley Hopkins, including his Correspondence with Coventry Patmore*, ed. C. C. Abbott, 2nd edn., OUP, 1970.
Sermons	*The Sermons and Devotional Writings of Gerard Manley Hopkins*, ed. C. Devlin, OUP, 1959.
Poems	*The Poems of Gerard Manley Hopkins*, ed. W. H. Gardner and N. H. MacKenzie, 4th edn., OUP, 1970.
NED	*A New English Dictionary on Historical Principles*, ed. James Murray *et al.*, 14 vols., Clarendon Press, 1888–1928.

INTRODUCTION

GERARD MANLEY HOPKINS was born on 28 July 1844 at Stratford in Essex. His father, Manley Hopkins, worked in the insurance profession as an average adjuster, and established his own firm shortly after his son's birth. He had been married for almost a year to Kate Hopkins, the daughter of a London doctor, when Gerard, their first son, was born. The family was finally to reach a total of eight children, three daughters and five sons.

The material circumstances of the Hopkinses always seem to have been comfortable and family life was sociable and cultured. Manley Hopkins wrote a number of books, including some volumes of highly conventional poetry, which had no obvious influence on his son's later work. Kate was musical and well read, and probably played the larger part in moulding Gerard's character. Both parents were devout Anglicans, and Manley described his wife's faith as being 'woven in with her very being'.[1] Two of their children became religious: Gerard, and one of his sisters, Millicent, who became a nun in the High Anglican community at Margaret Street in London. Their shocked reaction at Gerard's conversion, however, and his uncharitable comments on his sister's vocation, suggests that it was a moderate Anglicanism, not Tractarianism, that they favoured.

This stimulating and artistic family background produced not only a great poet (and talented artist) in Gerard, but also a successful artist and a distinguished Chinese scholar in two of his brothers. The eldest son was perhaps making an indirect comment on the happiness of his own family life when he remarked, after sixteen years as a Jesuit: 'Every one should marry . . . a single life is a difficult, not altogether a natural life.'[2]

In 1852 they moved from Stratford to Hampstead which became the family home for the next thirty years. Gerard was a boarder from 1854 to 1863 at Highgate School, a small public school of Elizabethan foundation which was steadily growing in reputation

1. *FL*, p. 435. For more about Mrs Hopkins and some other important figures in her son's correspondence, see the Biographical Appendix.
2. *LB*, pp. 193–4 and this selection, p. 129.

under an energetic but authoritarian headmaster, the Reverend John Dyne. The strong will of master and pupil clashed on more than one occasion and Hopkins wrote later, 'The truth is I had no love for my schooldays';[3] nevertheless he won school prizes for poetry and for work, and in 1862 a closed exhibition in classics to Balliol College, Oxford. It was at Highgate that he and Richard Dixon, Anglican priest and poet, first came across one another; the memory of this seventeen years later led to the opening of a rich and revealing correspondence between the two men.

When he went up to Oxford in April 1863, he found everything 'delightful',[4] responding immediately to its social and cultural attractions. His tutors Jowett and Pater were men of redoubtable intellect and little more than formal religion, while in complete and stimulating contrast many of his friends were profoundly influenced by Tractarianism, some wavering on the brink of Catholicism, 'ready to go at a touch'.[5] His decision in July 1866 to become a Catholic was made after months of anxious thought, and whatever indirect part his friends had in his conversion, it must essentially be seen as a personal and deliberate step.

Having made the all-important decision, he turned for further advice to John Henry Newman, England's most famous convert, now living in semi-retirement in Birmingham as Headmaster of his own school, the Oratory. He received Hopkins into the Church on 21 October, but recommended him not to come to any rash decision about a vocation and to make it his first duty to achieve a good examination result (he had already gained a first in Mods in December 1864). His parents were shocked and pained at the news of his reception, which they had tried to prevent until the last minute. For a time it seemed as if their relationship with their son was to be permanently affected as they implored him to change his mind: 'Every new letter I get', he wrote to his mother, 'breaks me down afresh, and this could not go on.'[6] But the natural strength of the family affections held under the strain; Gerard's conversion was accepted, and his relationship with his parents and the rest of the family remained close for the rest of his life, despite his various postings to different parts of the country.

But in many ways, of course, things could never be the same again, and by becoming a Catholic Gerard had initiated a funda-

3. *LD*, p. 12.   4. p. 15.   5. pp. 28–9.   6. p. 33.

mental change in his life which would be finally sealed when he joined the Jesuits. *The Times* described the period as one when 'We seemed . . . to have reached a vantage ground where the old antagonisms between Roman Catholic and Protestant were to be finally laid aside',[7] but there were still many areas of English life where Catholics were at a disadvantage. Manley Hopkins was anxious to stop his son 'throwing' his life 'away in the cold limbo which Rome assigns to her English converts';[8] in fact Gerard's thoughts were on the priesthood even during the period of conversion, and at Easter 1867 he went into retreat at Belmont Abbey in Herefordshire to consider his suitability for the Benedictine life.

Still undecided in the summer (when he took a First in Greats), he accepted Newman's invitation to teach at the Oratory until he had made up his mind. He also hoped, as he told his friend Alexander Baillie, that he would have time 'to read almost every thing that has ever been written',[9] but as it turned out, life at the Oratory was far too busy, and although he enjoyed the pupils he was happy to leave. In April 1868 another retreat, this time with the Jesuits at Manresa House, Roehampton, convinced him where his vocation lay, and the following month he was accepted as a novice to start in September. Despite a steady increase in numbers during the nineteenth century, the English Province of the Society of Jesus was still regarded with suspicion by many Englishmen and was the occasional object of attack in sections of the press. Typical of this attitude were the remarks made after Hopkins's death by someone who had known him at Highgate:

Humanly speaking he made a grievous mistake in joining the Jesuits for on further acquaintance his whole soul must have revolted against a system which has killed many and many a noble soul . . . To get on with the Jesuits you must become on many grave points a machine, without will, without conscience, and that to his nature was an impossibility.[10]

Hopkins himself remarked of his acceptance by the Society: 'I do not think there is another prospect so bright in the world',[11] and whatever his misgivings about his success as a priest, he remained unwaveringly loyal for the rest of his life.

In May too he took the decision to destroy his poetry because it

7. Quoted in E. R. Norman, *Anti-Catholicism in Victorian England*, p. 95.
8. *FL*, p. 435.   9. Ibid. 228.   10. Ibid. 396.   11. Ibid. 49.

would 'interfere with my state and vocation', [12] and wrote nothing
for the next seven years. He had come to look upon poetry as a mis-
use of time and a channel for the indulgence of the senses incompat-
ible with the priesthood (although no rule in the Constitutions of
the Society of Jesus warns against the writing of verse). Later he
modified this extreme view of his religious duties, although he
never fully convinced himself that poetry was a fit occupation for a
priest.

Before entering the Society in September, he took his last holiday
as a layman with his friend Edward Bond, and most of July was
spent in Switzerland. As an admirer of Ruskin, who had celebrated
the mountains so enthusiastically, Hopkins was naturally attracted
by the Alps, and it was also his last opportunity to visit a country
whose laws forbade the entry of Jesuits. This holiday is immortal-
ized in the pages of the Journal in some of the richest and most
personal prose in the language. There is nothing elegiac in the tone
of his last writing as a layman; rather, it confirms his own claim that
since his decision to join the Society, 'I have enjoyed the first com-
plete peace of mind I have ever had.' [13]

His new life began on 7 September 1868 when he joined six other
novices at Manresa House at the beginning of eight years of training
for the priesthood. Within a fortnight he was immersed in the most
intense of Jesuit experiences, the thirty-day retreat based on the
Spiritual Exercises of the order's founder, and over the next two
years the work of spiritual formation was continued through the
means of the liturgy, prayer, spiritual reading, and talks by the
novice-master. Obedience, as described in the Jesuit Constitutions,
was a fundamental principle:

[We must convince ourselves] that all orders are good ... denying with
what is called 'blind obedience' every opinion and judgment we may have
which runs counter to them ... It should be as if [we] were a dead body
which lets itself be carried to any place and handled in any way ... [14]

The daily timetable was strict, with novices rising at 5.30 and in bed
by 10. Their studies were varied by manual work in the house or
garden, walks on Wimbledon Common, and weekly catechizing
of local Catholic children. Even the lavatories fell under their care –

12. *LB*, p. 24.   13. p. 37.   14. See Rules 31–6.

as Hopkins observed in a later sermon: 'A man with a dung-fork in his hand ... gives [God] glory.'[15]

In September 1870 he went to St. Mary's Hall, Stonyhurst, in north-east Lancashire, for the next stage of his training, called Philosophy. Although next door to the famous Jesuit public school, the seminary was a virtually independent community consisting of about forty Jesuit staff and scholastics. Studies included logic, mathematics, psychology and ethics. He discovered for himself the philosophy of Duns Scotus with its encouraging confirmation of his own joy in the individuality of things, and enjoyed long walks in the beautiful scenery of Ribblesdale, but complaints of weariness are among the first signs of what was later to become a regular cry: 'Life here though it is hard is God's will for me.'[16] At the end of December 1872 he had to have an operation for piles, and stayed for some weeks with his parents at Hampstead.

Instead of being sent straight on to Theology, the last period of training, he was given the comparative rest of teaching Classics and English to the young novices at Roehampton. He told Bridges afterwards that he taught 'so badly and so painfully',[17] a characteristic piece of self-criticism (although he never had the reputation in the Society of being a good teacher), but it was a year which allowed him much variety of recreation. Roehampton, in its semi-rural surroundings yet near the city that he loved as much as Dr Johnson, was an ideal location. In the Journal he beautifully records the changing of the seasons and describes visits to galleries and museums, Parliament and Law Courts. He renewed his friendship with Bridges which had lapsed two years before when Hopkins had rashly proclaimed: 'Horrible to say, in a manner I am a Communist.'[18] The reality, which was his disapproval of social conditions created by the industrial society, was not quite so radical.

He went to St. Beuno's College, near St. Asaph, at the end of August 1874 to begin his three years of Theology, 'lectures in dogmatic theology, moral ditto, canon law, church history, scripture, Hebrew and what not.'[19] Out of class there were debates, spelling-bees, learning Welsh, and more long walks in the beautiful Vale of Clwyd. He gave up learning the language as a serious study, on the rector's advice, as it was not 'purely for the sake of labouring

15. p. 108.   16. p. 50.   17. *LB*, p. 30.   18. p. 55.   19. p. 60.

among the Welsh',[20] but the same rector, Fr Jones, must take credit
for encouraging the composition of one of the great poems of
modern literature. *The Wreck of the Deutschland*, inspired by the
drowning of five German nuns in December 1875, was the symbol
of a revolutionary change in its author's feelings about his vocation
as a poet. For the moment at least he was prepared to accept that
man, who in St. Ignatius's words, 'was created to praise, do rever-
ence to and serve God our Lord',[21] could do so as well through
poetry as in the priesthood, and that the two vocations were not,
after all, mutually exclusive.

The *Month* refused the poem with its strange scansion marks and
written in a style that would have disconcerted most Victorian
editors, let alone a Jesuit one. The response of Hopkins's friends,
Bridges and Patmore, was similarly negative, and even Canon
Dixon implied that the *Loss of the Eurydice* would be more interest-
ing to contemporary readers. In face of this disappointment, the
poet maintained: 'I do not write for the public.'[22] It was a stoicism
which at times expressed itself as an almost morbid fear of offending
his superiors by allowing his name to appear in print. Paradoxic-
ally, in writing to Dixon, he laid great stress on the importance of
public recognition:

... I knew what I should feel myself in your position—if I had written
and published works the extreme beauty of which the author himself the
most keenly feels and they had fallen out of sight at once and been ...
almost wholly unknown ... [Want of fame] may do [men] harm ... For
disappointment and humiliation embitter the heart and make an aching in
the very bones ...[23]

Hopkins *knew* the feeling, but scrupulously refused it moral
approval, an instance of that divided self which haunted him
throughout his life.

Eight years training came to an end with his ordination in
September 1877, and it was now the Provincial's responsibility to
decide how his talents could best serve the Society. That he found
this difficult to do is evident from the bewildering number of
appointments that Hopkins held over the next seven years in
parishes and schools all over the country. He went first to Mount

20. *Journal*, p. 258.   21. *Spiritual Exercises*, ed. Rickaby, p. 18.
22. p. 66.   23. See the letter for 13 June 1878, pp. 70–1.

St. Mary's, the boarding school near Sheffield, where he was given a 'mess of employments'[24] and his 'muse turned utterly sullen in the Sheffield smoke-ridden air'.[25] After six months he was sent in April 1878 to teach at Stonyhurst for the summer term. In August he was preacher at Farm Street Church in Mayfair, and by November he was working in the parish of St. Aloysius in Oxford. His happiness and success at Oxford as a student were not repeated as a priest: he did not feel at ease with the parishioners, nor with Fr Parkinson, his superior, the type of English convert gentleman, and the change in his own circumstances since his Balliol days created an awkwardness with former acquaintances.

In October he was moved again, this time to the very different surroundings of Bedford Leigh, an industrial parish near Manchester. Surprisingly, despite the 'mills' and 'coalpits' and the air 'charged with smoke as well as damp',[26] he was delighted by the 'charming and cheering happiness'[27] of his parishioners who were treated to some of his most direct and appealing sermons. But the posting was unfortunately only temporary, and from the end of December 1879 until August 1881 he worked in the parish of St. Francis Xavier's in the centre of Liverpool. For the most part it was a depressing experience: the appalling conditions, both material and moral, that he came across in the slums, were proof to him of the irreparable harm to English life caused by the big cities – London was perhaps an emotional exception – and his own lack of success as special preacher deepened a growing sense of personal failure. He had to spend three months in yet another slum parish in Glasgow before, in October, he was able to return to his beloved Roehampton for the welcome relief of the Tertianship. This obligatory year of spiritual rejuvenation for every Jesuit is deliberately delayed for some years after ordination, in order, as he told Dixon, 'to enable us to recover that fervour which may have cooled through application to study and contact with the world'.[28] He enjoyed the spiritual peace and relaxation from pressure which he found in these months, and his letters to Dixon range over a wide variety of topics, including more personal reflections over doubts at his worthiness as a priest and time misspent in composing poetry.

He completed his Tertianship in August 1882 and, despite the

24. p. 68. 25. *LB*, p. 48. 26. p. 80.
27. *LB*, p. 97. 28. p. 99.

Provincial's private doubts about his suitability, he was sent to teach classics at Stonyhurst. If any school was to suit his particular gifts, this was the most likely: with as many pupils as its 300 years of history, it had a reputation for academic standards that encouraged suggestions of its future as a new Catholic university. Hopkins's duties were to teach the Philosophers, laymen of university age who were studying for University of London degrees as an alternative to Oxford and Cambridge, attendance at which was banned by the Hierarchy.

His seventeen months at Stonyhurst were not particularly successful. At best his feelings for his work were lukewarm: 'I like my pupils and do not wholly dislike the work';[29] at worst he felt drained of all interest and energy, 'always tired, always jaded'.[30] Poetic inspiration was virtually dead and he was unable to concentrate on writing those scholarly articles which the Provincial had encouraged and which Hopkins felt it was his duty to write. Ironically, his most attractive piece of work appeared in the scientific journal *Nature*, where he described in a letter recent spectacular sunsets he had observed around Stonyhurst in terms that recall the rich and sensuous observation of the Journal.

At the beginning of 1884 he was given what was to be his final appointment in the Society, the Chair of Classics at University College, Dublin. The tangled history of this institution requires some comment if Hopkins's position over the next five years is to be fully understood. The original Catholic University of Ireland, an establishment distinct from Protestant Trinity and the non-denominational Queen's Colleges, had been founded under Newman's leadership in 1854. It received no state aid, and after Newman's resignation in 1858 financial problems and the indecisive policy of the Irish bishops led to a serious decline in prestige and influence. By the Royal University bill of 1879, all Irish colleges, except Trinity, were brought together under one examining institution, and limited financial aid was offered to the Catholic members. In 1883 the Jesuits agreed to take over University College, St. Stephen's Green, the central institution for the Catholic colleges. The policy of Fr Delany, its President, was, with the approval of the majority of the Royal University Senate, to concentrate at St. Stephen's Green all the salaried teaching fellowships (Hopkins's chair and fellowship went together), so that other Catholic institutions around the country teaching for the Royal University exams had no state support.

In appointing his staff, Fr Delany had written to Fr Purbrick, the English Provincial, asking for permission to approach Hopkins. He received the reply: 'Fr Hopkins is very clever and a good scholar . . . but I should do you no kindness in sending you a man so eccentric. I am trying him this year in coaching B.A.'s at Stonyhurst, but with fear and trembling.'[31] The impression Hopkins made on his anxious Provincial must be judged from the point of view of a religious superior concerned at maintaining the conventional image of a conservative order and at using each member's talents to that person's and the Society's best advantage. The anecdotes about Hopkins passed down to posterity hardly reflect a disturbingly eccentric character; what must have been most worrying to Purbrick was the failure as yet to find a suitable post for someone of such intellectual potential. Perhaps University College, Dublin, could provide it . . . ?

He allowed Delany to approach Hopkins, who reluctantly accepted the appointment as a duty which his superiors wished him to undertake. In February 1884 he began his work at St. Stephen's Green inauspiciously with the resignation of Dr Walsh, soon to be Archbishop of Dublin, from the Royal University Senate because his own nominee from Blackrock College had not been offered the Fellowship in Classics. In other ways, too, Hopkins quickly realized the differences between Irish and English university life. The library was in a deplorable condition, and opportunities for writing and research by the staff were severely handicapped by excessive teaching and examining duties. The rector of the College publicly admitted that the amount of examining work tended to lower the professors 'to the condition of college grinders, and to extinguish all ardour for original research'.[32] Hopkins was responsible for six examinations a year, sometimes with as many as 300 candidates at each; the burden was overwhelming, the cause of tragic desperation on many occasions for someone of such a conscientious turn of mind. Moreover, his failure to realize plans to write a number of

31. Quoted in Fr T. Morrissey, S.J., 'Some Jesuit Contributions to Irish Education' (unpublished thesis), p. 512.
32 *Irish Ecclesiastical Review*, Jan. 1884, p. 68.

scholarly articles and his disappointment at the slow progress of his
verse made him brand himself a 'eunuch'.[33] As a priest, too, if one
is to take the self-criticism of the Tullamore retreat notes at face
value, he felt that he had failed to live up to his vocation.

Politics was another source of frustration. A sincere patriot
believing in the ideal of English imperialism, he was by no means a
jingo and had no faith in 'spoon or brag'.[34] He differed sharply from
his conservative friends in recognizing the expediency and even
justice of granting Ireland Home Rule, but still saw poetry as a
'patriotic duty', declaring that when Wordsworth composed his
masterpiece, the *Immortality Ode*, 'St. George and St. Thomas of
Canterbury wore roses in heaven for England's sake'.[35] The failure
of the English in Ireland became part of his profound disillusion
with his own life, and like another benighted cleric in that country,
Jonathan Swift, his thoughts sometimes turned to madness: 'I can
not always last like this: in mind or body or both I shall give way'.[36]

But to see him simply as a lonely tragic figure trapped in perm-
anent exile is to gloss over much that was happy and creative. He
had good friends in both Ireland and England, and at this period as
well as throughout his career he was generously treated by the
Society in the matter of holidays. The fresh and sensitive informal
literary criticism in the Dublin letters offers insights which are as
personal and unconventional as *Tom's Garland* and *Harry Plough-
man*. Hopkins's humour, too little acknowledged, is still delightful,
with a gift for the delicate phrase which he demonstrates in his
anecdote of the drunken organist who was 'a clever young fellow
and thoroughly understood the properties of narrow-necked
tubes'.[37]

At the end of April 1889 he fell ill of what he thought was
'rheumatic fever',[38] but which by the end of the first week in May
was diagnosed as typhoid. On 8 June in the presence of his parents
he died in Dublin. He least of all would have regarded the unhappi-
ness of much of his later life as a matter of great consequence, and
been more than satisfied that his poems did at last win that fame
which he thought all great art deserved.

Stonyhurst College, April 1980   GERALD ROBERTS

33. *LB*, p. 270, and see *Poems*, pp. 106–7.
34. p. 162.   35. pp. 143 and 146.   36. p. 161.   37. p. 155.   38. *FL*, p. 195.

EDITOR'S NOTE

WITH nearly 1,500 pages of text to choose from in the Oxford University Press editions of Hopkins's letters, sermons, journal, and miscellaneous writings, the difficulties of the anthologizer are obvious. In this selection I have tried to bring out the richness of Hopkins's personality and the attractiveness and variety of his prose. The letters, naturally I think, play the major part, but I am bound to have disappointed some Hopkins admirers by the omission of favourite passages; I can only apologize by hoping that this selection will encourage all readers to turn to the full editions of Abbott, Devlin, and House and Storey.

The arrangement in chronological order seems to me the natural one for appreciating continuity and development in Hopkins's life and personality.

The text is that of the standard editions, but I have silently, and perhaps arbitrarily, emended certain of Hopkins's spellings to bring them into line with modern practice. I have however left unaltered 'misspellings' which seem to me deliberate and characteristic of the author, e.g. 'guage', 'cieling'.

A brief bibliography appears at the end of the book. I should say here that I have been especially helped by Fr Thomas's *Hopkins the Jesuit* and the Oxford University Press House and Storey edition of the Journal, an inexhaustible source of Hopkinsiana.

I am very grateful for the use of facilities at the following libraries and the patient assistance of staff: University of Lancaster, the British Library, the National Library of Ireland. Many individuals have been kind enough to respond to demands which I have made on their knowledge, notably: Fr A. Bischoff and Fr T. Gornall, both of the Society of Jesus; Mrs B. Hardwick; Lord Blake; Mr D. Henry; Dr C. Harris; Dr N. Wright. But I must especially thank Fr F. Turner and Fr T. Smalley of Stonyhurst, and Fr F. McGrath of Dublin, all of the Society of Jesus, for help and interest well beyond the call of duty.

G.L.R.

SELECTED PROSE

To C. N. Luxmoore

Oak Hill, Hampstead, N.W. 7 May 1862

. . . You ask whether I am 'still cock of the walk at Elgin'. Why no. I am no longer an Elginite – I am a dayboarder. Fancy that of me! But it arose thus. Last quarter while working for the Exhibition I petitioned Dyne for a private room to work in, representing to him the great disadvantage I was at compared with my rivals and indeed the whole sixth, (for even the Grove-Bankites have their quiet sixth-form room to hold three), in this respect. I alone in fact was forced to work for the exhibition and keep order etc. at once, and in a noisy room. He quite readily and ungrudgingly (though to be sure Mrs Rich pays him for her rooms, and he has no right to do what he likes with them) granted me one of her rooms – the sitting room, but Mrs Chapple exchanged it for the bedroom. Dyne added un-asked that I might have a fire every evening; so I was really quiet and comfortable for a little time. So far, so good, but shortly after-wards I got nearly expelled, deprived of the testimonial which enables one to try for the ex. and degraded to the bottom of the pre-fects for the most trifling ludicrous little thing which I cannot relate at present and actually was turned out of the room and had to make 6 apologies to avoid the other punishments being inflicted. Dyne and I had a terrific altercation. I was driven out of patience and checked him wildly, and he blazed into me with his riding-whip. However Nesfield and Mrs C. soon gave me back my room on their own responsibility, repenting, I believe, of their shares in my punish-ment. Shortly after this Bord's cards were discovered but happily in that matter I was found irreproachable, but not so in the next case, when like a fool I seized one of the upstairs candles on Sunday night when they had taken ours away too soon and my room was denied me for a week. Nesfield presently offered it me back as a favour, but in such a way that I could not take it. Before, however, it was time for me to resume possession I was in a worse row than ever about absolutely nothing, with the chill off, and an accident. Clarke, my co-victim, was flogged, struck off the confirmation list and fined £1;

I was deprived of my room for ever, sent to bed at half past nine till further orders, and ordered to work *only* in the school room, not even in the school library and might not sit on a window sill on the staircase to read. Dyne had repeatedly said he hoped I might not be at the top of the school after the exam., so you may suppose, when he took these last measures, I drew my own conclusions. Next – was late on Sunday; I was exemplary on other days but took Sunday as a 'day of rest' too literally, consequently the fifth time, Dyne having heard, sent me to bed at nine and for the third time this quarter threatened expulsion, deprivation . . .

To his Mother

Balliol College, Oxford. 22 April 1863

. . . My rooms are, I suppose you know, in the roof, which slopes up to the middle of the cieling. Running up and down between lectures is exhausting. However from four of my six windows I have the best views in Balliol, and my staircase has the best scout in the college, Henry. My rooms are three, bedroom, sitting-room and cellar. I have no scout's hole, and no oak to sport when necessary . . .

This is the programme of my day – 7.15, get up, dress; 8, chapel; 8.30, breakfast; 10, lecture; 11, second ditto; 12, sometimes third ditto; 1–2, buttery open for lunch; afternoon, boating or walking and following your own devices; 5, evening chapel, which I have never yet attended; 5.30, the hall; 6, the Union; 7 to bed-time, tea and preparing lectures . . .

Yesterday afternoon [Strachan-Davidson] and I went boating on the upper river. We took a sailing boat, skulled up and sailed down. We then took canoes. I know nothing so luxuriously delicious as a canoe. It is a long light covered boat, the same shape both ways, with an opening in the middle where you recline, with your feet against one board, your back against a cushion on another. You look, contrary of course to ordinary boats, in the direction in which you are going, and move with a single paddle – a rod with a broad round blade at either end which you dip alternately on either side. The motion is Elysian. Strachan Davidson's canoe being low in the water and the wind being very high and making waves, he shipped much water, till he said that it was more pleasant than safe, and had to get to shore and bale out the water, which had nearly sunk him. I, rejoicing in the security of a boat high in the water and given me because large and safe, was meanwhile washed onto the opposite lee shore where I was comfortable but embarrassed, and could not get off for some time. Altogether it was Paradisaical. A canoe in the Cherwel must be the summit of human happiness. On Saturday morning I breakfasted with Palmer, on Sunday Papa and I with Bond, on Tuesday I with Jowett. Jowett is my tutor; when you can get him to talk he is amusing, but when the opposite, it is terribly embarrassing ... This afternoon I walked with Addis to Littlemore Church which Newman's mother built, and where was Newman's last sermon before the exodus. It is quite dark when you enter, but the eye soon becomes accustomed to it. Every window is of the richest stained glass; the east end, east window, altar and reredos are exquisite; the decorations being on a small scale, but most elaborate and perfect. It is a pity Margaret St. Church could not have borrowed something from it. I can not go on describing all Oxford, its inhabitants and its neighbourhood, but to be short, everything is delightful, I have met with much attention and am perfectly comfortable ...

To Baillie

Manor Farm, Shanklin, Isle of Wight. 10/13 July 1863

... About Millais' Eve of S. Agnes, you ought to have known me well enough to be sure I should like it. Of course I do intensely – not wholly perhaps as Keats' Madeline but as the conception of her by a genius. I think over this picture, which I could only unhappily see once, and it, or the memory of it, grows upon me. Those three pictures by Millais in this year's Academy have opened my eyes. I see that he is the greatest English painter, one of the greatest of the world. Eddis, the painter, said to me that he thought some of its best men – he instanced Millais – were leaving the school. Very unfairly, as you will see. If Millais drops his mannerisms and becomes only so far prominent from others' styles as high excellence stands out from mediocrity, then how unfair to say he is leaving his school, when that school, represented in the greatest perfection by him, passing through stage after stage, is at last arriving at Nature's self, which is of no school – inasmuch as different schools represent Nature in their own more or less truthful different ways, Nature meanwhile having only one way . . .

I am sketching (in pencil chiefly) a good deal. I venture to hope you will approve of some of the sketches in a Ruskinese point of view: – if you do not, who will, my sole congenial thinker on art? There are the most deliciously graceful Giottesque ashes (should one say *ashs*?) here – I do not mean Giottesque though, Peruginesque, Fra-Angelical(!), in Raphael's earlier manner. I think I have told you that I have particular periods of admiration for particular things in Nature; for a certain time I am astonished at the beauty of a tree, shape, effect etc, then when the passion, so to speak, has subsided, it is consigned to my treasury of explored beauty, and acknowledged with admiration and interest ever after, while something new takes its place in my enthusiasm. The present fury is the ash, and perhaps barley and two shapes of growth in leaves and one in tree boughs and also a conformation of fine-weather cloud . . .

EARLY DIARIES

1863

Note on water coming through a lock.

There are openings near the bottom of the gates (which allow the water to pass through at all times, I suppose). Suppose three, as there often are. The water strikes through these with great force and extends itself into three fans. The direction of the water is a little oblique from the horizontal, but the great force with which it runs keeps it almost uncurved except at the edges. The end of these fans is not seen for they strike them under a mass of yellowish boiling foam which runs down between the fans, and meeting covers the whole space of the lock-entrance. Being heaped up in globes and bosses and round masses the fans disappear under it. This turpid mass smooths itself as the distance increases from the lock. But the current is strong and if the basin into which it runs has curving banks it strikes them and the confusion of the already folded and doubled lines of foam is worse confounded.

1864

Note on green wheat. The difference between this green and that of long grass is that first suggests silver, latter azure. Former more opacity, body, smoothness. It is the exact complement of carnation. Nearest to emerald of any green I know, the real emerald *stone*. It is lucent. Perhaps it has a chrysoprase bloom. Both blue greens.

*

There was neither rain nor snow, it was cold but not frosty: it had been a gloomy day with all the painful dreariness which December can wear over Clapham. M.C. came in, a little warmed by her walk. She had made a call, she had met the Miss Finlaysons, she had done some shoppings, she had been round half the place and seen the nakedness of the land, and now it struck her how utterly hateful was Clapham. Especially she abominated the Berlin wool shop, where Mrs Vandelinde and her daughter called her 'Miss' and there was a continual sound of sliding glass panels and a smell of Berlin wool.

*

March 19, Saturday, 1864, walked to Edgware from Hampstead and home by Hendon, stopping at Kingsbury water a quarter of an hour or so. Saw what was probably a heron: it settled on a distant elm, was driven away by two rooks, settled on a still more distant, the same thing happened, the rooks pursuing it. It then flew across the water, circled about, and flew Hampsteadwards away . . .

*

Poetry at Oxford.
It is a happy thing that there is no royal road to poetry. The world should know by this time that one cannot reach Parnassus except by flying thither. Yet from time to time more men go up and either perish in its gullies fluttering *excelsior* flags or else come down again with full folios and blank countenances. Yet the old fallacy keeps its ground. Every age has its false alarms.

To E. H. Coleridge

Oxford Union Society. 1 June 1864

. . . I hope you will come up soon, for one reason because you do not appear to me very Catholic, and I think you could no longer be

in that state of mind when you are come to the head and fount of
Catholicism in England and the heart of our Church. Beware of
doing what I once thought I could do, *adopt an enlightened Christ-
ianity*, I may say, horrible as it is, *be a credit to religion*. This fatal
state of mind leads to infidelity, if consistently and logically deve-
loped. The great aid to belief and object of belief is the doctrine of
the Real Presence in the Blessed Sacrament of the Altar. Religion
without that is sombre, dangerous, illogical, with that it is – not to
speak of its grand consistency and certainty – *loveable*. Hold that
and you will gain all Catholic truth.

Yours affectionately,

GERARD M. HOPKINS

TO BAILLIE

Blunt House, Croydon. 10/11 Sept. 1864

DEAR BAILLIE, – Your letter has been sent to me from Hampstead.
It has just come, and I do a rare thing with me, begin at once on an
answer. I have just finished *The Philippics* of Cicero and an hour
remains before bedtime; no one except Wharton would begin a new
book at that time of night, so I was reading *Henry IV*, when your
letter was brought in – a great enjoyment.

The letter-writer on principle does not make his letter only an
answer; it is a work embodying perhaps answers to questions put by
his correspondent but that is not its main motive. Therefore it is as
a rule not well to write with a received letter fresh on you. I sup-
pose the right way is to let it sink into you, and reply after a day or
two. I do not know why I have said all this.

Do you know, a horrible thing has happened to me. I have begun
to *doubt* Tennyson. (Baillejus ap. Hopk.) It is a great *argumentum*,
a great clue, that our minds jump together even if it be a leap into
the dark. I cannot tell you how amused and I must say pleased and
comforted by this coincidence I am. A little explanation first. You
know I do not mistrust my judgment so soon as you do; I say it to
the praise of your modesty. Therefore I do not think myself 'getting
into my dotage' for that, and I will shew why. I think (I am assum-
ing a great deal in saying this I fear) I may shew, judging from my
own mind, how far we are both of us right in this, and on what, if

I may use the word, more *enlightened* ground we may set our admiration of Tennyson. I have been thinking about this on and off since I read *Enoch Arden* and the other new poems, so that my judgment is more digested than if the ideas had only struck me while answering you. I was shaken too you know by Addis, which makes a good deal of difference.

I am meditating an essay, perhaps for the *Hexameron,* on some points of poetical criticism, and it is with reference to this a little that I have composed my thoughts on Tennyson. I think then the language of verse may be divided into three kinds. The first and highest is poetry proper, the language of inspiration. The word inspiration need cause no difficulty. I mean by it a mood of great, abnormal in fact, mental acuteness, either energetic or receptive, according as the thoughts which arise in it seem generated by a stress and action of the brain, or to strike into it unasked. This mood arises from various causes, physical generally, as good health or state of the air or, prosaic as it is, length of time after a meal. But I need not go into this; all that it is needful to mark is, that the poetry of inspiration can only be written in this mood of mind, even if it only last a minute, by poets themselves. Everybody of course has like moods, but not being poets what they then produce is not poetry. This second kind I call *Parnassian.* It can only be spoken by poets, but it is not in the highest sense poetry. It does not require the mood of mind in which the poetry of inspiration is written. It is spoken *on and from the level* of a poet's mind, not, as in the other case, when the inspiration which is the gift of genius, raises him above himself. For I think it is the case with genius that it is not when quiescent so very much above mediocrity as the difference between the two might lead us to think, but that it has the power and privilege of rising from that level to a height utterly far from mediocrity: in other words that its greatness is *that it can be* so great. You will understand. *Parnassian* then is that language which genius speaks as fitted to its exaltation, and place among other genius, but does not sing (I have been betrayed into the whole hog of a metaphor) in its flights. Great men, poets I mean, have each their own dialect as it were of Parnassian, formed generally as they go on writing, and at last, – this is the point to be marked, – they can see things in this Parnassian way and describe them in this Parnassian tongue, without further effort of inspiration. In a poet's particular

kind of Parnassian lies most of his style, of his manner, of his man-
nerism if you like. But I must not go farther without giving you
instances of Parnassian. I shall take one from Tennyson, and from
Enoch Arden, from a passage much quoted already and which will
be no doubt often quoted, the description of Enoch's tropical island.

> The mountain wooded to the peak, the lawns
> And winding glades high up like ways to Heaven,
> The slender coco's drooping crown of plumes,
> The lightning flash of insect and of bird,
> The lustre of the long convolvuluses
> That coil'd around the stately stems, and ran
> Ev'n to the limit of the land, the glows
> And glories of the broad belt of the world,
> All these he saw.

Now it is a mark of Parnassian that one could conceive oneself
writing it if one were the poet. Do not say that *if* you were Shake-
spear you can imagine yourself writing Hamlet, because that is just
what I think you cannot conceive. In a fine piece of inspiration
every beauty takes you as it were by surprise, not of course that you
did not think the writer could be so great, for that is not it, – indeed
I think it is a mistake to speak of people admiring Shakespear more
and more as they live, for when the judgment is ripe and you have
read a good deal of any writer including his best things, and care-
fully, then, I think, however high the place you give him, that you
must have rated him equally with his merits however great they be;
so that all after admiration cannot increase but keep alive this esti-
mate, make his greatness stare into your eyes and din it into your
ears, as it were, but not make it greater, – but to go on with the
broken sentence, every fresh beauty could not in any way be pre-
dicted or accounted for by what one has already read. But in Par-
nassian pieces you feel that if you were the poet you could have gone
on as he has done, you see yourself doing it, only with the difference
that if you actually try, to find you cannot write his Parnassian.
Well now to turn to the piece above. The glades being 'like ways to
Heaven' is, I think, a new thought, it is an inspiration. Not so the
next line, that is pure Parnassian. If you examine it the words are
choice and the description is beautiful and unexceptionable, but it
does not *touch* you. The next is more Parnassian still. In the next

lines I think the picture of the convolvuluses does touch; but only the picture: the words are Parnassian. It is a very good instance, for the lines are undoubtedly beautiful, but yet I could scarcely point anywhere to anything more idiomatically Parnassian, to anything which I more clearly see myself writing *qua* Tennyson, than the words

> The glows
> And glories of the broad belt of the world.

What Parnassian is you will now understand, but I must make some more remarks on it. I believe that when a poet palls on us it is because of his Parnassian. We seem to have found out his secret. Now in fact we have not found out more than this, that when he is not inspired and in his flights, his poetry does run in an intelligibly laid down path. Well, it is notorious that Shakespear does not pall, and this is because he uses, I believe, so little Parnassian. He does use some, but little. Now judging from my own experience I should say no author palls so much as Wordsworth; this is because he writes such an 'intolerable deal of' Parnassian.

If with a critical eye and in a critical appreciative mood you read a poem by an unknown author or an anonymous poem by a known, but not at once recognizable, author, and he is a real poet, then you will pronounce him so at once, and the poem will seem truly inspired, though afterwards, when you know the author, you will be able to distinguish his inspirations from his Parnassian, and will perhaps think the very piece which struck you so much at first mere Parnassian. You know well how deadened, as it were, the critical faculties become at times, when all good poetry alike loses its clear ring and its charm; while in other moods they are so enlivened that things that have long lost their freshness strike you with their original definiteness and piquant beauty.

I think one had got into the way of thinking, or had not got out of the way of thinking, that Tennyson was always new, *touching*, beyond other poets, not pressed with human ailments, never using Parnassian. So at least I used to think. Now one sees he uses Parnassian; he is, one must see it, what we used to call Tennysonian. But the discovery of this must not make too much difference. When puzzled by one's doubts it is well to turn to a passage like this. Surely your maturest judgment will never be fooled out of saying

that this is divine, terribly beautiful – the stanza of *In Memoriam*
beginning with the quatrain

> O Hesper o'er the buried sun,
>   And ready thou to die with him,
>   Thou watchest all things ever dim
> And dimmer, and a glory done.

I quote from memory. Inconsequent conclusion: Shakespear is and
must be utterly the greatest of poets.

Just to end what I was saying about poetry. There is a higher sort
of Parnassian which I call *Castalian*, or it may be thought the lowest
kind of inspiration. Beautiful poems may be written wholly in it. Its
peculiarity is that though you can hardly conceive yourself having
written in it, if in the poet's place, yet it is too characteristic of the
poet, too so-and-so-all-over-ish, to be quite inspiration. E.g.

>   Yet despair
> Touches me not, though pensive as a bird
> Whose vernal coverts winter hath laid bare.

This is from Wordsworth, beautiful, but rather too essentially
Wordsworthian, too persistently his way of looking at things. The
third kind is merely the language of verse as distinct from that of
prose, Delphic, the tongue of the Sacred *Plain*, I may call it, used in
common by poet and poetaster. Poetry when spoken is spoken in it,
but to speak it is not necessarily to speak poetry. I may add there is
also *Olympian*. This is the language of strange masculine genius
which suddenly, as it were, forces its way into the domain of poetry,
without naturally having a right there. Milman's poetry is of this
kind I think, and Rossetti's *Blessèd Damozel*. But unusual poetry has
a tendency to seem so at first . . .

EARLY DIARIES

1865

Sunrise at Chagford. There was a remarkable fan of clouds traced
in fine horizontals, which afterwards lost their levels, some becom-
ing oblique. Below appearing bright streaks which crowded up one
after another. A white mist in the churchyard, trees ghostly in it.

Sunset here also. Over the nearest ridge of Dartmoor. Sky orange, trail of Bronze-lit clouds, stars and streaks of brilliant electrum underneath, but not for this, but effect of dark intensified foreground. Long rounded ridge of Dartmoor deep purple, then trees on the descending hill, and a field with an angle so that the upper level was lighter green the lower darker, then a purplish great brown field, then the manufactory with grey white timbers (it is built of wood) and grey shingle (?) roofs.

Grey sky at Hampstead lately. Clouds showing beautiful and rare curves like curds, comparable to barrows, arranged of course in parallels.

Rain railing off something.

The butterfly perching in a cindery dusty road and pinching his scarlet valves. Or wagging, one might say. And also valvèd eyes.

Mallowy red of sunset and sunrise clouds.

1866

For Lent. No pudding on Sundays. No tea except if to keep me awake and then without sugar. Meat only once a day. No verses in Passion Week or on Fridays. No lunch or meat on Fridays. Not to sit in armchair except can work in no other way. Ash Wednesday and Good Friday bread and water.

JOURNAL

3 May

Cold. Morning raw and wet, afternoon fine. Walked then with Addis, crossing Bablock Hythe, round by Skinner's Weir through many fields into the Witney road. Sky sleepy blue without liquidity. From Cumnor Hill saw St. Philip's and the other spires through blue haze rising pale in a pink light. On further side of the Witney road hills, just fleeced with grain or other green growth, by their dips and waves foreshortened here and there and so differenced in brightness and opacity the green on them, with delicate effect. On left, brow of the near hill glistening with very bright newly turned sods and a scarf of vivid green slanting away beyond the skyline, against which the clouds shewed the slightest tinge of rose or purple. Copses in grey-red or grey-yellow – the tinges immediately forerunning the opening of full leaf. Meadows skirting Seven-bridge road voluptuous green. Some oaks are out in small leaf. Ashes not out, only tufted with their fringy blooms. Hedges springing richly. Elms in small leaf, with more or less opacity. White poplars most beautiful in small grey crisp spray-like leaf. Cowslips capriciously colouring meadows in creamy drifts. Bluebells, purple orchis. Over the green water of the river passing the slums of the town and under its bridges swallows shooting, blue and purple above and shewing their amber-tinged breasts reflected in the water, their flight unsteady with wagging wings and leaning first to one side then the other. Peewits flying. Towards sunset the sky partly swept, as often, with moist white cloud, tailing off across which are morsels of grey-black woolly clouds. Sun seemed to make a bright liquid hole in this, its texture had an upward northerly sweep or drift from the W, marked softly in grey. Dog violets. Eastward after sunset range of clouds rising in bulky heads moulded softly in tufts or bunches of snow – so it looks – and membered somewhat elaborately, rose-coloured. Notice often imperfect fairy rings. Apple and other fruit trees blossomed beautifully. A. talking about the whole story of the home affairs. His idea was (when he went down three years ago and was all the Long preparing for confession) that 7 years was a moderate time during which to fast within the boundaries of life and abstain from communicating. Being not allowed to read he took long walks, and it must have been on one of these that he fainted as he once told me.

Yellow and green in the fields charming. Ferryman said 'I can't justly tell you', and they call *weir* as if *wire*.

I think that thread in smooth rivers is made by water being drawn or retained at right angles to the current.

To Newman

Oak Hill, Hampstead. 28 Aug. 1866

REVEREND SIR, – I address you with great hesitation knowing that you are in the midst of yr. own engagements and because you must be much exposed to applications from all sides. I am anxious to become a Catholic, and I thought that you might possibly be able to see me for a short time when I pass through Birmingham in a few days, I believe on Friday. But I feel most strongly the injustice of intruding on yr. engagements or convenience and therefore, if that is the case, I shall think it a favour if you will kindly let me know that you are unable to see me. I do not want to be helped to any con-clusions of belief, for I am thankful to say my mind is made up, but the necessity of becoming a Catholic (although I had long foreseen where the only consistent position wd. lie) coming upon me suddenly has put me into painful confusion of mind about my immediate duty in my circumstances. I wished also to know what it wd. be morally my duty to hold on certain formally open points, because the same reasoning which makes the Tractarian ground contradictory wd. almost lead one also to shrink from what Mr. Oakley calls a minimising Catholicism. I say this much to take fr. you any hesitation in not allowing me to come to Birmingham if duties shd. stand in the way: you will understand that by God's mercy I am clear as to the sole authority of the Church of Rome. While much in doubt therefore as to my right to trouble you by this application, I wd. not deny at the same time that I shd. feel it the greatest privilege to see you. If it were so, I shd. hope not to detain you long. I may perhaps in some way introduce myself by remind-ing you of an intimate college friend of mine, William Addis, who once had the pleasure of spending an hour with you at the Oratory; I think also he has written to you since: I have little doubt that in not a very long time he will become a Catholic. If I shd. be so happy as to hear before Friday that you cd. spare time to see me, I shd. hope to be at Birmingham that day and sleep there, or if you had any convenient time in the two or three weeks after that I shd. like to come over fr. Rochdale where I shall be staying at Dr. Molesworth's. But in ending I wd. again say that I beg you will have no hesitation, as I have no doubt you will not, in declining to see me if you think best.

Believe me, Reverend Sir, your obedient servant.

GERARD M. HOPKINS

To Bridges

Oak Hill, Hampstead, 22/24 Sept. 1866

... Dr Newman was most kind, I mean in the very best sense, for his manner is not that of solicitous kindness but genial and almost, so to speak, unserious. And if I may say so, he was so sensible. He asked questions which made it clear for me how to act; I will tell you presently what that is: he made sure I was acting deliberately and wished to hear my arguments; when I had given them and said I cd. see no way out of them, he laughed and said 'Nor can I': and he told me I must come to the church to accept and believe – as I hope I do. He thought there appeared no reason, if it had not been for matters at home of course, why I shd. not be received at once, but in no way did he urge me on, rather the other way. More than once when I offered to go he was good enough to make me stay talking. Amongst other things he said that he always answered those who thought the learned had no excuse in invincible ignorance, that on the contrary they had that excuse the most of all people. It is needless to say he spoke with interest and kindness and appreciation of all that Tractarians reverence. This much pleased me, namely a bird's-eye view of Oxford in his room the frame of which he had lettered *Fili hominis, putasne vivent ossa ista? Domine Deus, tu nosti*. This speaks for itself. He told me what books to get and then left me at lunch-time to Mr John Walford – discovered at football. Mr Walford gave me lunch in the refectory and shewed all the school and the oratory, then walked back and took me to St. Chad's cathedral. He told me to remember him very kindly to you and to say how glad he shd. be to see you on yr. way to Oxford, if you liked it. You have much common interest fr. Eton etc, and of course he wd. avoid all religious subjects, I am sure.

I am to go over fr. Oxford to the Oratory for my reception next term – early in the term I must make it, and since a Retreat is advisable for a convert, Dr Newman was so very good as to offer me to come there at Xtmas, which wd. be the earliest opportunity for it. He thought it both expedient and likely that I shd. finish my time at Oxford, and next term at all events I shall be there, since I shall announce my conversion to my parents by letter at the time of my reception. And now I have even almost ceased to feel anxiety.

[24 Sept.] You were surprised and sorry, you said, and possibly hurt that I wd. not tell you of my conversion till my going to Birmingham made it impossible any longer to conceal it. I was never sorry for one minute: it wd. have been culpably dishonourable and ungrateful, as I said before, not to have done one's best to conceal it: but I do not mean that, but this – the happiness it has been the means of bringing me I cd. not have conceived: I can never thank you enough for yr. kindness at that time. Notwithstanding my anxiety, which on the day we filled the aquarium was very great indeed, it gives me more delight to think of the time at Rochdale than any other time whatever that I can remember. I did not see Mrs. Molesworth at the last: will you give her for me my very greatest thanks for her kindness? Dr Molesworth I did say Goodbye to. I am most distressed to think that the news of my conversion, if they hear it, may give them pain and alarm for you, but you must remember that when I came to Rochdale I did not look upon my reception as to be so soon as it really was to be. You see the point of what was on my mind at the vicarage was chiefly this, that my wishes about you cd. not be gained except at your own and their trouble and grief. This will make it plain how I feel that wherever I go I must either do no good or else harm. . . .

To the Rev E. W. Urquhart

Hampstead. 24 Sept. 1866

. . . You are the only friend whom I have deliberately told of my conversion, though I let Macfarlane and Garrett, with whom I was staying at the time, know it through my incaution. Fr. Bridges I hid it with difficulty while I stayed at Rochdale, till my going to Birmingham made concealment useless. His kindness at that time when he did not know what was the matter with me I perpetually thank God for. One of my brothers knows it; he forced it from me by questions. Dr. Newman of course and one or two other Catholics know, but no one else: Addis does not. I shd. have told him but I did not want by introducing a train of thoughts and difficulties about himself to break up his pleasure at Birchington, which he was enjoying when he wrote, he said, most deeply. But now I shall let one friend after another hear till the time of my reception. I hope the painful time of yr. hesitation may be short: one is sure in these cases that one is not alone but then, if ever, the saints and one's guardian angel are praying for one. If it is a relief possibly to write I shall be so glad to be hearing fr. you. But I am so sanguine, that I can scarcely believe your next letter will not put all doubt at an end and explain *Magnificavit Dominus facere nobiscum; facti sumus laetantes.* I wd. write more if I were your friend in the same way that Challis or Gurney are, but I hope that I can sympathise as much as Challis will, for Gurney of course we cannot bring in here. Believe me yr. affectionate friend,

GERARD HOPKINS

P.S. I am so glad, do you know, that my conversion is surprising to you (though I am sorry that you shd. have had a shock from it), because although my actual conversion was two months ago yet the silent conviction that I was to become a Catholic has been present to me for a year perhaps, as strongly, in spite of my resistance to it when it formed itself into words, as if I had already determined it . . .

TO NEWMAN

18 New Inn Hall Street, Oxford. St. Theresa, 1866

VERY REVEREND FATHER, – I have been up at Oxford just long enough to have heard fr. my father and mother in return for my letter announcing my conversion. Their answers are terrible: I cannot read them twice. If you will pray for them and me just now I shall be deeply thankful. But what I am writing for is this – they urge me with the utmost entreaties to wait till I have taken my degree – more than half a year. Of course it is impossible, and since it is impossible to wait as long as they wish it seems to me useless to wait at all. Wd. you therefore wish me to come to Birmingham at once, on Thursday, Friday, or Saturday? You will understand why I have any hesitation at all, namely because if immediately after their letters urging a long delay I am received without any, it will be another blow and look like intentional cruelty. I did not know till last night the rule about *communicatio in sacris* – at least as binding catechumens, but I now see the alternative thrown open, either to live without Church and sacraments or else, in order to avoid the Catholic Church, to have to attend constantly the services of that very Church. This brings the matter to an absurdity and makes me think that any delay, whatever relief it may be to my parents, is impossible. I am asking you then whether I shall at all costs be received at once.

Strange to say of four conversions mine is the earliest and yet my reception will be last. I think that I said that my friend William

Garrett was converted and received shortly after hearing of my conversion; just before term began another friend, Alexander Wood, wrote to me in perplexity, and when I wrote back to his surprise telling him I was a convert he made up his own mind the next morning and is being received today; by a strange chance he met Addis in town and Addis, who had put off all thought of change for a year, was by God's mercy at once determined to see a priest, and was received at Bayswater the same evening – Saturday. All our our minds you see were ready to go at a touch and it cannot but be that the same is the case with many here. Addis' loss will be deep grief to Dr Pusey I think: he has known him so long and stayed with him at Chale in a retreat.

I shall ask F. William Neville to open and answer this in your absence.

Monsignor Eyre seemed to say that I ought not to make my confession by means of a paper as I have been used to do. Will you kindly say whether you wd. prefer it so or not?

Believe me, dear Father, your affectionate son in Christ.

GERARD M. HOPKINS

P.S. And if you shd. bid me be received at once will you kindly name the day? The liberality of the college authorities will throw no hindrance in the way.

To his Father

23 New Inn Hall Street, Oxford. 16/17 Oct. 1866

MY DEAR FATHER, – I must begin with a practical immediate point. The Church strictly forbids all communion in sacred things with non-Catholics. I have only just learnt this, but it prevents me going to chapel, and so yesterday I had to inform the Dean of the Chapel. Today the Master sent for me and said he cd. not grant me leave of absence without an application from you. As the College last term passed a resolution admitting Catholics and took a Catholic into residence it has no right to alter its principle in my case. I wish you therefore not to give yourself the pain of making this application, even if you were willing: I am of age moreover and am alone concerned. If you refuse to make the application, the Master explains that he shall lay my case before the common-room. In this case there is very little doubt indeed that the Fellows wd. take the reasonable course and give me leave of absence fr. chapel, and if not, I am quite contented: but in fact I am satisfied as to the course our Fellows will take and the Master will at the last hesitate to lay the matter before them perhaps even. I want you therefore to write at once, if you will, – not to the Master who has no right to ask what he does, but to me, with a refusal: no harm will follow.

The following is the position of things with me. You ask me to suspend my judgment for a long time, or at the very least more than half a year, in other words to stand still for a time. Now to stand still is not possible, thus: I must either obey the Church or disobey. If I disobey, I am not suspending judgment but deciding, namely to take backward steps fr. the grounds I have already come to. To stand still if it were possible might be justifiable, but to go back nothing can justify. I must therefore obey the Church by ceasing to attend any service of the Church of England. If I am to wait then I must either be altogether without services and sacraments, which you will of course know is impossible, or else I must attend the services of the Church – still being unreceived. But what can be more contradictory than, in order to avoid joining the Church, attending the services of that very Church? Three of my friends, whose conversions were later than mine, Garrett, Addis, and Wood, have already been received, but this is by the way. Only one thing remains to be done: I cannot fight against God who calls me to His Church: if I were to delay and die in the meantime I shd. have no plea why my soul was not forfeit. I have no power in fact to stir a finger: it is God Who makes the decision and not I.

But you do not understand what is involved in asking me to delay and how little good you wd. get from it. I shall hold as a Catholic what I have long held as an Anglican, that literal truth of our Lord's words by which I learn that the least fragment of the consecrated elements in the Blessed Sacrament of the Altar is the whole Body of Christ born of the Blessed Virgin, before which the whole host of saints and angels as it lies on the altar trembles with adoration. This belief once got is the life of the soul and when I doubted it I shd. become an atheist the next day. But, as Monsignor Eyre says, it is a gross superstition unless guaranteed by infallibility. I cannot hold this doctrine confessedly except as a Tractarian or a Catholic: the Tractarian ground I have seen broken to pieces under my feet.

What end then can be served by a delay in wh. I shd. go on believing this doctrine as long as I believed in God and shd. be by the fact of my belief drawn by a lasting strain towards the Catholic Church?

About my hastiness I wish to say this. If the question which is the Church of Christ? cd. only be settled by laborious search, a year and ten years and a lifetime are too little, when the vastness of the subject of theology is taken into account. But God must have made his Church such as to attract and convince the poor and unlearned as well as the learned. And surely it is true, though it will sound pride to say it, that the judgment of one who has seen both sides for a week is better than his who has seen only one for a lifetime. I am surprised you shd. say fancy and aesthetic tastes have led me to my present state of mind: these wd. be better satisfied in the Church of England, for bad taste is always meeting one in the accessories of Catholicism. My conversion is due to the following reasons mainly (I have put them down without order) – (i) simple and strictly drawn arguments partly my own, partly others', (ii) common sense, (iii) reading the Bible, especially the Holy Gospels, where texts like 'Thou art Peter' (the evasions proposed for this alone are enough to make one a Catholic) and the manifest position of St. Peter among the Apostles so pursued me that at one time I thought it best to stop thinking of them, (iv) an increasing knowledge of the Catholic system (at first under the form of Tractarianism, later in its genuine place), which only wants to be known in order to be loved – its consolations, its marvellous ideal of holiness, the faith and devotion of its children, its multiplicity, its array of saints and martyrs, its consistency and unity, its glowing prayers, the daring majesty of its claims, etc etc. You speak of the claims of the Church of England, but it is to me the strange thing that the Church of England makes no claims: it is true that Tractarians make them for her and find them faintly or only in a few instances borne out for them by her liturgy, and are strongly assailed for their extravagances while they do it. Then about applying to Mr Liddon and the Bp. of Oxford. Mr Liddon writes begging me to pause: it wd. take too long to explain how I did not apply to him at first and why it wd. have been useless. If Dr Pusey is in Oxford tomorrow I will see him, if it is any satisfaction to you. The Bishop is too much engaged to listen to individual difficulties and those who do apply to him may get such answers as young Mr Lane Fox did, who gave up £30,000 a year just lately to become a Catholic. He wrote back about a cob which he wanted to sell to the Dean of some place and wh. Lane Fox was to put his own price on and ride over for the Bishop to the place of sale. In fact Dr Pusey and Mr Liddon were the only two men in the world who cd. avail to detain me: the fact that they were Anglicans kept me one, for arguments for the Church of England I had long ago felt there were none that wd. hold water, and when that influence gave way everything was gone.

You are so kind as not to forbid me your house, to which I have no claim, on condition, if I understand, that I promise not to try to convert my brothers and sisters. Before I can promise this I must get permission, wh. I have no doubt will be given. Of course this promise will not apply after they come of age. Whether after my reception you will still speak as you do now I cannot tell.

You ask me if I have had no thought of the estrangement. I have had months to think of everything. Our Lord's last care on the cross was to commend His mother to His Church and His Church to His mother in the person of St. John. If even now you wd. put yourselves into that position wh. Christ so unmistakeably gives us and ask the Mother of sorrows to remember her three hours' compassion at the cross, the piercing of the sword prophesied by Simeon, and her seven dolours, and her spouse Joseph, the lily of chastity, to remember the flight into Egypt, the searching for his Foster-Son at twelve years old, and his last ecstasy with Christ at his death-bed, the prayers of this Holy Family wd. in a few days put an end to estrangements for ever. If you shrink fr. doing this, though the Gospels cry aloud to you to do it, at least for once – if you like, only once – approach Christ in a new way in which you will at all events feel that you are exactly in unison with me, that is, not vaguely, but casting yourselves into His sacred broken Heart and His five adorable Wounds. Those who do not pray to Him in His Passion pray to God but scarcely to Christ. I have the right to propose this, for I have tried both ways, and if you will not give one trial to this way you will see you are prolonging the estrangement and not I.

After saying this I feel lighter-hearted, though I still can by no means make my pen write what I shd. wish. I am your loving son,

GERARD M. HOPKINS

P.S. I am most anxious that you shd. not think of my future. It is likely that the positions you wd. like to see me in wd. have no attraction for me, and surely the happiness of my prospects depends on the happiness to me and not on intrinsic advantages. It is possible even to be very sad and very happy at once and the time that I was with Bridges, when my anxiety came to its height, was I believe the happiest fortnight of my life. My only strong wish is to be independent.

If you are really willing to make the application to the Master, well and good; but I do not want you to put yourself to pain. I have written a remonstrance to him.

Many thanks to Arthur for his letter.

To his Mother

Oxford Union Society. 20 Oct. 1866

... I am to be received into the church tomorrow at Birmingham by Dr Newman. It is quite the best that any hopes should be ended quickly, since otherwise they wd. only have made the pain longer. Until then the comforts you take are delusive, after it they will be real. And even for me it is almost a matter of necessity, for every new letter I get breaks me down afresh, and this cd. not go on. Your letters, wh. shew the utmost fondness, suppose none on my part and the more you think me hard and cold and that I repel and throw you off the more I am helpless not to write as if [it] were true. In this way I have no relief. You might believe that I suffer too. I am your very loving son,

GERARD M. HOPKINS

Journal

22 Aug. 1867

Bright. – Walked to Finchley and turned down a lane to a field where I sketched an appletree. Their sprays against the sky are gracefully curved and the leaves looping over, edge them, as it looks, with rows of scales. In something the same way I saw some tall young slender wych-elms of thin growth the leaves of which enclosed the light in successive eyebrows. From the spot where I sketched – under an oak, beyond a brook, and reached by the above

green lane between a park-ground and a pretty field – there was a
charming view, the field, lying then on the right of the lane, being a
close-shaven smoothly-rounded shield of bright green ended near
the high road by a row of viol-headed or flask-shaped elms – not
rounded merely but squared – of much beauty – dense leafing, rich
dark colour, ribs and spandrils of timber garlanded with leaf
between tree and tree. But what most struck me was a pair of ashes
in going up the lane again. The further one was the finer – a globeish
just-sided head with one launching-out member on the right; the
nearer one was more naked and horny. By taking a few steps one
could pass the further behind the nearer or make the stems close,
either coincidingly, so far as disagreeing outlines will coincide, or
allowing a slit on either side, or again on either side making a
broader stem than either would make alone. It was this which was so
beautiful – making a noble shaft and base to the double tree, which
was crested by the horns of the nearer ash and shaped on the right
by the bosom of the hinder one with its springing bough. The out-
line of the double stem was beautiful to whichever of the two sides
you slid the hinder tree – in one (not, I think, in both) shaft-like
and narrowing at the ground. Besides I saw how great the richness
and subtlety is of the curves in the clusters, both in the forward bow
mentioned before and in some most graceful hangers on the other
side: it combines somewhat-slanted outward strokes with rounding,
but I cannot very well characterise it now. – Elm-leaves: they shine
much in the sun – bright green when near from underneath but
higher up they look olive: their shapelessness in the flat is from their
being made, διὰ τὸ πεφυκέναι, to be dimpled and dog's-eared:
their leaf-growth is in this point more rudimentary than that of oak,
ash, beech, etc that the leaves lie in long rows and do not subdivide
or have central knots but tooth or cog their woody twigs.

To the Rev E. W. Urquhart

The Oratory, Edgbaston, Birmingham. 30 Sept. 1867

Dear Urquhart, – How badly you must think I have remembered
my promise to write soon. If I had only done so the first week I was
here it wd. have been well: ever since then I have scarcely had a
minute of leisure.

First I must tell you that I had a wild tear to catch the train and there was a pain in my back for many days after it. At Exeter station I saw Tracy of Ch. Ch. and Mr Oxenham of Torquay together; the latter had on a remarkable cap like an ancient helmet with *bucculae*, if you know what they were.

My box came all right. I went, the day before the boys came back, to Oxford to get my things and there Wharton entertained me very kindly. I had to borrow one of Mrs Ridley's boxes. For the first week I was in the Oratory as a guest: now I am in the house where Walford was and do not see anything of the Oratory. Fancy me getting up at a quarter past six: it is however done with a melancholy punctuality nearly every morning. The boys' mass is at seven; then what they call Preparation fr. 7.45 to 8.30; then breakfast in Hall, so to speak; at 9.30 school till 12; dinner in Hall at 1; school fr. 2 to 3; then the boys and sometimes I go to their field, which they call Bosco, for a game, just now hockey but soon football; at 6 tea in Hall; from 6.30 to 8.30 school. My class is the fifth but besides this my work includes two private pupils who come to me fr. 8.45 to 10 on all nights but Saturday and fr. 5 to 6 on the half-holidays Tuesday, Thursday, and Saturday. With reading the class books and looking over exercises (which takes a long time) I find all my time occupied. Today however is Sunday and the boys are playing fives like good ones: I wish they wd. play all the other numbers on the clock all the other days of the week. The fifth, the head class, has only five boys; thus I have seven. I feel as if they were all my children, a notion encouraged by their innocence and backwardness. They never swear beyond Con-found you, you young fool, and that only one of them. The masters' table appears to be the dregs of Great Britain, indeed one of us is a Dutchman but I cannot spell his name: when I say dregs I only mean that they come fr. all quarters indiscriminately and I include myself: it is sweepings, not dregs I mean. They are nice souls and one of them, a very young man, I like particularly. I see no papers: if democracy shd. be established or Mr Disraeli take that title I was mentioning of Earl Mount Horeb, Baron Bashan, will you let me hear of it? I get no letters, which may depend upon or merely synchronise with my not writing any. I see I have not given you a proper notion altogether of my employment, for I have my private pupils oftener. But F. Ambrose is going to make an arrangement by which I shall get some time for private

reading. Today I have been hearing a quartet on violins and violin-
cello by the music master, one of my p.p.s, one of my fifth form
boys, and Dr Newman. The country round is really very good for
so near Birmingham. I wonder if there is anything I cd. do, though
the income were less, wh. wd. give me more time, for I feel the want
of that most of all. – All but the last few words of this were written
on Michaelmas day: it is now Monday. Last night I saw Mr Thomas
Pope, until this term one of the masters here, received into the
congregation of the Oratory and we have had a half-holiday for it
today.

Now goodbye. Many thanks for my pleasant stay at Bovey. You
may yet, I hope, be a Catholic. You know what my specific is, if you
wd. only make up yr. mind to apply it.

Believe me yr. affectionate friend,

GERARD M. HOPKINS

TO BAILLIE

The Oratory. 12 Feb. 1868

... I must say that I am very anxious to get away from this place.
I have become very weak in health and do not seem to recover
myself here or likely to do so. Teaching is very burdensome,
especially when you have much of it: I have. I have not much time
and almost no energy – for I am always tired – to do anything on
my own account. I put aside that one sees and hears nothing and
nobody here. Very happily Challis of Merton is now here; else the
place were without reservation 'damned, shepherd'. (This is not
swearing.) I ought to make the exception that the boys are very nice
indeed. I am expecting to take orders and soon, but I wish it to be
secret till it comes about. Besides that it is the happiest and best way
it practically is the only one. You know I once wanted to be a
painter. But even if I could I wd. not I think, now, for the fact is
that the higher and more attractive parts of the art put a strain upon
the passions which I shd. think unsafe to encounter. I want to
write still and as a priest I very likely can do that too, not so freely
as I shd. have liked, e.g. nothing or little in the verse way, but no
doubt what wd. best serve the cause of my religion. But if I am a
priest it will cause my mother, or she says it will, great grief and this

preys on my mind very much and makes the near prospect quite black. The general result is that I am perfectly reckless about things that I shd. otherwise care about, uncertain as I am whether in a few months I may not be shut up in a cloister, and this state of mind, though it is painful coming to, when reached gives a great and real sense of freedom. Do you happen to know of any tutorship I cd. take for a few months after Easter? as I am anxious to leave this place then and also not to leave it without having secured something to live upon till, as seems likely, I take minor orders ...

To the Rev E. W. Urquhart

Oak Hill, Hampstead, N.W. 13 June 1868

... About the end of the month I am going to Switzerland for a month with Edward Bond and when I return shall be admitted at once to the Jesuit noviciate at Roehampton. It is enough to say that the sanctity has not departed fr. the order to have a reason for joining it. Since I made up my mind to this I have enjoyed the first complete peace of mind I have ever had. I am quite surprised – not that on reflection it is surprising – at the kind and contented way my parents have come to take the prospect.

With regard to the rejoinder you speak for I think argument is not only useless but tends to encourage the way of thinking of yr. position as if intellectual and not moral hindrance stood between you and the Catholic Church. If I tell you the truth it is that you are trying the forbearance of God and that the most terrible things our Lord uttered were spoken to some who had to all appearance more excuse than you. The way you write, peculiar so far as I know among your school to yourself, whether blindness or as I suppose irony, I can only call desperate. I know that living a moral life, with the ordinances of religion and yourself a minister of them, with work to do and the interest of a catholicwards movement to support you, it is most natural to say *all things continue as they were* and most hard to realise the silence and the severity of God, as Dr Newman very eloquently and persuasively has said in a passage of the Anglican Difficulties; but this plea or way of thinking – all things continuing as they were – is the very character of infidelity. The difference between a state of grace and a state of reprobation, that difference to wh. all other differences of humanity are as the splitting of straws, makes no change in the outer world; faces, streets, and sunlight look just the same: it is therefore the more dangerous and terrible. And if God says that without faith it is impossible to please Him and will not excuse the best of heathens with the best of excuses for the want of it what is to be said of people who knowing it live in avowed doubt whether they are in His church or not? Will it comfort you at death not to have despaired of the English Church if by not despairing of it you are out of the Catholic Church? – a contingency which by the fact of doubt you contemplate. Will God thank you for yr. allegiance and will He excuse you for it? He asks obedience before everything else. Make half an hour's meditation on death and suppose you have received what you call the last sacrament: it will then occur – *perhaps* this is not a sacrament and if not it is a mockery to me and God; secondly, if it is, *perhaps* it is received in schism and I have wounded my soul with the 'instrument of salvation': this *perhaps* which gives little trouble on an ordinary Sunday will be very terrible then. Then if you add – but will not God allow for the possible mistake because I cd. not help being deceived? you will be able to answer – *certainly not*: I always knew there was a doubt. Dare to think of this fixedly even for three minutes if you will not make the longer meditation. And above all things say *Domine, quid vis ut faciam?* Say it and force yourself to mean it. Until you prefer God to the world and yourself you have not made the first step. You see I do not apologise for this language: it is, I think, now my right and my duty to use it. In conclusion I earnestly beg you to say *Domine, quid vis ut faciam?* and, if you will, ask our Lady's help. Believe me yr. affectionate friend—

GERARD M. HOPKINS

JOURNAL

1868

July 3. Dull morning; then fine; rain in evening. – The sea under dark clouds became quite black – fat and black but not dark – and when we were over a bank took white crests. – Saw some hops trellised. The Belgian hop-poles much higher than ours. – The leafage in England this year picked, nice, and scanty.

Started with Ed. Bond for Switzerland. We went by Dover and Ostende to Brussels.

July 4. Dull, with rain. After sunset, when we were on the further side of the river at Cologne, spanning the town the cathedral, and other towers [were] long girders or meridians of pale grey cloud, one within the other.

Yes, the cathedral is very meagre.

July 5. To mass at the cathedral. Then up the Rhine to Mainz. The Rhine hills are shaped in strict planes and coigns. Where the banks are flat mossy or velvet eyots of poplar edged with osier rise plump from the river.

The day was, I think, dull.

Watching from close the motion of a flag in the wind.

July 6. Rainy till lately (5 o'clock), when a low rainbow backed by the Black Forest hills, which were partly dimmed out with wet mist, appeared, and – what I never saw before – rays of shadow crossed it, all its round, and where they crossed it paled the colour. It was a 'blue bow'. That evening saw a shepherd *leading* his flock through the town.

By railway to Basel. Beautiful view from the train of the hills near Mülheim etc. They were clothed with wood and at the openings in this and indeed all upward too they were characterised by vertical stemming, dim in the distance. Villages a little bare like Brill rise in blocks of white and deep russet tiling. The nearer hills terraced with vine-yards deep and vertical, the pale grey shaven poles close on the railway leaning capriciously towards one another. – Here we met the young Englishman who had been to see Charlotte Bronte's school in Brussels. – The whole country full of walnut and cherry trees; oleanders in bloom; creeper is trained on houses and even the stations and waves in the wind.

But Basel at night! with a full moon waking the river and sending up straight beams from the heavy clouds that overhung it. We saw this from the bridge. The river runs so strong that it keeps the bridge shaking. Then we walked about the place and first of all had the adventure of the little Englishwoman with her hat off. We went through great spacious streets and places dead still and came to fountains of the clearest black water through which pieces of things at the bottom gleamed white. We got up to a height where a bastion-shaped vertical prominence shaded with chestnut trees looked down on the near roofs, which then in the moonlight were purple and velvety and edged along with ridges and chimneys of chalk whie. At woman came to a window with a candle and some mess she was making, and then that was gone and there was no light anywhere but the moon. We heard music indoors about. We saw the courtyard of a charming house with some tree pushing to the windows and a fountain. A church too of immensely high front all dead and flush to the top and next to it three most graceful flamboyant windows. Nothing could be more taking and fantastic than this stroll.

July 7. Fine morning; rain between Basel and Lucerne and in the evening.

We saw the Munster and the Museum – where is a noble dead Christ by the younger Holbein, but the other Holbeins were unimpressive; also a crucifixion by a German in which the types of the two thieves, especially the good thief – a young man with a moustache and a modern air – were in the wholeness and general scape of the anatomy original and interesting. (The prominence of the peculiar square-scaped drapery etc in Holbein and his contemporaries is remarkable – e.g. as a determination of German art.) There was one of those drawings in white upon black, purple, or bronze paper – I do not know the technical name – by Dürer – the crucifixion: the angel who is taking the soul of the good thief has the drapery flying in two coils and the last of these coils shellrayed ...

Storks' nests on the church roofs.

By rail through beautiful country to Lucerne: the Reuss deep green: our first view of Alps. Saw Thorvaldsen's monument in the evening, with the bats flitting round the pond.

Swiss trees are, like English, well inscaped – in quains.

July 8. Fine.

From Lucerne by steamer to Küssnacht, thence walk across to Immensee, thence by steamer over lake of Zug to Arth, whence up the Rigi. – The normal colour of the lake water, from near at least, bottle blue; from some way up we saw it with the sea shoaling colours, purple and blue, the purple expressing the rose of the chord to the eye (– in the same way as the same colour in a rose fading expresses the blue of the chord – the converse case: in fact it may perhaps be generalised that when this happens the modulation in question is the flat of the next term and not the sharp of the former one). From the top the lakes egg-blue, blue strongly modulated to green. – At sunset featherbed sky with a fluffy and jointed rib-cloud: I noticed one 'flock' of which I made a drawing was a long time with little change. – Huddling and precipitation of the fir woods down one side of the Rossberg following the fall of water like the sheep-flock at Shanklin did.

July 9. Before sunrise looking out of window saw a noble scape of stars – the Plough all golden falling, Cassiopeïa on end with her bright quains pointing to the right, the graceful bends of Perneus underneath her, and some great star whether Capella or not I am not sure risen over the brow of the mountain. Sunrise we saw well: the north landscape was blighty but the south, the important one, with the Alps, clear; lower down all was mist and flue of white cloud, which grew thicker as day went on and like a junket lay scattered on the lakes. The sun lit up the bright acres of the snows at first with pink but afterwards clear white: the snow of the Bernese Highland remained from its distance pinkish all day. – The mountain ranges, as any series or body of inanimate like things not often seen, have the air of persons and of interrupted activity; they are multitudinous too, and also they express a second level with an upper world or shires of snow. – In going down between Pilatus and a long streak of cloud the blue sky was greenish. Since, I have found this colour is seen in looking from the snow to the sky but why I do not understand: can there possibly be a rose hue suppressed in the white (– *purpurea candidior nive*)? ...

July 20. Fine.

Walked down to the Rhone glacier. It has three stages – first a smoothly-moulded bed in a pan or theatre of thorny peaks, swells of ice rising through the snow-sheet and the snow itself tossing and fretting into the sides of the rock walls in spray-like points: this is the first stage of the glaciers generally; it is like bright-plucked water swaying in a pail –; second, after a slope nearly covered with landslips of moraine, was a ruck of horned waves steep and narrow in the gut: now in the upper Grindelwald glacier between the bed or highest stage was a descending limb which was like the rude and knotty bossings of a strombus shell –; third the foot, a broad limb opening out and reaching the plain, shaped like the fan-fin of a dolphin or a great bivalve shell turned on its face, the flutings in either case being suggested by the crevasses and the ribs by the risings between them, these being swerved and inscaped strictly to the motion of the mass. Or you may compare the three stages to the heel, instep, and ball or toes of a foot. – The second stage looked at from nearer appeared like a box of plaster of Paris or starch or toothpowder, a little moist, tilted up and then struck and jarred so that the powder broke and tumbled in shapes and rifts.

We went into the grotto and also the vault from which the Rhone flows. It looked like a blue tent and as you went further in changed to lilac. As you come out the daylight glazes the groins with gleaming rosecolour. The ice inside has a branchy wire texture. The man shewed us the odd way in which a little piece of ice will stick against the walls – as if drawn by a magnet.

Standing on the glacier saw the prismatic colours in the clouds, and worth saying what sort of clouds: it was fine shapeless skins of fretted make, full of eyebrows or like linings of curled leaves which one finds in shelved corners of a wood.

I had a trudge over the glacier and a tumble over the side moraine, which was one landslip of limestone. It was neighboured however by hot sweet smells and many flowers – small crimson pinks, the brown tulip-like flower we have seen so often, another which we first saw yesterday like Solomon's seal but rather coarser with a spike of greenish veiny-leaved blossom, etc.

At the *table d'hôte* of the inn there I first saw that repulsive type of French face. It is hard to seize what it is. The outline is oval but cut away at the jaws; the eyes are big, shallow-set, close to the eyebrows, and near, the upper lid straight and long, the lower brought down to a marked corner in the middle, the pupils large and clear; the nostrils prominent; the lips fleshy, long, and unwaved, with a vertical curling at the end (in one case at any rate); the nose curved hollow or so tending; the head large; the skin fair – white and scarlet colour.

We drove down the Rhone valley to Visp and soon entered a Catholic canton. The churches here have those onion steeples nearly all, the onion being in some cases newly covered with bright tin or lead: they remind one of tinselled humming-tops too. – They enclose the head of the cross in a triangle ... it looks like a beacon at sea.

Soon we saw the vines trellised. – Hemp swaying in its sweet-smelling thickset beds. – That sprayed silvery weed something like tamarisk leaned over the road: what is it? Maize very high. –

Spanish chestnuts: their inscape here bold, jutty, somewhat oak-like, attractive, the branching visible and the leaved peaks spotted so as to make crests of eyes.

Plushy look and very rich warm green of mountain grass, noticed especially at the Rhone glacier.

In the valley a girl with spindle and distaff tending cows.

July 21. Bright.

We walked up the valley of the Visp to Zermatt, a beautiful valley and the river in torrent.

Vines, as I have often seen, like the fretting of pike-blades.

Chalky blue of cornflowers.

We lunched at St. Niclaus and shortly after leaving it saw the Little Matterhorn and the Breithorn closing the valley. The latter is like a broad piece of hacked or knocked flint-stone – flint of the half-chalky sort, for the mountain is covered with snow, while the breaks of rock remind one of the dark eyes or spots in the white; and this resemblance did not disappear even at much nearer.

Tall larches by the river.

Coffee-foam waterfalls ran into the Visp, which above one of these being paler and becoming at the place a little smoother – for else it never for a hand's breadth could recover from one crumpled sheet of jolting foam – looked like a strew of waving poppy-leaf.

Note how river billows all look back.

Not unapparent that the Matterhorn is like a Greek galley stranded, a reared-up rostrum – the sharp quains or arrêtes the gunwales, the deck of the forecastle looking upon Zermatt, the figure-head looking the other way reaching up in the air, the cutwater and ram descending and abutting on a long reef – the gable-length of the mountain.

July 22. Morning fine; in the afternoon rain as we went up the Riffel; fine evening.

Up the Riffel from which, the point of view somewhat changing, the Matterhorn looks like a sea-lion couchant or a sphinx, and again like the hooded-snake frontal worn by the Egyptian kings.

After a dinner up a height from which we saw a little less fully the Gornergrat prospect – on the extreme left (beyond which the Gornergrat heights rose) Monte Rosa, then the Lyskamm, then the Jumeaux, then the Breithorn, and, after the break made by the Riffelhorn immediately before us, the Matterhorn. (The Little

Matterhorn is thus eclipsed.) Of these the first four names are round-headed; the Little Matterhorn couples the two inscapes, being a sharpened bolt rising from a flattened shoulder; in the Great Matterhorn the shoulder – not what is specially so called, which rises to within a little of the summit, but a much lower ridge – is unimportant, the stem of the mountain edged and sharpened to an unparalleled degree – a mere fang –, but still lancet-shaped, convex: the range on the other side of Zermatt and skirting the Zermatt valley are concave, cusped; they run like waves in the wind, ricked and sharply inscaped – first on the left and furthest the Dent Blanche; next in two crests which gracefully accent a shell head the Gabelhorn; then the Rothhorn, a rickety crest pitching over, acutely leaved or notched; then the Weisshorn, of which the lines are the ideal inflexions of a mountain-peak; after that, across the Zermatt valley, the Mischabel and the view intercepted.

The Monte Rosa range are dragged over with snow like cream. As we looked at them the sky behind them became dead purple, the effect unique; and then the snow according to its lie and its faces differenced itself, the upward-looking faces taking shade, the vertical light, like lovely damask. Above the Breithorn Antares sparkled like a bright crab-apple tingling in the wind.

JOURNAL (*Roehampton*)

23 Dec. 1869

Yesterday morning I was dreaming I was with George Simcox and was considering how to get away in time to ring the bells here which as porter I had to ring (I was made porter on the 12th of the month, I think, and had the office for a little more than two months). I knew that I was dreaming and made this odd dilemma in my dream: either I am not really with Simcox and then it does not matter what I do, or if I am, waking will carry me off without my needing to do anything – and with this I was satisfied.

Another day in the evening after Litanies as Father Rector was giving the points for meditation I shut my eyes, being very tired, and without ceasing to hear him began to dream. The dream-images seemed to rise and overlie those which belonged to what he was saying and I saw one of the Apostles – he was talking about the

Apostles – as if pressed against by a piece of wood about half a yard long and a few inches across, like a long box with two of the long sides cut off. Even then I could not understand what the piece of wood did encumbering the apostle. Now this piece of wood I had often seen in an outhouse and being that week 'A Secretis' I had seen it longer together and had been that day wondering what it was: in reality it is used to hold a little heap of cinders against the wall which keep from the frost a piece of earthenware pipe which there comes out and goes in again making a projection in the wall. It is just the things which produce dead impressions, which the mind, either because you cannot make them out or because they were perceived across other more engrossing thoughts, has made nothing of and brought into no scaping, that force themselves up in this way afterwards . . .

One day in the Long Retreat (which ended on Xmas Day) they were reading in the refectory Sister Emmerich's account of the Agony in the Garden and I suddenly began to cry and sob and could not stop. I put it down for this reason, that if I had been asked a minute beforehand I should have said that nothing of the sort was going to happen and even when it did I stood in a manner wondering at myself not seeing in my reason the traces of an adequate cause for such strong emotion – the traces of it I say because of course the cause in itself is adequate for the sorrow of a lifetime. I remember much the same thing on Maundy Thursday when the presanctified Host was carried to the sacristy. But neither the weight nor the stress of sorrow, that is to say of the thing which should cause sorrow, by themselves move us or bring the tears as a sharp knife does not cut for being pressed as long as it is pressed without any shaking of the hand but there is always one touch, something striking sideways and unlooked for, which in both cases undoes resistance and pierces, and this may be so delicate that the pathos seems to have gone directly to the body and cleared the understanding in its passage. On the other hand the pathetic touch by itself, as in dramatic pathos, will only draw slight tears if its matter is not important or not of import to us, the strong emotion coming from a force which was gathered before it was discharged: in this way a knife may pierce the flesh which it had happened only to graze and only grazing will go no deeper . . .

TO HIS MOTHER

The Seminary, Stonyhurst, near Blackburn. 10 Sept. 1870

MY DEAREST MOTHER, – I took my vows on the morning of the 8th and came here next day, yesterday. It is vacation time: the scholastics are still in their holidays till the 2nd of October. I will tell you more about the place when I know more but it is certain that it is an excellent country for walks, beauty, and general interest. On our way we dined at Manchester and saw our new church which is building. It is so big as to be a sort of cathedral, but I did not think very highly of it. We disembarked at Whalley, a little place in a valley of the moors with an abbey ruin and otherwise worth seeing and we were driven four miles over the Hodder and Calder rivers ('yon brig's over the Cauder' a little native told me) up and down hill to this house. 'The yellow moonlight slept on all the hills': I could not even on one, the one we stand upon, all night nearly. The window of the room I am in commands a beautiful range of moors dappled with light and shade. It has rained many times already and I know it will go on so to the end of the chapter. I can feel that summer is but diluted here. They say it is mild in winter compared with places more south and I partly believe it; that is I believe it is mild in winter compared with places more north. But a Scotchman told me Argyleshire was the mildest part of Great Britain and that trees etc grow there which will grow no where else. At all events both are near the sea and in the eye of the west wind. Three of my companions had been a year with me in the noviceship and I found others among the seminarians and one of them in particular a most charming fellow: there was moonlight, supper, and a pleasant sociable bustle which made a welcome. By daylight I feel the strangeness of the place and the noviceship after two years seems like a second home: it made me sad to look at the crucifix and things Fr Gallwey gave me when I was going. He was very kind. But the brotherly charity of everyone here can be felt at once: indeed it is always what you take for granted. I can speak more freely now because I have bound myself to our Lord for ever to be poor, chaste, and obedient like Him and it delights me to think of it. I must now make haste and conclude. I will write again soon. With best love to all believe me always your loving son

GERARD HOPKINS

JOURNAL

Sept. 24 – First saw the Northern Lights. My eye was caught by beams of light and dark very like the crown of horny rays the sun makes behind a cloud. At first I thought of silvery cloud until I saw that these were more luminous and did not dim the clearness of the stars in the Bear. They rose slightly radiating thrown out from the earthline. Then I saw soft pulses of light one after another rise and pass upwards arched in shape but waveringly and with the arch broken. They seemed to float, not following the warp of the sphere as falling stars look to do but free though concentrical with it. This busy working of nature wholly independent of the earth and seeming to go on in a strain of time not reckoned by our reckoning of days and years but simpler and as if correcting the preoccupation of the world by being preoccupied with and appealing to and dated to the day of judgment was like a new witness to God and filled me with delightful fear.

Oct. 20 – Laus Deo – the river today and yesterday. Yesterday it was a sallow glassy gold at Hodder Roughs and by watching hard the banks began to sail upstream, the scaping unfolded, the river was all in tumult but not running, only the lateral motions were perceived, and the curls of froth where the waves overlap shaped and turned easily and idly. – I meant to have written more. – Today the river was wild, very full, glossy brown with mud, furrowed in permanent billows through which from head to head the water swung with a great down and up again. These heads were scalped with rags of jumping foam. But at the Roughs the sight was the burly water-backs which heave after heave kept tumbling up from the broken foam and their plump heap turning open in ropes of velvet.

Oct. 25 – A little before 7 in the evening a wonderful Aurora, the same that was seen at Rome (shortly after its seizure by the Italian government) and taken as a sign of God's anger. It gathered a little below the zenith, to the S.E. I think – a knot or crown, not a true circle, of dull blood-coloured horns and dropped long red beams down the sky on every side, each impaling its lot of stars. An hour or so later its colour was gone but there was still a pale crown in the same place: the skies were then clear and ashy and fresh with stars and there were flashes of or like sheet-lightning. The day had been very bright and clear, distances smart, herds of towering pillow clouds, one great stack in particular over Pendle was knoppled all over in fine snowy tufts and pencilled with bloom-shadow of the greatest delicacy. In the sunset all was big and there was a world of swollen cloud holding the yellow-rose light like a lamp while a few sad milky blue slips passed below it. At night violent hailstorms and hail again next day, and a solar halo. Worth noticing too perhaps the water-runs were then mulled and less beautiful than usual.

Dec. 19 or thereabouts a very fine sunrise: the higher cloud was like seams of red candle-wax.

On April 29 or thereabouts *at sunset* in the same quarter of the sky I saw, as far as I could remember it, almost the very same scape, the same colour and so on, down to a wavy wisp or rather seam above the rest – and this made by the sun shining from the West instead of the East. It was not so brilliant though.

The winter was long and hard. I made many observations on freezing. For instance the crystals in mud. – Hailstones are shaped like the cut of diamonds called brilliants. – I found one morning the ground in one corner of the garden full of small pieces of potsherd from which there rose up (and not dropped off) long icicles carried on in some way each like a forepitch of the shape of the piece of potsherd it grew on, like a tooth to its root for instance, and most of them bended over and curled like so many tusks or horns or / best of all and what they looked likest when they first caught my eye / the first soft root-spurs thrown out from a sprouting chestnut. This bending of the icicle seemed so far as I could see not merely a resultant, where the smaller spars of which it was made were still straight, but to have flushed them too. – The same day and others the garden mould very crisp and meshed over with a lace-work of needles leaving (they seemed) three-cornered openings: it looked greyish and like a coat of gum on wood. Also the smaller crumbs and clods were lifted fairly up from the ground on upright ice-pillars, whether they had dropped these from themselves or drawn them from the soil: it was like a little Stonehenge – Looking down into the thick ice of our pond I found the imprisoned air-bubbles nothing at random but starting from centres and in particular one most beautifully regular white brush of them, each spur of it a curving string of beaded and diminishing bubbles – The pond, I suppose from over pressure when it was less firm, was mapped with a puzzle of very slight clefts branched with little sprigs: the pieces were odd-shaped and sized – though a square angular scaping could be just made out in the outline but the cracks ran deep through the ice markedly in planes and always the planes of the cleft on the surface. They remained and in the end the ice broke up in just these deep pieces.

To Baillie

Stonyhurst. 10 April 1871

My Dear Baillie, – Your letters are always welcome but often or always it is more pleasant to get them than easy to see how they are to be answered. So with today's dinner and tomorrow's twelve months' butcher's bill. My time is short both for writing and reading, so that I can seldom write and when I do I have nothing to say. Don't you know, it is mainly about books and so on that I shd. be writing and I read so few. I am going through a hard course of scholastic logic (not just at present: it is holidays) which takes all the fair part of the day and leaves one fagged at the end for what remains. This makes the life painful to nature. I find now too late *how* to read – at least some books, e.g. the classics: now I see things, now what I read tells, but I am obliged to read by snatches. – I will not go a step further till I have explained that down to the bottom of the last page I was writing with the worst of steel pens and most of it with a dreadfully cold hand but now the grey goose and I are come to terms at the point of the knife – this to forestall your cuts and snarls at my material worsening.

I will tell you something about this place. Perpetual winter smiles. In the first place we have the highest rain-guage in England, I believe: this our observatory shews and a local rhyme expresses as much. Early in the year they told me there wd. be no spring such as we understood it in the south. When I asked about May they told me they had hail in May. Of June they told me it had one year been so cold that the procession could not be held on Corpus Christi. The country is also very bare and bleak – what its enemies say of

Scotland, only that a young Campbell at Roehampton shewed me that Argyleshire was the warmest part of Great Britain, that green-house fuchsias grew in the open air, and that the pomegranate was for ever on the bough. But nevertheless it is fine scenery, great hills and 'fells' with noble outlines often, subject to charming effects of light (though I am bound to say that total obscuration is the commonest effect of all), and three beautiful rivers. The clouds in particular are more interesting than in any other place I have seen. But they must be full of soot, for the fleeces of the sheep are quite black with it. We also see the northern lights to advantage at times. There is good fishing for those who do not see that after bad fishing the next worst thing is good fishing. At the College close by is a big library.

Let me see what books I can speak of. – I find nothing or nothing that I cd. at present say shortly and if I keep this longer I might perhaps never send it. I am glad to hear literary etc news as I am here removed from it and get much behind. I hope you find yourself happy in town: this life here though it is hard is God's will for me as I most intimately know, which is more than violets knee-deep. This sprig of rhetoric brings me to a close. Believe me always your affectionate friend—

GERARD M. HOPKINS

JOURNAL

[April 15] The white violets are broader and smell; the blue, scentless and finer made, have a sharper whelking and a more winged recoil in the leaves.

Take a *few* primroses in a glass and the instress of – brilliancy, sort of starriness: I have not the right word – so simple a flower gives is remarkable. It is, I think, due to the strong swell given by the deeper yellow middle.

'The young lambs bound As to the tabour's sound'.
They toss and toss: it is as if it were the earth that flung them, not themselves. It is the pitch of graceful agility when we think that. – April 16 – Sometimes they rest a little space on the hind legs and the fore-feet drop curling in on the breast, not so liquidly as we see it in the limbs of foals though.

Bright afternoon; clear distances; Pendle dappled with tufted shadow; west wind; interesting clouding, flat and lying in the warp of the heaven but the pieces with rounded outline and dolphin-backs shewing in places and all was at odds and at Z's, one piece with another. Later beautifully delicate crisping. Later rippling ...

April 21 – We have had other such afternoons, one today – the sky a beautiful grained blue, silky lingering clouds in flat-bottomed loaves, others a little browner in ropes or in burly-shouldered ridges swanny and lustrous, more in the Zenith stray packs of a sort of violet paleness. White-rose cloud formed fast, not in the same density – some caked and swimming in a wan whiteness, the rest soaked with the blue and like the leaf of a flower held against the light and diapered out by the worm or veining of deeper blue between rosette and rosette. Later / moulding, which brought rain: in perspective it was vaulted in very regular ribs with fretting between: but these are not ribs; they are a 'wracking' install made of these two realities – the frets, which are scarves of rotten cloud bellying upwards and drooping at their ends and shaded darkest at the brow or tropic where they double to the eye, and the whiter field of sky shewing between: the illusion looking down the 'wagon' is complete. These swaths of fretted cloud move in rank, not in file.

April 22 – But such a lovely damasking in the sky as today I never felt before. The blue was charged with simple instress, the higher, zenith sky earnest and frowning, lower more light and sweet. High up again, breathing through woolly coats of cloud or on the quains and branches of the flying pieces it was the true exchange of crimson, nearer the earth / against the sun / it was turquoise, and in the opposite south-western bay below the sun it was like clear oil but just as full of colour, shaken over with slanted flashing 'travellers', all in flight, stepping one behind the other, their edges tossed with bright ravelling, as if white napkins were thrown up in the sun but not quite at the same moment so that they were all in a scale down the air falling one after the other to the ground.

April 27 – Went to see Sauley Abbey (Cistercian): there is little to see.

Mesmerised a duck with chalk lines drawn from her beak sometimes level and sometimes forwards on a black table. They explain that the bird keeping the abiding offscape of the hand grasping her neck fancies she is still held down and cannot lift her head as long as she looks at the chalk line, which she associates with the power that holds her. This duck lifted her head at once when I put it down on the table without chalk. But this seems inadequate. It is most likely the fascinating instress of the straight white stroke.

To Kate Hopkins

Stonyhurst. 25 April, 1871

My Dear Katie, – Many thanks for your letter, which I was delighted to get. When it first came to hand I stood balancing in my mind who it could be from, there was such a youngladyship and grownupdom about the address, until I remembered that you were older than you used to be. As for me, I will say no more than this, that I have prescribed myself twenty four hourglasses a day (which I take even during sleep, such is the force of habit) and that even this does not stop the ravages of time.

What month in the year it may be at Hampstead I will not be sure; with us it is a whity-greeny January. What with east winds, cloud, and rain I think it will never be spring. If we have a bright afternoon the next morning it is winter again.

We were all vaccinated the other day. The next day a young Portuguese came up to me and said 'Oh misther 'Opkins, do *you* feel the cows in *yewer* arm?' I told him I felt the horns coming through. I do I am sure. I cannot remember now whether one ought to say the calf of the arm or the calf of the leg. My shoulder is like a shoulder of beef. I dare not speak above a whisper for fear of bellowing – there now, I was going to say I am obliged to speak low for fear of lowing. I dream at night that I have only two of my legs in bed. I think there is a split coming in both my slippers. Yesterday I could not think why it was that I would wander about on a wet grass-plot: I see now. I chew my pen a great deal. The long and short of it is that my left forequarter is swollen and painful (I meant to have written arm but I cowld not). Besides the doctor has given us medicine, so that I am in a miserable way just now.

From cows I will turn to lambs. Our fields are full of them. When they were a little younger and nicer and sillier they wd. come gambolling up to one as if one were their mother. One of them sucked my finger and my companion took another up in his arms.

The ewes then came up and walked round us making suspicious sheep's eyes at us, as people say. Now, when they are not sucking the breast (to do which they make such terrific butts and digs at the old dam that two of them together will sometimes lift her off her hind legs) they spend their time in bounding and spinning round as if they were tumblers. The same thing is I daresay to be seen (and earlier than this) about Hampstead: still as many of these lambs are ours I cannot pass it by and must tell you of it in black and white.

One thing made me very sad the day we were vaccinated. I was coming away: I left a number of my companions in a room in the infirmary – some had come from the doctor and others were waiting for their turn – all laughing and chatting. As I came down one of the galleries from the room I saw one of our young men standing there looking at a picture. I wondered why he stayed by himself and did not join the rest and then afterwards I remembered that he had had the smallpox and was deeply marked with it and all his good looks gone which he would have had and he did not want to face the others at that time when they were having their fun taking safe precautions against catching what it was too late for him to take any precautions against.

I want to know two things by the next person who writes – first some particulars from Arthur about the American yacht Sappho which seems to have had such great successes last year and next whether it is true that the cuckoo has come unusually early this year, as I heard said. It has not come here yet and I do not know if it will.

With best love to all believe me your loving brother

GERARD M. HOPKINS

JOURNAL

[May 9] This day and May 11 the bluebells in the little wood between the College and the highroad and in one of the Hurst Green cloughs. In the little wood / opposite the light / they stood in blackish spreads or sheddings like the spots on a snake. The heads are then like thongs and solemn in grain and grape-colour. But in the clough / through the light / they came in falls of sky-colour washing the brows and slacks of the ground with vein-blue, thickening at the double, vertical themselves and the young grass and brake fern combed vertical, but the brake struck the upright of

all this with light winged transomes. It was a lovely sight. – The
bluebells in your hand baffle you with their inscape, made to every
sense: if you draw your fingers through them they are lodged and
struggle / with a shock of wet heads; the long stalks rub and click
and flatten to a fan on one another like your fingers themselves
would when you passed the palms hard across one another, making
a brittle rub and jostle like the noise of a hurdle strained by leaning
against; then there is the faint honey smell and in the mouth the
sweet gum when you bite them. But this is easy, it is the eye they
baffle. They give one a fancy of panpipes and of some wind instru-
ment with stops – a trombone perhaps. The overhung necks – for
growing they are little more than a staff with a simple crook but in
water, where they stiffen, they take stronger turns, in the head like
sheephooks or, when more waved throughout, like the waves
riding through a whip that is being smacked – what with these over-
hung necks and what with the crisped ruffled bells dropping mostly
on one side and the gloss these have at their footstalks they have an
air of the knights at chess. Then the knot or 'knoop' of buds some
shut, some just gaping, which makes the pencil of the whole spike,
should be noticed: the inscape of the flower most finely carried out
in the siding of the axes, each striking a greater and greater slant, is
finished in these clustered buds, which for the most part are not
straightened but rise to the end like a tongue and this and their
tapering and a little flattening they have made them look like the
heads of snakes.

TO BRIDGES

Stonyhurst. 2 Aug. 1871

MY DEAR BRIDGES, – Our holidays have begun, so I will write
again. I feel inclined to begin by asking whether you are secretary
to the International as you seem to mean me to think nothing too
bad for you but then I remember that you never relished 'the
intelligent artisan'. I must tell you I am always thinking of the Com-
munist future. The too intelligent artisan is master of the situation I
believe. Perhaps it is what everyone believes, I do not see the papers
or hear strangers often enough to know. It is what Carlyle has long
threatened and foretold. But his writings are, as he might himself

say, 'most inefficacious-strenuous heaven-protestations, caterwaul, and Cassandra-wailings'. He preaches obedience but I do not think he has done much except to ridicule instead of strengthening the hands of the powers that be. Some years ago when he published his *Shooting Niagara* he did make some practical suggestions but so vague that they should rather be called '*too* dubious moonstone-grindings and on the whole impracticable-practical unveracities'. However I am afraid some great revolution is not far off. Horrible to say, in a manner I am a Communist. Their ideal bating some things is nobler than that professed by any secular statesman I know of (I must own I live in bat-light and shoot at a venture). Besides it is just. – I do not mean the means of getting to it are. But it is a dreadful thing for the greatest and most necessary part of a very rich nation to live a hard life without dignity, knowledge, comforts, delight, or hopes in the midst of plenty – which plenty they make. They profess that they do not care what they wreck and burn, the old civilisation and order must be destroyed. This is a dreadful look out but what has the old civilisation done for them? As it at present stands in England it is itself in great measure founded on wrecking. But they got none of the spoils, they came in for nothing but harm from it then and thereafter. England has grown hugely wealthy but this wealth has not reached the working classes; I expect it has made their condition worse. Besides this iniquitous order the old civiliza-tion embodies another order mostly old and what is new in direct entail from the old, the old religion, learning, law, art, etc and all the history that is preserved in standing monuments. But as the working classes have not been educated they know next to nothing of all this and cannot be expected to care if they destroy it. The more I look the more black and deservedly black the future looks, so I will write no more . . .

JOURNAL

[July 19, 1872] Stepped into a barn of ours, a great shadowy barn, where the hay had been stacked on either side, and looking at the great rudely arched timberframes – principals(?) and tie-beams, which make them look like bold big *A*s with the cross-bar high up – I thought how sadly beauty of inscape was unknown and buried away from simple people and yet how near at hand it was if they had eyes to see it and it could be called out everywhere again . . .

After the examinations we went for our holiday out to Douglas in the Isle of Man. Aug. 3 – At this time I had first begun to get hold of the copy of Scotus on the Sentences in the Baddely library and was flush with a new stroke of enthusiasm. It may come to nothing or it may be a mercy from God. But just then when I took in any inscape of the sky or sea I thought of Scotus . . .

Aug. 10 – I was looking at high waves. The breakers always are parallel to the coast and shape themselves to it except where the curve is sharp however the wind blows. They are rolled out by the shallowing shore just as a piece of putty between the palms whatever its shape runs into a long roll. The slant ruck or crease one sees in them shows the way of the wind. The regularity of the barrels surprised and charmed the eye; the edge behind the comb or crest was as smooth and bright as glass. It may be noticed to be green behind and silver white in front: the silver marks where the air begins, the pure white is foam, the green / solid water. Then looked at to the right or left they are scrolled over like mouldboards or feathers or jibsails seen by the edge. It is pretty to see the hollow of the barrel disappearing as the white combs on each side run along the wave gaining ground till the two meet at a pitch and crush and overlap each other.

About all the turns of the scaping from the break and flooding of wave to its run out again I have not yet satisfied myself. The shores are swimming and the eyes have before them a region of milky surf but it is hard for them to unpack the huddling and gnarls of the water and law out the shapes and the sequence of the running: I catch however the looped or forked wisp made by every big pebble the backwater runs over – if it were clear and smooth there would be a network from their overlapping, such as can in fact be seen on smooth sand after the tide is out –; then I saw it run browner, the foam dwindling and twitched into long chains of suds, while the strength of the backdraught shrugged the stones together and clocked them one against another . . .

April 8 [1873] – The ashtree growing in the corner of the garden was felled. It was lopped first: I heard the sound and looking out and seeing it maimed there came at that moment a great pang and I wished to die and not to see the inscapes of the world destroyed any more.

April 17 – To Whitewell with Mr Clarke. Saw a shoal of salmon in the river and many hares on the open hills. Under a stone hedge was a dying ram: there ran slowly from his nostril a thick flesh-coloured ooze, scarlet in places, coiling and roping its way down, so thick that it looked like fat . . .

June 16 – Still brighter and warmer, southern-like. Shadows sharp in the quarry and on the shoulders of our two young white pigeons. There is some charm about a thing such as these pigeons or trees when they dapple their boles in wearing its own shadow. I was on the fells with Mr Strappini. They were all melled and painted with colour and full of roaming scents, and winged silver slips of young brake rising against the light trim and symmetrical and gloried from within reminded me of I do not remember what detail of coats of arms, perhaps the lilies of Eton College, Meadows smeared yellow with buttercups and bright squares of rapefield in the landscape. Fine-weather bales of cloud. Napkin folds brought out on the Parlick ridge and capfulls of shadow in them. A cuckoo flew by with a little bird after it as we lay by the quarry at Kemble End.

As I passed the stables later and stayed to look at the peacocks John Myerscough came out to shew me a brood of little peafowl (though it could not be found at that time) and the kindness touched my heart.

I looked at the pigeons down in the kitchen yard and so on. They look like little gay jugs by shape when they walk, strutting and jod-jodding with their heads. The two young ones are all white and the pins of the folded wings, quill pleated over quill, are like crisp and shapely cuttleshells found on the shore. The others are dull thundercolour or black-grape-colour except in the white pieings, the quills and tail, and in the shot of the neck. I saw one up on the eaves of the roof: as it moved its head a crush of satin green came and went, a wet or soft flaming of the light.

Sometimes I hear the cuckoo with wonderful clear and plump and fluty notes: it is when the hollow of a rising ground conceives them and palms them up and throws them out, like blowing into a big humming ewer – for instance under Saddle Hill one beautiful day and another time from Hodder wood when we walked on the other side of the river . . .

July 22 – Very hot, though the wind, which was south, dappled very sweetly on one's face and when I came out I seemed to put it on like a gown as a man puts on the shadow he walks into and hoods or hats himself with the shelter of a roof, a penthouse, or a copse of trees, I mean it rippled and fluttered like light linen, one could feel the folds and braids of it – and indeed a floating flag is like wind visible and what weeds are in a current; it gives it thew and fires it and bloods it in. – Thunderstorm in the evening, first booming in gong-sounds, as at Aosta, as if high up and so not reechoed from the hills; the lightning very slender and nimble and as if playing very near but after supper it was so bright and terrible some people said they had never seen its like. People were killed, but in other parts of the country it was more violent than with us. Flashes lacing two clouds above or the cloud and the earth started upon the eyes in live veins of rincing or riddling liquid white, inched and jagged as if it were the shivering of a bright riband string which had once been kept bound round a blade and danced back into its pleatings. Several strong thrills of light followed the flash but a grey smother of darkness blotted the eyes if they had seen the fork, also dull furry thickened scapes of it were left in them.

July 24 – A Blandyke. Mr Colley and I crossed the river at Hacking boat, went up the fell opposite near the Nab, walked some way, and coming down at Billington recrossed at the Troughs and so home. But the view was dim. A farmer on the other side at the Troughs talked of the driver of the mower (he had one) 'a-peerkin' on the seat', being perched on the seat, and said the hay was to be 'shaked'. The ferryman told us how in the hot days working in the hay he had 'Sûpped beer till' he 'could sûp no more' . . .

July 9 [Roehampton, 1874]. To the Oratory. Addis was away but Fr Law was kind and hospitable. I met Mr David Lewis, a great Scotist, and at the same time old Mr Brande Morris was making a retreat with us: I got to know him, so that oddly I made the acquaintance of two and I suppose the only two Scotists in England in one week.

Heat has come on now. The air is full of the sweet acid of the limes. The trees themselves are starrily tasselled with the blossom. I remark that our cedars, which had a warp upward in the flats of leaf, in getting their new green turn and take a soft and beautiful warp downwards: whether it is the lushness or the weight of the young needles or both I cannot tell. They are now very beautiful in shape and colour.

July 12. I noticed the smell of the big cedar, not just in passing it but always at a patch of sunlight on the walk a little way off. I found the bark smelt in the sun and not in the shade and I fancied too this held even of the smell it shed in the air.

July 13 – The comet – I have seen it at bedtime in the west, with head to the ground, white, a soft well-shaped tail, not big: I felt a certain awe and instress, a feeling of strangeness, flight (it hangs like a shuttlecock at the height, before it falls), and of threatening.

By the by Mr Knowles was here lately to see Fr Johnson. He has now left the Society.

July 14 – To the House of Commons. The debate was on the Schools Endowment bill moved by Lord Sandon, who spoke well; so did, not *so* well, Mr Forster in reply. We heard Newdigate. Gladstone was preparing to speak and writing fast but we could not stay to hear him. Lowe, who sat next him, looked something like an apple in the snow.

July 23 – To Beaumont: it was the rector's day. It was a lovely day: shires-long of pearled cloud under cloud, with a grey stroke underneath marking each row; beautiful blushing yellow in the straw of the uncut ryefields, the wheat looking white and all the ears making a delicate and very true crisping along the top and with just enough air stirring for them to come and go gently; then there were fields reaping. All this I would have looked at again in returning but during dinner I talked too freely and unkindly and had to do penance going home. One field I saw from the balcony of the house behind an elmtree, which it threw up, like a square of pale goldleaf, as it might be, catching the light.

Our schools at Roehampton ended with two days of examination before St. Ignatius' feast the 31st. I was very tired and seemed deeply cast down till I had some kind words from the Provincial. Altogether perhaps my heart has never been so burdened and cast down as this year. The tax on my strength has been greater than I have felt before: at least now at Teignmouth I feel myself weak and can do little. But in all this our Lord goes His own way.

To his Father

St. Beuno's, St. Asaph, North Wales. 29 Aug. 1874

MY DEAREST FATHER, – I came here yesterday, to begin my studies in theology. I had expected to have another year's teaching at Roehampton, but now my ordination and profession will be earlier. The house stands on a steep hillside, it commands the long-drawn valley of the Clwyd to the sea, a vast prospect, and opposite is Snowdon and its range, just now it being bright visible but coming and going with the weather. The air seems to me very fresh and wholesome. Holidays till the 2nd of October. After that hours of study very close – lectures in dogmatic theology, moral ditto, canon law, church history, scripture, Hebrew and what not. I have half a mind to get up a little Welsh: all the neighbours speak it. I have said nothing about the house. It is built of limestone, decent outside, skimpin within, Gothic, like Lancing College done worse. The staircases, galleries, and bopeeps are inexpressible: it takes a fortnight to learn them. Pipes of affliction convey lukewarm water of affliction to some of the rooms, others more fortunate have fires. The garden is all heights, terraces, Excelsiors, misty mountain tops, seats up trees called Crows' Nests, flights of steps seemingly up to heaven lined with burning aspiration upon aspiration of scarlet geraniums: it is very pretty and airy but it gives you the impression that if you took a step farther you would find yourself somewhere on Plenlimmon, Conway Castle, or Salisbury Craig. With best love to detachments stationed at Hampstead believe me your loving son,

GERARD M. HOPKINS S.J.

JOURNAL

Sept. 6 – With Wm Kerr, who took me up a hill behind ours (ours is Mynefyr), a furze-grown and heathy hill, from which I could look round the whole country, up the valley towards Ruthin and down to the sea. The cleave in which Bodfari and Caerwys lie was close below. It was a leaden sky, braided or roped with cloud, and the earth in dead colours, grave but distinct. The heights by Snowdon were hidden by the clouds but not from distance or dimness. The nearer hills, the other side of the valley, shewed a hard and beautifully detached and glimmering brim against the light, which was lifting there. All the length of the valley the skyline of hills was flowingly written all along upon the sky. A blue bloom, a sort of meal, seemed to have spread upon the distant south, enclosed by a basin of hills. Looking all round but most in looking far up the valley I felt an instress and charm of Wales. Indeed in coming here I began to feel a desire to do something for the conversion of Wales. I began to learn Welsh too but not with very pure intentions per-

haps. However on consulting the Rector on this, the first day of the
retreat, he discouraged it unless it were purely for the sake of
labouring among the Welsh. Now it was not and so I saw I must
give it up. At the same time my music seemed to come to an end.
Yet, rather strangely, I had no sooner given up these two things
(which disappointed me and took an interest away – and at that
time I was very bitterly feeling the weariness of life and shed many
tears, perhaps not wholly into the breast of God but with some un-
manliness in them too, and sighed and panted to Him), I had no
sooner given up the Welsh than my desire seemed to be for the
conversion of Wales and I had it in mind to give up everything else
for that; nevertheless weighing this by St. Ignatius' rules of election
I decided not to do so.

To his Mother

St. Beuno's. 20 Sept. 1874

My Dearest Mother, – I have been in an eight days' retreat end-
ing on Friday night. On Friday, Saturday, and today ordinations
have been going on here; sixteen priests were ordained this morn-
ing. I received the tonsure and the four minor orders yesterday. The
tonsure consisted of five little snips but the bishop must have found
even that a hard job, for I had cut my hair almost to the scalp, as it
happened, just before. The four minor orders are those of Door-
keepers, Readers, Exorcists, and Acolytes: their use is almost
obsolete. The holy orders are of Subdeacons, Deacons, and Priests.

I have got a yearning for the Welsh people and could find it in my
heart to work for their conversion. However on consideration it
seems best to turn my thoughts elsewhere. I say this because,
though I am not my own master, yet if people among us shew a zeal
and aptitude for a particular work, say foreign missions, they can
commonly get employed on them. The Welsh round are very civil
and respectful but do not much come to us and those who are con-
verted are for the most part not very stanch. They are much swayed
by ridicule. Wesleyanism is the popular religion. They are said to
have a turn for religion, especially what excites outward fervour,
and more refinement and pious feeling than the English peasantry
but less steadfastness and sincerity. I have always looked on myself

as half Welsh and so I warm to them. The Welsh landscape has a great charm and when I see Snowdon and the mountains in its neighbourhood, as I can now, with the clouds lifting, it gives me a rise of the heart. I ought to say that the Welsh have the reputation also of being covetous and immoral: I add this to forestall your saying it, for, as I say, I warm to them – and in different degrees to all the Celts.

The Provincial was here a few days ago. It seems he wrote a letter giving me leave to spend a week with you at Lyme on my way or beside my way here, but I had already started. You will be vexed at this; at the same time it shews how thoughtful he is.

I fear my music has come to an end. I am very sorry, though practising (and I made singularly little way: I think I must be musically deficient somewhere) was a burden and here especially so, with a grunting harmonium that lived in the sacristy.

With best love to all believe me your loving son

GERARD M. HOPKINS S.J. . . .

JOURNAL

Oct. 8 – Bright and beautiful day. Crests of snow could be seen on the mountains. Barraud and I walked over to Holywell and bathed at the well and returned very joyously. The sight of the water in the well as clear as glass, greenish like beryl or aquamarine, trembling at the surface with the force of the springs, and shaping out the five foils of the well quite drew and held my eyes to it. Within a month or six weeks from this (I think Fr di Pietro said) a young man from Liverpool, Arthur Kent(?), was cured of rupture in the water. The strong unfailing flow of the water and the chain of cures from year to year all these centuries took hold of my mind with wonder at the bounty of God in one of His saints, the sensible thing so naturally and gracefully uttering the spiritual reason of its being (which is all in true keeping with the story of St. Winefred's death and recovery) and the spring in place leading back the thoughts by its spring in time to its spring in eternity: even now the stress and buoyancy and abundance of the water is before my eyes.

Oct. 12 – The bp came, so we got a half holiday and I went with Rickaby to Cwm. We came back by the woods on the Rhuallt and the view was so like Ribblesdale from the fells that you might have thought you were there. The sky was iron grey and the valley, full of Welsh charm and graceful sadness, all in grave colours lay like a painted napkin.

Oct. 19 – I was there again with Purbrick, at the scaffolding which is left as a mark of the survey at the highest point. We climbed on this and looked round: it was a fresh and delightful sight. The day was rainy and a rolling wind; parts of the landscape, as the Orms' Heads, were blotted out by rain. The clouds westwards were a pied piece – sail-coloured brown and milky blue; a dun yellow tent of rays opened upon the skyline far off. Cobalt blue was poured on the hills bounding the valley of the Clwyd and far in the south spread a bluish damp, but all the nearer valley was showered with tapered diamond flakes of fields in purple and brown and green.

No. 8 – Walking with Wm. Splaine we saw a vast multitude of starlings making an unspeakable jangle. They would settle in a row of trees; then, one tree after another, rising at a signal they looked like a cloud of specks of black snuff or powder struck up from a brush or broom or shaken from a wig; then they would sweep round in whirlwinds – you could see the nearer and farther bow of the rings by the size and blackness; many would be in one phase at once, all narrow black flakes hurling round, then in another; then they would fall upon a field and so on. Splaine wanted a gun; then 'there it would rain meat' he said. I thought they must be full of enthusiasm and delight hearing their cries and stirring and cheering one another.

Nov. 11 – Bitter north wind, hail and sleet. On the hills snow lying and the mountains covered from head to foot. But they could scarcely be seen till next day, a Blandyke, which was fine and clear. I went with Mr Hughes up Moel y Parch, from the top of which we had a noble view, but the wind was very sharp. Snowdon and all the range reminded me of the Alps: they looked like a stack of rugged white flint, specked and streaked with black, in many places chiselled and channelled. Home by Caerwys wood, where we saw two beautiful swans, as white as they should be, restlessly steering and 'canting' in the water and following us along the shore: one of them several times, as if for vexation, caught and gnawed at the stone quay of the sluice close under me.

To his Mother

St. Beuno's. 26 June 1876

My Dearest Mother, – I am glad to say that I have again heard from Lionel.

You ask about my poem on the Deutschland. You forget that we have a magazine of our own, the *Month*. I have asked Fr Coleridge the editor, who is besides my oldest friend in the Society, to take it, but I had to tell him that I felt sure he wd. personally dislike it very much, only that he was to consider not his tastes but those of the *Month's* readers. He replied that there was in America a new sort of poetry which did not rhyme or scan or construe; if mine rhymed and scanned and construed and did not make nonsense or bad morality he did not see why it shd. not do. So I sent it. Hitherto he has not answered; which is a sign it cannot appear in the July number but otherwise seems to shew he means to take it.

June 28 – I have heard from him this morning. The poem was too late for July but will appear in the August number. He wants me however to do away with the accents which mark the scanning. I would gladly have done without them if I had thought my readers would scan right unaided but I am afraid they will not, and if the lines are not rightly scanned they are ruined. Still I am afraid I must humour an editor, but some lines at all events will have to be marked.

Whom did Ernest Coleridge marry?

You must never say that the poem is mine.

With best love to all I am your loving son

GERARD M. HOPKINS S.J.

There is a lamentable account in the *Graphic* of the sweeping away of the old civilisation in Japan . . .

To Bridges

St. Beuno's. 21 Aug. 1877

Dearest Bridges, – Your letter cannot amuse Father Provincial, for he is on the unfathering deeps outward bound to Jamaica: I shd. not think of telling you anything about his reverence's goings and comings if it were not that I know this fact has been chronicled in the Catholic papers.

Enough that it amuses me, especially the story about Wooldridge and the Wagnerite, wh. is very good.

Your parody reassures me about your understanding the metre. Only remark, as you say that there is no conceivable licence I shd. not be able to justify, that with all my licences, or rather laws, I am stricter than you and I might say than anybody I know. With the exception of the *Bremen* stanza, which was, I think, the first written after 10 years' interval of silence, and before I had fixed my principles, my rhymes are rigidly good – to the ear – and such rhymes as *love* and *prove* I scout utterly. And my quantity is not like 'Fĭftў̄-twō Bĕdfŏrd Squāre', where *fĭftў* might pass but *Bĕdfŏrd* I should never admit. Not only so but Swinburne's dactyls and anapaests are halting to my ear: I never allow e.g. *I* or *my* (that is diphthongs, for $I = a + i$ and $my = ma + i$) in the short or weak syllables of those feet, excepting before vowels, semi-vowels, or *r*, and rarely then, or when the measure becomes (what is the word?) molossic – thus: ᴗ–ᴗ|ᴗ–ᴗ|ᴗ–ᴗ , for then the first short is almost long. If you look again you will see. So that I may say my apparent licences are counterbalanced, and more, by my strictness. In fact all English verse, except Milton's, almost, offends me as 'licentious'. Remember this.

I do not of course claim to have invented *sprung rhythms* but only *sprung rhythm:* I mean that single lines and single instances of it are not uncommon in English and I have pointed them out in lecturing – e.g. 'why should this ⦙ desert be?' – which the editors have variously amended; 'There to meet ⦙ with Macbeth' or 'There to meet with Mac ⦙ beth'; Campbell has some throughout the *Battle of the Baltic* – 'and their fleet along the deep ⦙ proudly shone' – and *Ye Mariners* – 'as ye sweep ⦙ through the deep' etc; Moore has some which I cannot recall; there is one in *Grongar Hill:* and, not to speak of *Pom pom*, in Nursery Rhymes, Weather Saws, and Refrains they are very common – but what I do in the *Deutschland* etc is to enfranchise them as a regular and permanent principle of scansion.

There are no outriding feet in the *Deutschland*. An outriding foot is, by a sort of contradiction, a recognized extra-metrical effect; it is and it is not part of the metre; not part of it, not being counted, but part of it by producing a calculated effect which tells in the general success. But the long, e.g. seven-syllabled, feet of the *Deutschland*, are strictly metrical. Outriding feet belong to counterpointed verse, which supposes a well-known and unmistakeable or unforgetable standard rhythm: the *Deutschland* is not counterpointed; counterpoint is excluded by sprung rhythm. But in some of my sonnets I have mingled the two systems: this is the most delicate and difficult business of all.

The choruses in *Samson Agonistes* are intermediate between counterpointed and sprung rhythm. In reality they are sprung, but Milton keeps up a fiction of counterpointing the heard rhythm (which is the same as the mounted rhythm) upon a standard rhythm which is never heard but only counted and therefore really does not exist. The want of a metrical notation and the fear of being thought to write mere rhythmic or (who knows what the critics might not have said?) even unrhythmic prose drove him to this. Such rhythm as French and Welsh poetry has is sprung, counterpointed upon a counted rhythm, but it differs from Milton's in being little calculated, not more perhaps than prose consciously written rhythmically, like orations for instance; it is in fact the *native rhythm* of the words used bodily imported into verse; whereas Milton's mounted rhythm is a real poetical rhythm, having its own laws and recurrence, but further embarrassed by having to count.

Why do I employ sprung rhythm at all? Because it is the nearest to the rhythm of prose, that is the native and natural rhythm of speech, the least forced, the most rhetorical and emphatic of all possible rhythms, combining, as it seems to me, opposite and, one wd. have thought, incompatible excellences, markedness of rhythm – that is rhythm's self – and naturalness of expression – for why, if it is forcible in prose to say 'lashed : rod',[1] am I obliged to weaken this in verse, which ought to be stronger, not weaker, into 'láshed birch-ród' or something?

My verse is less to be read than heard, as I have told you before; it is oratorical, that is the rhythm is so. I think if you will study what I have here said you will be much more pleased with it and may I say? converted to it.

You ask may you call it 'presumptious jugglery'. No, but only for this reason, that *presumptious* is not English.

I cannot think of altering anything. Why shd. I? I do not write for the public. You are my public and I hope to convert you.

You say you wd. not for any money read my poem again. Never-

theless I beg you will. Besides money, you know, there is love. If it
is obscure do not bother yourself with the meaning but pay atten-
tion to the best and most intelligible stanzas, as the two last of each
part and the narrative of the wreck. If you had done this you wd.
have liked it better and sent me some serviceable criticisms, but now
your criticism is of no use, being only a protest memorialising me
against my whole policy and proceedings.

I may add for your greater interest and edification that what
refers to myself in the poem is all strictly and literally true and did
all occur; nothing is added for poetical padding.

Believe me your affectionate friend

GERARD M. HOPKINS S.J.

To his Mother

St. Beuno's. 9 Oct. 1877

MY DEAREST MOTHER, – I am glad that my dear grandfather's end
was peaceful and that all his children could be present to witness the
last moments of an affectionate and generous father. But there is one
circumstance about it which gives me the deepest consolation: I
shall communicate it to you, think of it what you like. I had for
years been accustomed every day to recommend him very earnestly
to the Blessed Virgin's protection; so that I could say, if such a
thing can ever be said without presumption, If I am disappointed
who can hope? As his end drew near I had asked some people to
pray for him and said to someone in a letter that I should take it as a
happy token if he died on Sunday the Feast of the Holy Rosary. It
is a day signalised by our Lady's overruling aid asked for and given
at the victory of Lepanto. This year the anniversary is better marked
than usual, for Lepanto was fought on the 7th of October but the
feast is kept on the first Sunday in the month whatever the day: this
time they coincide. I receive it without questioning as a mark that
my prayers have been heard and that the queen of heaven has saved
a Christian soul from enemies more terrible than a fleet of infidels.
Do not make light of this, for it is perhaps the seventh time that I
think I have had some token from heaven in connection with the
death of people in whom I am interested.

Since Saturday week I have been sick in bed, today I am up for the first time, in a few days' time I shall be completely recovered, and am then to go to Mount St. Mary's College, Chesterfield, Derbyshire (Chesterfield is the address). I cannot write more about it now. The work is nondescript – examining, teaching, probably with occasional mission work and preaching or giving retreats attached: I shall know more when I am there. The number of scholars is about 150, the community moderately small and family-like, the country round not very interesting but at a little distance is fine country, Sheffield is the nearest great town. The people call the place Spink Hill, Eckington is the station.

Believe me your loving son

GERARD M. HOPKINS S.J.

TO HIS MOTHER

Mount St. Mary's College, Chesterfield. 27 Jan. 1878

MY DEAREST MOTHER, – I know it is a very long time since I wrote and so it is a goodish long one since any of you did either. I am so fallen into a mess of employments that I have given up doing every-thing whatever but what is immediately before me to do. One of the masters has fallen ill, it would appear for a long spell, and I have taken his place without diminution of my former occupations. Unluckily Sunday brings me little leisure but is a busy day, for I have work both in the school and at the church, where I help the parish priest.

During the holidays the boys did not go home but presented plays and concerts every night. Their acting was creditable and Berkeley my particular pupil is a born actor, a very amusing low comedian and still better in tragedy; his Lady Macbeth, in spite of being turned into 'Fergus' Macbeth's younger brother, was quite a 'creation'. I wrote them a prologue to Macbeth: it was a scene of a farce and consisted in the speaker seeming to forget all the points, but Berkeley did it so naturally that he overshot the mark and most part of the audience thought he had forgotten in earnest and that his strange behaviour was due to 'refreshments' behind the scenes. On Twelfth Night they had a mumming, which is the custom. The country lads also go about mumming in red and yellow paper clothes at Xmas, but very soberly. Our boys gave two performances in aid of the poor schools, the country people came, laughed prodigiously at the jokes and sometimes at the wrong places and wept freely at the pathetic scenes.

The little charges thrown on me by their master's illness have written me an account of the Earthquake of Lisbon: 'It was a fine bright day' they say 'when at ten o'clock a picture of extreme suddenness came on'. After the earthquake 'an old ruffian of a mob ran about killing everyone he met'. Finally 'this catastrophe has left many a mark on the minds of learned men'. A batch of copybooks lies before me with no doubt more of the same sort on the Earl of Nithsdale's escape...

To Bridges

Stonyhurst College. 13/21 May 1878

... I enclose you my Eurydice, which the *Month* refused. It is my only copy. Write no bilgewater about it: I will presently tell you what that is and till then excuse the term. I must tell you I am sorry you never read the Deutschland again.

Granted that it needs study and is obscure, for indeed I was not over-desirous that the meaning of all should be quite clear, at least unmistakeable, you might, without the effort that to make it all out would seem to have required, have nevertheless read it so that lines and stanzas should be left in the memory and superficial impressions deepened, and have liked some without exhausting all. I am sure I have read and enjoyed pages of poetry that way. Why, sometimes one enjoys and admires the very lines one cannot understand, as for instance 'If it were done when 'tis done' sqq., which is all obscure and disputed, though how fine it is everybody sees and nobody disputes. And so of many more passages in Shakspere and others. Besides you would have got more weathered to the style and its features – not really odd. Now they say that vessels sailing from the port of London will take (perhaps it should be / used once to take) Thames water for the voyage: it was foul and stunk at first as the ship worked but by degrees casting its filth was in a few days very pure and sweet and wholesomer and better than any water in the world. However that may be, it is true to my purpose. When a new thing, such as my ventures in the Deutschland are, is presented us our first criticisms are not our truest, best, most homefelt, or most lasting but what the ignorant and the ruck say. This was so with you. The Deutschland on her first run worked very much and unsettled you, thickening and clouding your mind with vulgar mud-bottom and common sewage (I see that I am going it with the image) and just then unhappily you *drew off* your criticisms all stinking (a necessity now of the image) and bilgy, whereas if you had let your thoughts cast themselves they would have been clearer in themselves and more to my taste too. I did not heed them therefore, perceiving they were a first drawing-off. Same of the Eurydice – which being short and easy please read more than once.

... To do the Eurydice any kind of justice you must not slovenly read it with the eyes but with your ears, as if the paper were declaiming it at you. For instance the line 'she had come from a cruise training seamen' read without stress and declaim is mere Lloyd's Shipping Intelligence; properly read it is quite a different thing. Stress is the life of it.

To Dixon

Stonyhurst. 13 June 1878

... When I spoke of fame I was not thinking of the harm it does to men as artists: it may do them harm, as you say, but so, I think, may the want of it, if 'Fame is the spur that the clear spirit doth raise To shun delights and live laborious days' – a spur very hard to find a substitute for or to do without. But I meant that it is a great danger in itself, as dangerous as wealth every bit, I should think, and as hard to enter the kingdom of heaven with. And even if it does not lead men to break the divine law, yet it gives them 'itching ears' and makes them live on public breath... Mr Coventry Patmore, whose fame again is very deeply below his great merit, seems to have said something very finely about the loss of fame in his lately published odes (*The Hidden Eros*) – I speak from an extract in a review.

What I do regret is the loss of recognition belonging to the work itself. For as to every moral act, being right or wrong, there belongs, of the nature of things, reward or punishment, so to every form perceived by the mind belongs, of the nature of things, admiration or the reverse. And the world is full of things and events, pheno-mena of all sorts, that go without notice, go unwitnessed. I think you have felt this, for you say, I remember, in one of the odes: 'What though the white clouds soar Unmarked from the horizon-shore?' or something like that. And if we regret this want of witness in brute nature much more in the things done with lost pains and disappointed hopes by man. But since there is always the risk of it, it is a great error of judgment to have lived for what may fail us ...

[June 15] ... It is sad to think what disappointment must many times over have filled your heart for the darling children of your mind. Nevertheless fame whether won or lost is a thing which lies in the award of a random, reckless, incompetent, and unjust judge, the public, the multitude. The only just judge, the only just literary critic, is Christ, who prizes, is proud of, and admires, more than any man, more than the receiver himself can, the gifts of his own making. And the only real good which fame and another's praise does is to convey to us, by a channel not at all above suspicion but from circumstances in this case much less to be suspected than the channel of our minds, some token of the judgment which a per-fectly just, heedful, and wise mind, namely Christ's, passes upon our doings. Now such a token may be conveyed as well by one as by many. Therefore, believing I was able to pass a fair judgment as people go, it seemed in the circumstances a charity to tell you what I thought. For disappointment and humiliation embitter the heart and make an aching in the very bones. As far as I am concerned I say with conviction and put it on record again that you have great reason to thank God who has given you so astonishingly clear an inward eye to see what is in visible nature and in the heart such a deep insight into what is earnest, tender, and pathetic in human life and feeling as your poems display.

Believe me, dear sir, very sincerely yours

GERARD HOPKINS S.J. ...

To Dixon

111 Mount Street, Grosvenor Square, W. 5 Oct. 1878

... I quite agree with what you write about Milton. His verse as one reads it seems something necessary and eternal (so to me does Purcell's music). As for 'proper hue', *now* it wd. be priggish, but I suppose Milton means *own hue* and they talk of *proper colours* in heraldry; not but what there is a Puritan touch about the line even so. However the word must once have had a different feeling. The Welsh have borrowed it for *pretty*; they talk of birds singing 'properly' and a little Welsh boy to whom I shewed the flowers in a green house exclaimed 'They *are* proper!' – Milton seems now coming to be studied better, and Masson is writing or has written his life at prodigious length. There was an interesting review by Matthew Arnold in one of the Quarterlies of 'a French critic on Milton' – Scherer I think. The same M. Arnold says Milton and Campbell are our two greatest masters of *style*. Milton's art is incomparable, not only in English literature but, I shd. think, almost in any; equal, if not more than equal, to the finest of Greek or Roman. And considering that this is shewn especially in his verse, his rhythm and metrical system, it is amazing that so great a writer as Newman should have fallen into the blunder of comparing the first chorus of the *Agonistes* with the opening of *Thalaba* as instancing the gain in smoothness and correctness of versification made since Milton's time – Milton having been not only ahead of his own time as well as all aftertimes in verse-structure but these particular choruses being his own highwater mark. It is as if you were to compare the Panathenaic frieze and a teaboard and decide in the teaboard's favour.

I have paid a good deal of attention to Milton's versification and collected his later rhythms: I did it when I had to lecture on rhetoric some years since. I found his most advanced effects in the *Paradise Regained* and, lyrically, in the *Agonistes*. I have often thought of writing on them, indeed on rhythm in general; I think the subject is little understood.

You ask, do I write verse myself. What I had written I burnt before I became a Jesuit and resolved to write no more, as not belonging to my profession, unless it were by the wish of my superiors; so for seven years I wrote nothing but two or three little presentation pieces which occasion called for. But when in the winter of '75 the Deutschland was wrecked in the mouth of the Thames and five Franciscan nuns, exiles from Germany by the Falck Laws, aboard of her were drowned I was affected by the account and happening to say so to my rector he said that he wished someone would write a poem on the subject. On this hint I set to work and, though my hand was out at first, produced one. I had long had haunting my ear the echo of a new rhythm which now I realised on paper. To speak shortly, it consists in scanning by accents or stresses alone, without any account of the number of syllables, so that a foot may be one strong syllable or it may be many light and one strong. I do not say the idea is altogether new; there are hints of it in music, in nursery rhymes and popular jingles, in the poets themselves, and, since then, I have seen it talked about as a thing possible in critics. Here are instances – 'Díng, dóng, béll; Pússy's ín the wéll; Whó pút her ín? Líttle Jóhnny Thín. Whó púlled her óut? Líttle Jóhnny Stóut.' For if each line has three stresses or three feet it follows that some of the feet are of one syllable only. So too 'Óne, twó, Búckle my shóe' passim. In Campbell you have 'Ánd their fléet alóng the déep próudly shóne' – 'Ít was tén of Ápril mórn bý the chíme' etc; in Shakspere 'Whý shd. thís désert bé?' corrected wrongly by the editors; in Moore a little melody I cannot quote; etc. But no one has professedly used it and made it the principle throughout, that I know of. Nevertheless to me it appears, I own, to be a better and more natural principle than the ordinary system, much more flexible, and capable of much greater effects. However I had to mark the stresses in blue chalk, and this and my rhymes carried on from one line into another and certain chimes suggested by the Welsh poetry I had been reading (what they call cynghanedd) and a great many more oddnesses could not but dismay an editor's eye, so that when I offered it to our magazine the Month, though at first they accepted it, after a time they withdrew and dared not print it. After writing this I held myself free to compose, but cannot find it in my conscience to spend time upon it; so I have done little and shall do less. But I wrote a shorter piece on the Eurydice, also in 'sprung rhythm', as I call it, but simpler, shorter, and without marks, and offered the Month that too, but they did not like it either. Also I have written some sonnets and a few other little things; some in sprung rhythm, with various other experiments – as 'outriding feet', that is parts of which do not count in the scanning (such as you find in Shakspere's later plays, but as a licence, whereas mine are rather calculated effects); others in the ordinary scanning counterpointed (this is counterpoint: 'Hóme to his móther's hóuse prívate retúrned' and 'Bút to vánquish by wísdom héllish wíles' etc); others, one or two, in common uncounterpointed rhythm. But even the impulse to write is wanting, for I have no thought of publishing.

I should add that Milton is the great standard in the use of counterpoint. In *Paradise Lost* and *Regained*, in the last more freely, it being an advance in his art, he employs counterpoint more or less everywhere, markedly now and then; but the choruses of *Samson Agonistes* are in my judgment counterpointed throughout; that is, each line (or nearly so) has two different coexisting scansions. But when you reach that point the secondary or 'mounted rhythm', which is necessarily a sprung rhythm, overpowers the original or conventional one and then this becomes superfluous and may be got rid of; by taking that last step you reach simple sprung rhythm. Milton must have known this but had reasons for not taking it ...

To Bridges

St. Giles's, Oxford. 29 Jan. 1879

Dearest Bridges, – Morals and scansion not being in one keeping, we will treat them in separate letters and this one shall be given to the first named subject: the Preface will wait.

You so misunderstand my words (it seems they ought never to have been written: if they meant what you take them to mean I should never have written them) that I am surprised, and not only surprised but put out. For amongst other things I am made to appear a downright fool.

Can you suppose I should send Pater a discipline wrapped up in a sonnet 'with my best love'? Would it not be mad? And it is much the same to burst upon you with an exhortation to mortification (under the name of 'sensible inconvenience') – which mortification too would be in your case aimless. So that I should have the two marks of the foolish counsellor – to advise what is bad to follow and what will not be followed.

But I said that my recommendation was not open to objection. I did not mean as the doctrine of the Real Presence, which is true and yet may be objected against; I meant what could not be and was not objected against. Unless you object to doing good and call it 'miserable' to be generous. All the world, so to speak, approves of charity and of the corporal works of mercy, though all the world does not practise what it approves of. Even Walt Whitman nurses the sick.

I spoke, then, of alms – alms whether in money or in medical or other aid, such as you from the cases you come across at the hospital might know to be called for. And I said 'sensible inconvenience'; that is, for instance, you might know of someone needing and deserving an alms to give which would require you in prudence to buy no books till next quarter day or to make some equivalent sacrifice of time. These are sensible inconveniences. And to submit to them you cannot, nevertheless, call the reverse of sensible. But to 'derweesh' yourself (please see the Cairo letter in the last *Athenaeum* – or possibly *Academy*), that would *not* be sensible and that is what you took me to mean and that is what it would have been supremely senseless of me to mean.

I added something about it needing the experience to know what it feels like to have put oneself out for charity's sake (or one might say for truth's sake, for honour's sake, for chastity's sake, for any virtue's sake). I meant: everybody knows, or if not can guess, how it feels to be short of money, but everybody may not know, and if not cannot well guess, how it feels to be short of money for charity's sake, etc as above.

All the above appears to me to be put plainly. It reads to me in the blustering bread-and-cheese style. You will ask why I was not as plain at first. Because the blustering bread-and-cheese style is not suited for giving advice, though it may be for defending it. Besides I did not foresee the misunderstanding. What I did fear, and it made me keep the letter back, was that you would be offended at my freedom, indeed that you would not answer at all. Whereas, for which I heartily thank you, you have answered three times.

It is true I also asked you to give me, if you liked, an account of your mind – which wd. call for, you say, self examination, and at all events one cannot say what one thinks without thinking. But this and the almsgiving are two independent things mentioned in one letter. No doubt I see a connection, but I do not need you to.

However if I must not only explain what I said but discover what I thought, my thoughts were these – Bridges is all wrong, and it will do no good to reason with him nor even to ask him to pray. Yet there is one thing remains – if he can be got to give alms, of which the Scripture says (I was talking to myself, not you) that they resist sins and that they redeem sins and that they will not let the soul go out into darkness, to give which Daniel advised Nabuchodonosor and Christ the Pharisees, the one a heathen, the other antichristians, and the whole scripture in short so much recommends; of which moreover I have heard so-and-so, whose judgment I would take against any man's on such a point, say that the promise is absolute and that there is for every one a fixed sum at which he will ensure his salvation, though for those who have sinned greatly it may be a very high sum and very distressing to them to give – or keep giving: and not to have the faith is worse then to have sinned deeply, for it is like not being even in the running. Yet I will advise something and it must improve matters and will lead to good. So with hesitation and fear I wrote. And now I hope you see clearly, and when you reply will make your objections, if any, to the practice of almsgiving, not to the use of hairshirts. And I take leave to repeat and you cannot but see, that it is a noble thing and not a miserable something or other to give alms and help the needy and stint ourselves for the sake of the unhappy and deserving. Which I hope will take the bad taste away. And at any rate it is good of you only to misunderstand and be vexed and not to bridle and drop correspondence . . .

To Bridges

St. Giles's, Oxford. 15 Feb. 1879

. . . When I say that I do not mean to publish I speak the truth. I have taken and mean to take no step to do so beyond the attempt I made to print my two wrecks in the *Month*. If some one in authority knew of my having some poems printable and suggested my doing it I shd. not refuse, I should be partly, though not altogether, glad. But that is very unlikely. All therefore that I think of doing is to keep my verses together in one place – at present I have not even correct copies –, that, if anyone shd. like, they might be published after my death. And that again is unlikely, as well as remote. I could add other considerations, as that if I meant to publish at all it ought to be more or ought at least to be followed up, and how can that be? I cannot in conscience spend time on poetry, neither have I the inducements and inspirations that make others compose. Feeling, love in particular, is the great moving power and spring of verse and the only person that I am in love with seldom, especially now, stirs my heart sensibly and when he does I cannot always 'make capital' of it, it would be a sacrilege to do so. Then again I have of myself made verse so laborious.

No doubt my poetry errs on the side of oddness. I hope in time to have a more balanced and Miltonic style. But as air, melody, is what strikes me most of all in music and design in painting, so design, pattern or what I am in the habit of calling 'inscape' is what I above all aim at in poetry. Now it is the virtue of design, pattern, or inscape to be distinctive and it is the virtue of distinctiveness to become queer. This vice I cannot have escaped . . .

To Dixon

St. Giles's, Oxford. 27 Feb./13 March 1879

. . . Marvel, of whom I have only read extracts, is a most rich and nervous poet. Thomas Vaughan's poems were reprinted not so long ago. He was a follower of Herbert both in life and style: he was in fact converted from worldly courses by reading Herbert's poems on a sickbed and even his muse underwent a conversion (for he had written before). He has more glow and freedom than Herbert but less fragrant sweetness. Somewhere he speaks of some spot 'primrosed and hung with shade' and one piece ends
> And here in dust and dirt, O here
> The lilies of his love appear.

(I am assuming that you have not got the book.) Still I do not think him Herbert's equal.

You call Tennyson 'a great outsider'; you mean, I think, to the soul of poetry. I feel what you mean, though it grieves me to hear him depreciated, as of late years has often been done. Come what may he will be one of our greatest poets. To me his poetry appears 'chryselephantine'; always of precious mental material and each verse a work of art, no botchy places, not only so but no half wrought or low-toned ones, no drab, no brown-holland; but the form, though fine, not the perfect artist's form, not equal to the material. When the inspiration is genuine, arising from personal feeling, as in *In Memoriam*, a divine work, he is at his best, or when he is rhyming pure and simple imagination, without afterthought, as in the *Lady of Shalott*, *Sir Galahad*, the *Dream of Fair Women*, or *Palace of Art*. But the want of perfect form in the imagination

comes damagingly out when he undertakes longer works of fancy,
as his Idylls: they are unreal in motive and incorrect, uncanonical
so to say, in detail and keepings. He shd. have called them *Charades
from the Middle Ages* (dedicated by permission to H.R.H. etc). The
Galahad of one of the later ones is quite a fantastic charade-playing
trumpery Galahad, merely playing the fool over Christian heroism.
Each scene is a triumph of language and of bright picturesque, but
just like a charade – where real lace and good silks and real jewelry
are used, because the actors are private persons and wealthy, but it
is acting all the same and not only so but the make-up has less
pretence of correct keeping than at Drury Lane. His opinions too
are not original, often not independent even, and they sink into
vulgarity: not only *Locksley Hall* but *Maud* is an ungentlemanly
row and *Aylmer's Field* is an ungentlemanly row and the *Princess*
is an ungentlemanly row. To be sure this gives him vogue, popu-
larity, but not that sort of ascendancy Goethe had or even Burns,
scoundrel as the first was, not to say the second; but then they spoke
out the real human rakishness of their hearts and everybody recog-
nised the really beating, though rascal, vein. And in his rhetorical
pieces he is at his worst, as the *Lord of Burleigh* and *Lady Clare
Vere de Vere* (downright haberdasher). But for all this he is a
glorious poet and all he does is chryselephantine. Though by the by
I owe him a grudge for *Queen Mary*, written to please the mob, and
for that other drama where a portent of a man in flaxen locks and
ring-mail mouths rationalism 'to torment us before the time' . . .

TO DIXON

St. Giles's, Oxford. 12 May 1879

. . . It was of course a very great pleasure to have so high an opinion
expressed of my poems and by you.

But for what concerns the notice you kindly offer to make of me
in your forthcoming volume, it would not at all suit me. For this
there are several reasons, any one sufficient; but it is enough to say
now that (1) I have no thought of publishing until all circumstances
favour, which I do not know that they ever will, and it seems that
one of them shd. be that the suggestion to publish shd. come from
one of our own people; (2) to allow such a notice would be on my

part a sort of insubordination to or doubledealing with my super-
iors. But nevertheless I sincerely thank you for your kind willing-
ness to do me a service.

The life I lead is liable to many mortifications but the want of
fame as a poet is the least of them. I could wish, I allow, that my
pieces could at some time become known but in some spontaneous
way, so to speak, and without my forcing.

Believe me, with many thanks for the kindness which your letters
always breathe, your sincere friend

GERARD M. HOPKINS S.J.

TO BRIDGES

St. Giles's, Oxford. 14 Aug. 1879

... I was almost a great admirer of Barnes' Dorset (not Devon)
poems. I agree with Gosse, not with you. A proof of their excellence
is that you may translate them and they are nearly as good – I say
nearly, because if the dialect plays any lawful part in the effect they
ought to lose something in losing that. Now Burns loses prodig-
iously by translation. I have never however read them since my
undergraduate days except the one quoted in Gosse's paper, the
beauty of which you must allow. I think the use of dialect a sort of
unfair play, giving, as you say, 'a peculiar but shortlived charm',
setting off for instance a Scotch or Lancashire joke which in
standard English comes to nothing. But its lawful charm and use I
take to be this, that it sort of guarantees the spontaneousness of the
thought and puts you in the position to appraise it on its merits as
coming from nature and not books and education. It heightens
one's admiration for a phrase just as in architecture it heightens
one's admiration of a design to know that it is old work, not new:
in itself the design is the same but as taken together with the design-
er and his merit this circumstance makes a world of difference.
Now the use of dialect to a man like Barnes is to tie him down to the
things that he or another Dorset man has said or might say, which
though it narrows his field heightens his effects. His poems used to
charm me also by their Westcountry 'instress', a most peculiar
product of England, which I associate with airs like Weeping

Winefred, Polly Oliver, or Poor Mary Ann, with Herrick and
Herbert, with the Worcestershire, Herefordshire, and Welsh
landscape, and above all with the smell of oxeyes and applelofts:
this instress is helped by particular rhythms and these Barnes
employs: as, I remember, in 'Linden Ore' and a thing with a refrain
like 'Alive in the Spring'.

   ... By the by, inversions – As you say, I do avoid them, because
they weaken and because they destroy the earnestness or in-
earnestness of the utterance. Nevertheless in prose I use them more
than other people, because there they have great advantages of
another sort. Now these advantages they should have in verse too,
but they must not seem to be due to the verse: that is what is so
enfeebling (for instance the finest of your sonnets to my mind has a
line enfeebled by inversion plainly due to the verse, as I said once
before ''Tis joy the falling of her fold to view' – but how it should
be mended I do not see). As it is, I feel my way to their use. How-
ever in a nearly finished piece I have a very bold one indeed. So
also I cut myself off from the use of *ere, o'er, wellnigh, what time, say
not* (for *do not say*), because, though dignified, they neither belong
to nor ever cd. arise from, or be the elevation of, ordinary modern
speech. For it seems to me that the poetical language of an age shd.
be the current language heightened, to any degree heightened and
unlike itself, but not (I mean normally: passing freaks and graces
are another thing) an obsolete one. This is Shakespeare's and Mil-
ton's practice and the want of it will be fatal to Tennyson's Idylls
and plays, to Swinburne, and perhaps to Morris ...

To Bridges

St. Joseph's, Bedford Leigh, Lancashire. 8 Oct. 1879

DEAREST BRIDGES, – I have left Oxford. I am appointed to Liver-
pool, I do not know for what work, but am in the meantime supply-
ing at the above address. Leigh is a town smaller and with less
dignity than Rochdale and in a flat; the houses red, mean, and two
storied; there are a dozen mills or so, and coalpits also; the air is
charged with smoke as well as damp; but the people are hearty.
Now at Oxford every prospect pleases and only man is vile, I mean
unsatisfactory to a Catholic missioner. I was yesterday at St.

Helen's, probably the most repulsive place in Lancashire or out of
the Black Country. The stench of sulphuretted hydrogen rolls in
the air and films of the same gas form on railing and pavement ...

To Bridges

Bedford Leigh. 22 Oct./18 Nov. 1879

... You seem to want to be told over again that you have genius
and are a poet and your verses beautiful. You have been told so, not
only by me but very spontaneously by Gosse, Marzials, and others;
I was going to say Canon Dixon, only, as he was acknowledging
your book, it was not so spontaneous as Gosse's case. You want
perhaps to be told more in particular. I am not the best to tell you,
being biassed by love, and yet I am too. I think then no one can
admire beauty of the body more than I do, and it is of course a
comfort to find beauty in a friend or a friend in beauty. But this
kind of beauty is dangerous. Then comes the beauty of the mind,
such as genius, and this is greater than the beauty of the body and
not to call dangerous. And more beautiful than the beauty of the
mind is beauty of character, the 'handsome heart'. Now every
beauty is not a wit or genius nor has every wit or genius character.
For though even bodily beauty, even the beauty of blooming
health, is from the soul, in the sense, as we Aristotelian Catholics
say, that the soul is the form of the body, yet the soul may have no
other beauty, so to speak, than that which it expresses in the sym-
metry of the body – barring those blurs in the cast which wd. not
be found in the die or the mould. This needs no illustration, as all
know it. But what is more to be remarked is that in like manner the
soul may have no further beauty than that which is seen in the
mind, that there may be genius uninformed by character. I some-
times wonder at this in a man like Tennyson: his gift of utterance is
truly golden, but go further home and you come to thoughts
commonplace and wanting in nobility (it seems hard to say it but I
think you know what I mean). In Burns there is generally recog-
nized on the other hand a richness and beauty of manly character
which lends worth to some of his smallest fragments, but there is a
great want in his utterance; it is never really beautiful, he had no eye
for pure beauty, he gets no nearer than the fresh picturesque

expressed in fervent and flowing language (the most strictly beautiful lines of his that I remember are those in Tam o'Shanter: 'But pleasures are like poppies spread' sqq. and those are not). Between a fineness of nature which wd. put him in the first rank of writers and a poverty of language which puts him in the lowest rank of poets, he takes to my mind, when all is balanced and cast up, about a middle place. Now after all this introduction I come to what I want to say. If I were not your friend I shd. wish to be the friend of the man that wrote your poems. They shew the eye for pure beauty and they shew, my dearest, besides, the character which is much more rare and precious. Did time allow I shd. find a pleasure in dwelling on the instances, but I cannot now. Since I must not flatter or exaggerate I do not claim that you have such a volume of imagery as Tennyson, Swinburne, or Morris, though the feeling for beauty you have seems to me pure and exquisite; but in point of character, of sincerity or earnestness, of manliness, of tenderness, of humour, melancholy, human feeling, you have what they have not and seem scarcely to think worth having (about Morris I am not sure: his early poems had a deep feeling). I may then well say, like St. Paul, *aemulor te Dei aemulatione*. To have a turn for sincerity has not made you sincere nor a turn for earnest / in earnest; Sterne had a turn for compassion, but he was not compassionate; a man may have natural courage, a turn for courage, and yet play the coward.

. . . I hardly know what you allude to at Oxford, it is better that I should not. I used indeed to fear when I went up about this time last year that people wd. repeat against me what they remembered to my disadvantage. But if they did I never heard of it. I saw little of University men: when you were up it was an exceptional occasion, which brought me into contact with them. My work lay in St. Clement's, at the Barracks, and so on. However it is perhaps well I am gone; I did not quite hit it off with Fr Parkinson and was not happy. I was fond of my people, but they had not as a body the charming and cheering heartiness of these Lancashire Catholics, which is so deeply comforting; they were far from having it. And I believe they criticised what went on in our church a great deal too freely, which is d – d impertinence of the sheep towards the shepherd, and if it had come markedly before me I shd. have given them my mind . . .

To Dixon

Bedford Leigh. 31 Oct. 1879

MY DEAR CANON, – Pray do not send the piece to the paper: I cannot consent to, I forbid its publication. You must see that to publish my manuscript against my expressed wish is a breach of trust. Ask any friend and he will tell you the same.

Moreover this kind of publication is very unlikely to do the good that you hope and very likely to do the harm that I fear. For who ever heard of fame won by publication in a local paper, and of one piece? If everything of its intrinsic goodness gravitated to fame your poems wd. long since have been famous. Were Tennyson, putting aside marks of style by which he might be recognised, to send something to the *Nineteenth Century* or best circulated London magazine *without his name* it wd. be forgotten in a month: now no name and an unknown name is all one. But what is not near enough for public fame may be more than enough for private notoriety, which is what I dread.

You say truly that our Society fosters literary excellence. Why then it may be left to look to its own interests. It could not approve of unauthorised publication, for all that we publish must be seen by censors first.

Then again if you were to print my piece you would surely not mutilate it. And yet you must; for with what grace could you, a clergyman of the Church of England, stand godfather to some of the stanzas in that poem? And besides I want to alter the last stanza.

Nov. 1 – This letter, which the pressure of parish work has delayed, will now, I daresay, be too late and the Eurydice may have appeared. You will see that your warmhearted but much mistaken kindness will be unavailing: if the paper takes the piece (which it is sure to misprint) few will read it and of those few fewer will scan it, much less understand or like it. (To be sure the scanning is plain enough, but people cannot, or they will not, take in anything however plain that departs from what they have been taught and brought up to expect: I know from experience). Indeed I am in hopes that the matter may even escape the notice of our own people.

Believe me affectionately your friend

GERARD M. HOPKINS S.J.

Sermon at Bedford Leigh

23 Nov. 1879

... Our Lord Jesus Christ, my brethren, is our hero, a hero all the world wants. You know how books of tales are written, that put one man before the reader and shew him off handsome for the most part and brave and call him My Hero or Our Hero. Often mothers make a hero of a son; girls of a sweetheart and good wives of a husband. Soldiers make a hero of a great general, a party of its leader, a nation of any great man that brings it glory, whether king, warrior, statesman, thinker, poet, or whatever it shall be. But Christ, he is the hero. He too is the hero of a book or books, of the divine Gospels. He is a warrior and a conqueror; of whom it is written he went forth conquering and to conquer. He is a king, Jesus of Nazareth king of the Jews, though when he came to his own kingdom his own did not receive him, and now, his people having cast him off, we Gentiles are his inheritance. He is a statesman, that drew up the New Testament in his blood and founded the Roman Catholic Church that cannot fail. He is a thinker, that taught us divine mysteries. He is an orator and poet, as in his eloquent words and parables appears. He is all the world's hero, the desire of nations. But besides he is the hero of single souls; his mother's hero, not out of motherly foolish fondness but because he was, as the angel told her, great and the son of the Most High and all that he did and said and was done and said about him she laid up in her heart. He is the true-love and the bridegroom of men's souls: the virgins follow him whithersoever he goes; the martyrs follow him through a sea of blood, through great tribulation; all his servants take up their cross and follow him. And those even that do not follow him, yet they look wistfully after him, own him a hero, and wish they dared answer to his call. Children as soon as they can understand ought to be told about him, that they may make him the hero of their young hearts. But there are Catholic parents that shamefully neglect their duty: the grown children of Catholics are found that scarcely know or do not know his name. Will such parents say they left instruction to the priest or the schoolmaster? Why, if they sent them very early to the school they might make

that excuse, but when they do not what will they say then? It is at
the father's or the mother's mouth first the little ones should learn.
But the parents may be gossiping or drinking and the children have
not heard of their lord and saviour. Those of you, my brethren, who
are young and yet unmarried resolve that when you marry, if God
should bless you with children, this shall not be but that you will
have more pity, will have pity upon your own.

There met in Jesus Christ all things that can make man lovely and
loveable. In his body he was most beautiful. This is known first by
the tradition in the Church that it was so and by holy writers agree-
ing to suit those words to him / Thou art beautiful in mould above
the sons of men: we have even accounts of him written in early
times. They tell us that he was moderately tall, well built and tender
in frame, his features straight and beautiful, his hair inclining to
auburn, parted in the midst, curling and clustering about the ears
and neck as the leaves of a filbert, so they speak, upon the nut. He
wore also a forked beard and this as well as the locks upon his head
were never touched by razor or shears; neither, his health being
perfect, could a hair ever fall to the ground. The account I have been
quoting (it is from memory, for I cannot now lay my hand upon it)
we do not indeed for certain know to be correct, but it has been
current in the Church and many generations have drawn our Lord
accordingly either in their own minds or in his images. Another
proof of his beauty may be drawn from the words *proficiebat
sapientia et aetate et gratia apud Deum et homines* (Luc. ii 52) / he
went forward in wisdom and bodily frame and favour with God
and men; that is / he pleased both God and men daily more and
more by his growth of mind and body. But he could not have
pleased by growth of body unless the body was strong, healthy, and
beautiful that grew. But the best proof of all is this, that his body
was the special work of the Holy Ghost. He was not born in
nature's course, no man was his father; had he been born as others
are he must have inherited some defect of figure or of constitution,
from which no man born as fallen men are born is wholly free
unless God interfere to keep him so. But his body was framed
directly from heaven by the power of the Holy Ghost, of whom it
would be unworthy to leave any the least botch or failing in his work.
So the first Adam was moulded by God himself and Eve built up by
God too out of Adam's rib and they could not but be pieces, both,

of faultless workmanship: the same then and much more must
Christ have been. His constitution too was tempered perfectly, he
had neither disease or the seeds of any: weariness he felt when he
was wearied, hunger when he fasted, thirst when he had long gone
without drink, but to the touch of sickness he was a stranger. I
leave it to you, brethren, then to picture him, in whom the fulness
of the godhead dwelt bodily, in his bearing how majestic, how
strong and yet how lovely and lissome in his limbs, in his look how
earnest, grave but kind. In his Passion all this strength was spent,
this lissomness crippled, this beauty wrecked, this majesty beaten
down. But now it is more than all restored, and for myself I make
no secret I look forward with eager desire to seeing the matchless
beauty of Christ's body in the heavenly light . . .

SERMON AT BEDFORD LEIGH

30 Nov. 1879

. . . Now, brethren, as the time of Christ's second coming is un-
certain so is the time of our death. Both are certain to come, both
are uncertain when. But one thing may be said of both and the
apostle says it: The night has got on, the day is nearer. This is, my
brethren, always true and always getting truer. Mark these two
things: every minute true, for it is at any minute true to say our life
has got some way on, our death made some approach, or again that
the world has gone on some time since Christ's first coming and
made some approach to his second; and also every minute truer for
every minute we and the world are older, every minute our death
and the world's end are nearer than before. For life and time are
always losing, always spending, always running down and running
out, therefore every hour that strikes is a warning of our end and
the world's end, for both these things are an hour nearer than
before. But there is a difference between our death and the world's
end: the world's end though every generation, one after another, is
warned of it, yet one only will be overtaken by it, the rest will have
passed away before; but death comes to everyone and none escapes.
Therefore God has given us more warnings of death: age is a warn-
ing, sickness is a warning, and the deaths of others that go before us

are a great warning. For the last day none have seen, but almost all men have seen death.

However, whether for the world's end or death, the apostle's warning is the same, to walk honestly, that is honourably, becomingly, wellbehavedly, as in the day, not etc. And Christ's warning is like it (Luke xxi 34.): But take heed to yourselves that your hearts be not loaded with overeating and drunkenness and cares of this life, and that day come upon you unawares. And these things that they warn us of, they abound; who needs the warning more than we? for the evils abound. Now more than ever is there riotous company, drunkenness, lewdness, strife, brawling, even bloodshed. To speak against all these things is too much. But look, brethren, at the order of them. First comes rioting or revelry, unruly company: here is the beginning of evil, bad company. Bad company seem hearty friends, goodnatured companions and such as a man should have: must not a man have his friend, his companion, unbend from his work at times, see company and life? Must he sit mum? must he mope at home? But, brethren, look at these things nearer. A friend is a friend, he loves you, he thinks of you and not only of his own pleasure. A rout of drinking companions do not love one another, they are selfish, they do not love their own, how can you think they care for strangers? Their own children may be hungry, their mothers or their wives in tears, their homes desolate and they are so good as to spend their time, their money, and their health with you. One of two things: you treat them or they you. If you treat them you like a fool spend your money on the worthless; if they treat you often you are eating their children's bread, you are draining the blood of their little ones. There is no friendship here, no love; there is no love, I say, where nothing comes in but selfishness.

And unruly company leads to drunkenness. Though many and many a tongue is now telling of it what tongue *can* tell the evils of drunkenness? – Drunkenness is shameful, it makes the man a beast; it drowns noble reason, their eyes swim, they hiccup in their talk, they gabble and blur their words, they stagger and fall and deal themselves dishonourable wounds, their faces grow blotched and bloated, scorpions are in their mind, they see devils and frightful sights. A little drunkenness is sad, a thing pitiful to see, and drunkenness confirmed and incurable is a world of woe. It defiles and dishonours the fresh blooming roses of youth, the strength of manhood, the grey hairs of age. It corrupts the children yet unborn, it gives convulsions to the poor sucking child. It is ugly in man, but in woman it is hideous beyond what words can say. And the world is laid waste with it.

It lays waste a home. There is no peace, there is no reverence or honour. The children are scandalised and taught to sin. Nay, it breaks home quite up, breaks the bond that God fastens, what he has joined it puts asunder, wife runs from drunken husband or husband from drunken wife.

It wastes, it spends, it brings on poverty. Times may be good, wages may abound, and yet in the house is seen want and slovenly disorder, for gold and silver and clothes and furniture and all are gone one way, down the belly. Or times may be bad and then surely there is nothing to spend on drink. But there is: feet may go bare and hearth be cold but the fire in the throat must be quenched with liquor or rather with liquor fanned to flame. And not only must the body want but the soul too is to fast and lose its food: the family cannot go to mass, obey the Church's commandment, worship God on his holy day in his holy place and be present at the great sacrifice; though it should cost not a penny they cannot do it, because the clothes are pawned.

And lastly drunkenness leads to worse sin than itself, leads to crimes – to cursing, blasphemy, abuse, the foul mouth; to all incontinence and impurity; to brawls and blows and bloodshed . . .

SERMON ON 'GOD'S KINGDOM' AT ST. FRANCIS XAVIER'S, LIVERPOOL

11 Jan. 1880

. . . Wherever there is a sovereign power, a king, an emperor, any kind of prince, ruler, governor, one such or more of them, or even a whole people selfgoverning and selfgoverned, there must always some understanding have gone before about the governing and the being governed – I mean those who are governed must have agreed to be governed and those who govern, they too must have accepted the task of government. Whether this understanding is well-known and a matter of history, as suppose the people have chosen a king and offered him the crown, or whether it is lost in the darkness of the past how it came about, nevertheless at any particular time when orderly government is going on there *is* such an agreement, there exists such an understanding: the subjects obey, at least they are not in rebellion; the rulers govern, at least they have not thrown up the reigns of power. For if the governed had never, neither at first nor after, submitted to be ruled / all would be riot, order could never have come about; if the ruling power had never, neither at first nor after, accepted the task of government how could he or his house or heirs or representatives be now upon the throne? The agreement, the understanding, the contract, must have somehow *come about*, and it will always have been brought about for the good of both parties, governor and governed, for their common good, their *common weal:* and this is what we call a commonwealth. For men are met in towns and assembled into states for their common well-being, to buy and sell, to marry and be given in marriage, for mutual defence, for learning's sake and company's sake, for a thousand reasons all gathered up in the words common weal or common-wealth. A leader and lawgiver for them there must be and they may choose one, but for the most part there is no need to enquire who was chosen or when, for people are born to things and rest content with them much as they are: look at ourselves, we have no two thoughts about the matter; we find the queen on her throne, houses of parliament, judges sitting or going, the army, the police, the postoffice at work; the common good is being provided for, we share it more or less, we share the common weal, we are part of the commonwealth; we may dislike this or that ministry or measure, move and agitate to get it changed, but as for refusing to be ruled at all and putting ourselves out of the commonwealth, to most people the very thought would never occur; they are born to share its advantages and therefore they suppose themselves born to share in its duties and be in its allegiance. I do not wish to speak of an oppressed country, where the burdens and not the blessings of government are felt, that sighs under a heavy yoke, but of a fairly well-governed one, and in such I say that those who find themselves born to the blessings and avail themselves of those blessings know they must be born to bear the burdens and that it is their duty to bear them.

Remark these two words, wellbeing or advantage and duty, for on them the commonwealth turns. The aim of every common-

wealth is the wellbeing, the welfare of all and this welfare of all is
secured by a duty binding all. For, as we have said, there is an
understanding, there is a contract, which once made, once allowed,
is in justice binding: he that undertook to govern bound himself to
look to the common good and for that he makes his laws; they that
undertook to be governed bound themselves to obey his laws and
perform what should be by them commanded. Hold fast this
thought, I say it once more: a commonwealth is the meeting of
many for their common good, for which good all are solemnly
agreed to strive and being so agreed are then in duty bound to
strive, the ruler by planning, the ruled by performing, the sovereign
by the weight of his authority, the subject by the stress of his
obedience.

Now what follows from this? – Something very beautiful and
noble and honourable. A covenant, a contract, an agreement, I mean
of course a lawful one, once made binds in justice and as it cannot
be broken without injustice and wrong, so it cannot be kept without
justice and right: therefore two that make and carry out a contract
are both just, both in the right. And mark this too, both *equally* just,
equally in their right. For this is the wonderful property of justice to
equalise those who share it: if I buy the baker's bread I cannot be
juster, righter, for paying my silver than he for delivering his
bread, nor yet he juster and righter for his bread than for my silver,
but the fair price having been asked and paid, we are both in our
duty, both in our rights, both equally in the right of it. So in the
commonwealth: the prince may have more prudence in planning the
campaign, the soldier more fortitude in storming the breach, but
justice, justice is halved between them or, if you like, whole in each
of them, the sovereign on his throne cannot be juster for claiming
obedience than the subject for yielding it. How bright a thing then is
good government and loyal submission, how bright a thing a well-
ordered commonwealth, where all the citizens, every least member
of the state, is glorified by one equal justice! every man a just man,
an honest man, an honourable man! for just means honest and
honest means deserving honour . . .

To his Mother

8 Salisbury Street, Liverpool. 2 March 1880

MY DEAREST MOTHER, – I wish you many happy returns of tomorrow: by great good luck, for we seldom have the opportunity of applying the mass to our own intentions, I was able to say mass for you this morning.

Every time I look at the stole you made I think it handsomer: I blessed it and handselled it on a poor consumptive girl yesterday. I believe however I could satisfy you that they can be made lighter, for I have a much lighter and more portable one: it is not, I think, of ribbon.

I wrote, as I do every year, to Cardinal Newman on his birthday the 21st of last month. I got by return of post a pretty little card of a spray of dogwood leaves, one green, two red and withered, symbolical perhaps of age, run through a card or piece of paper on which was written 'Many, many thanks. Pardon so brief an answer. J.H.N.', with a date.

The Musgrove Incident – Every week one of our community goes to Lydiate, to a Catholic country house the residence of the Lightbound family, so as to say mass next morning and return. It came to be my turn some weeks ago. I was returning to town in company with John Lightbound the only unmarried son. There entered the railway carriage a tall fine venerable-looking old gentleman with a benevolent air and silvery beautiful locks and beard, Mr Musgrove, in whose office John Lightbound is and considers as the greatest being in the world 'under the deity'. It was Thursday the eve of the Liverpool election. Mr Musgrove is a Radical. He handed about a portrait of Lord Ramsay, saying 'The future member for Liverpool'. 'I hope' said I 'that this is *not* the portrait of the future member for Liverpool'. From that we fell, pleasantly at first, into politics, but I talked so outrageously against Liberals and worse that Mr Musgrove was shocked and hurt and in a beautiful but alarming and no-joke-ative way, began addressing himself in such Noachian and Abramitical Methusalem-like strains to two little lads in the carriage, about their living to see something or other and marking his words, that it was very touching and brought on a creeping in the midriff. On alighting Mr Musgrove made off ahead and my host and the lads', the two infant Samuels', father told me how dangerous it was to broach politics to strangers. So it is and I was compunctious enough all that day; at last I wrote John Lightbound a letter to make my apologies to Mr Musgrove and said how wrong I had been. I got an answer to say that Mr Musgrove had been hurt indeed but now wd. think no more of the matter. However I was at Lydiate again last week and everything happened as before: Mr Musgrove got in and sat in the same corner, looking all sacred and silvery, and I was in my corner, but he wd. make me no sign of recognition. He had *not* forgiven me. Left to myself I shd. have accosted him and humbled myself till he had given in, but John Lightbound, as a kind of priest who had studied his theology and knew more than I cd. be supposed to do about the deity and propitiatory rites and ceremonies, wd. not have anything more said. I am very sorry, for Mr Musgrove appeared at the very time I was outraging him, a kind and good man and a gentleman; but what more could I do? I think it was for him to speak and shew he bore no malice...

To his Mother

Liverpool. 30 April, 1880

MY DEAREST MOTHER, – It is quite a long time since I wrote. Since then I have been knocked up, the work of Easter week (worse than Holy Week) was so hard, and I had happened to catch a bad cold, which led to earache and deafness: I felt wretched for some time. Neither am I very strong now and as long as I am in Liverpool I do not see how I can be; not that I complain of this, but I state it. There are many Italians here, organ grinders and so on; I do not know how they can bear such an air and sky. No, I see nothing of the Spring but some leaves in streets and squares. It is good, and all advise it, to get out of town and breathe fresh air at New Brighton or somewhere else, but I find it almost impossible. I have done it but once, barring the necessary run to Lydiate. I did not tell you then of the friendly scene of reconciliation between Mr Musgrove and me, which I had determined to bring about next time we shd. meet, and luckily I was with the more genial Randal Lightbound, not with

Mr Musgrove's highpriest John. It took place on a bitter cold morn-
ing by a glowing waiting-room fire at Town Green station. I
advanced and eat humblepie ravenously, Mr M. was very good-
natured and himself finished the dish. He must, as you say, be
radiant now. John Lightbound has never since alluded to my affair:
it stirs memories too sacred and terrible.

Gloomy as I felt over the elections there are one or two circum-
stances which reconcile me. And I tell myself that I ought to have
no politics and that I have burned my fingers, not only with Mr
Musgrove, where I was to blame, but elsewhere too, where I was
not.

I heard one time you had a sore mouth. I suppose it is gone, but
sometimes they last long.

I will add some lines for Grace. Work and sickness have stood in
the way of the music.

With best love to all, believe me your loving son
                                    GERARD M. HOPKINS S.J.

To Baillie

Liverpool. 22 May 1880

DEAREST BAILLIE, – I do not know how it is, when your letters give
me so much pleasure to get, I am so slow in answering them. At
least I can say my Liverpool work is very harassing and makes it
hard to write. Tonight I am sitting in my confessional, but the
faithful are fewer than usual and I am unexpectedly delivered from a
sermon which otherwise I should have had to be delivered of. Here
comes someone.

You say it is something of an affectation for me to run up the
Lancashire people and run down 'Oxonians' – unpleasant word, let
us say the Oxford ones. I do not remember quite what I said; are
you sure it was, as you assume, of Gown, not Town I was speaking?
Now I do like both. Not to love my University would be to undo
the very buttons of my being and as for the Oxford townspeople I
found them in my 10 months' stay among them very deserving of
affection – though somewhat stiff, stand-off, and depressed. And in
that stay I saw very little of the University. But I could not but feel
how alien it was, how chilling, and deeply to be distrusted. I could

have wished, and yet I could not, that there had been no one that
had known me there. As a fact there were many and those friendly,
some cordially so, but with others I cd. not feel at home. With the
Lancastrians it is the reverse; I felt as if [I] had been born to deal
with them. Religion, you know, enters very deep; in reality it is
the deepest impression I have in speaking to people, that they are or
that they are not of my religion. And then it is sweet to be a little
flattered and I can truly say that except in the most transparently
cringing way I seldom am. Now these Lancashire people of low
degree or not of high degree are those who most have seemed to me
to welcome me and make much of me. This is, I suppose, what was
on my mind.

. . . June 9 – I had written a great deal more, about this place (to
which I came on Dec. 30), but have suppressed it all after keeping
it by me and reading it with my head first on one side, then on the
other, at various distances and in various lights, many times over.
I do not think I can be long here; I have been long nowhere yet. I
am brought face to face with the deepest poverty and misery in my
district. On this theme I could write much, but it would do no
good.

What you write of Apuleius is interesting. But when you have a
parish you can no longer read nor have intellectual interests . . .

Notes on *Principium sive Fundamentum*

'Homo creatus est' – Aug. 20 1880: during this retreat, which I am
making at Liverpool, I have been thinking about creation and this
thought has led the way naturally through the exercises hitherto. I
put down some thoughts. – We may learn that all things are created
by consideration of the world without or of ourselves the world
within. The former is the consideration commonly dwelt on, but
the latter takes on the mind more hold. I find myself both as man
and as myself something most determined and distinctive, at pitch,
more distinctive and higher pitched than anything else I see; I find
myself with my pleasures and pains, my powers and my experiences,
my deserts and guilt, my shame and sense of beauty, my dangers,
hopes, fears, and all my fate, more important to myself than any-
thing I see. And when I ask where does all this throng and stack of

being, so rich, so distinctive, so important, come from / nothing I
see can answer me. And this whether I speak of human nature or of
my individuality, my selfbeing. For human nature, being more
highly pitched, selved, and distinctive than anything in the world,
can have been developed, evolved, condensed, from the vastness of
the world not anyhow or by the working of common powers but
only by one of finer or higher pitch and determination than itself
and certainly than any that elsewhere we see, for this power had to
force forward the starting or stubborn elements to the one pitch
required. And this is much more true when we consider the mind;
when I consider my selfbeing, my consciousness and feeling of
myself, that taste of myself, of *I* and *me* above and in all things,
which is more distinctive than the taste of ale or alum, more dist-
inctive than the smell of walnutleaf or camphor, and is incommunic-
able by any means to another man (as when I was a child I used to
ask myself: What must it be to be someone else?). Nothing else in
nature comes near this unspeakable stress of pitch, distinctiveness,
and selving, this selfbeing of my own. Nothing explains it or
resembles it, except so far as this, that other men to themselves have
the same feeling. But this only multiplies the phenomena to be
explained so far as the cases are like and do resemble. But to me
there is no resemblance: searching nature I taste *self* but at one
tankard, that of my own being. The development, refinement, con-
densation of nothing shews any sign of being able to match this to
me or give me another taste of it, a taste even resembling it . . .

To Bridges

Liverpool. 26 Jan. 1881

DEAREST BRIDGES, – This is that promised letter, begun on St.
Agnes' Eve, an Eve as bitter as in Keats, but found fault with and
begun again. The weather we are undergoing in Liverpool is not
remarkable except for its severity, or so at least I wrote at first, but
since then I have been into the country a little way and seen deep
frozen snowdrifts – yet these parts have felt the storm as little, I
think, as any – and I am shortly going down to see the ice in the
Mersey and the infinite flocks of seagulls of which I hear. But how-
ever I want you, as you are χιονουργός or χιονότεχνος, a snow-

wright or snowsmith or whatever one should say, to write me a graphic account of what London and its neighbourhood have been and looked like at this time.

Jan. 27 – Well, I went. The river was coated with dirty yellow ice from shore to shore; where the edges could be seen it seemed very thick; it was not smooth but many broken pieces framed or pasted together again; it was floating down stream with the ebb tide; it everywhere covered the water, but was not of a piece, being continually broken, ploughed up, by the plying of the steam ferry-boats, which I believe sometimes can scarcely make their way across. The gulls were pampered; throngs of people were chucking them bread; they were not at all quick to sight it and when they did they dipped towards it with infinite lightness, touched the ice, and rose again, *but generally missed the bread*: they seem to fancy they cannot or ought not to rest on ground. – However I hear the Thames is frozen and an ox roasted whole. Today there is a thaw, and the frostings, which have been a lovely fairyland on the pub-licans' windows, are vanished from the panes . . .

To his Mother

Liverpool. 2 March 1881

My Dearest Mother, – I wish you many very happy returns of tomorrow.

I am very sad at heart about the battle of Majuba. It is a deep disgrace, a stain upon our arms; which indeed have not shone of late. The effect will, I am afraid, be felt all over the empire. Would that we had some great statesman, a patriot and not a truckler to Russia or the Freemasons. I do hope we shall not be guilty of the folly of giving up Candahar.

I was at Hallé's last concert last night and will presently send Grace the book with my MS notes made at the time. There is to be another concert for his benefit next Tuesday – Berlioz' Faust, which must be a very striking, indeed a terror-striking, work. The band is to be increased and the prices are higher. I should much like to hear it, but fear it would be too much to go to two concerts two Tuesdays running.

The weather is very nasty.

Lenten work will no doubt be hard.

I have not heard Grace's hymns satisfactorily played yet.

With best love to all, I am your loving son

GERARD HOPKINS S.J.

TO BRIDGES

Liverpool. 27 April/1 May, 1881

May 1 – The procession was not so very good: some people had thought it shd. be on Monday and so everybody and every horse did not come. A busman or cabman consoled me by declaiming in a voice hoarse with professional passion that he cd. not get on for this damned show. While I admired the handsome horses I remarked for the thousandth time with sorrow and loathing the base and bespotted figures and features of the Liverpool crowd. When I see the fine and manly Norwegians that flock hither to embark for America walk our streets and look about them it fills me with shame and wretchedness. I am told Sheffield is worse though. We have been shamefully beaten by the Boers (at Majuba it was simply that our troops funked and ran), but this is not the worst that is to be . . .

TO DIXON

Manresa House, Roehampton, London, S.W. 12/17 Oct. 1881

. . . But Browning has, I think, many frigidities. Any untruth to nature, to human nature, is frigid. Now he has got a great deal of what came in with Kingsley and the Broad Church school, a way of talking (and making his people talk) with the air and spirit of a man bouncing up from table with his mouth full of bread and cheese and saying that he meant to stand no blasted nonsense. There is a whole volume of Kingsley's essays which is all a kind of munch and a not standing of any blasted nonsense from cover to cover. Do you know what I mean? The *Flight of the Duchess*, with the repetition of 'My friend', is in this vein. Now this is *one* mood or vein of human nature, but they would have it all and look at all human nature through it. And Tennyson in his later works has been 'carried away with their dissimulation.' The effect of this style is a frigid bluster. A true humanity of spirit, neither mawkish on the one hand nor blustering on the other, is the most precious of all qualities in style, and this I prize in your poems, as I do in Bridges'. After all it is the breadth of his human nature that we admire in Shakespeare.

I read some, not much of the *Ring and the Book*, but as the tale was not edifying and one of our people, who had been reviewing it, said that further on it was coarser, I did not see, without a particular object, sufficient reason for going on with it. So far as I read I was greatly struck with the skill in which he displayed the facts from different points of view: this is masterly, and to do it through three volumes more shews a great body of genius. I remember a good case of 'the impotent collection of particulars' of which you speak in the description of the market place at Florence where he found the book of the trial: it is a pointless photograph of still life, such as I remember in Balzac, minute upholstery description; only that in Balzac, who besides is writing prose, all tells and is given with a reserve and simplicity of style which Browning has not got. Indeed I hold with the oldfashioned criticism that Browning is not really a poet, that he has all the gifts but the one needful and the pearls without the string; rather one should say raw nuggets and rough diamonds. I suppose him to resemble Ben Jonson, only that Ben Jonson has more real poetry.

As for Carlyle; I have a letter by me never sent, in answer to a pupil of mine, who had written about him, and I find I there say just what you do about his incapacity of general truths. And I always thought him morally an imposter, worst of all imposters a false prophet. And his style has imposture or pretence in it. But I find it difficult to think there is imposture in his genius itself. However I must write no more criticism.

I see you do not understand my position in the Society. This Tertianship or Third Year of Probation or second Noviceship, for it is variously called in the Institute, is not really a noviceship at all in the sense of a time during which a candidate or probationer makes trial of our life and is free to withdraw. At the end of the noviceship proper we take vows which are perpetually binding and renew them every six months (not *for* every six months but for life) till we are professed or take the final degree we are to hold, of which in the Society there are several. It is in preparation for these last vows that

we make the tertianship; which is called a *schola affectus* and is
meant to enable us to recover that fervour which may have cooled
through application to study and contact with the world. Its exer-
cises are however nearly the same as those of the first noviceship.
As for myself, I have not only made my vows publicly some two
and twenty times but I make them to myself every day, so that I
should be black with perjury if I drew back now. And beyond that I
can say with St. Peter: To whom shall I go? *Tu verba vitae aeternae
habes.* Besides all which, my mind is here more at peace than it has
ever been and I would gladly live all my life, if it were so to be, in as
great or a greater seclusion from the world and be busied only with
God. But in the midst of outward occupations not only the mind is
drawn away from God, which may be at the call of duty and be
God's will, but unhappily the will too is entangled, worldly interests
freshen, and worldly ambitions revive. The man who in the world
is as dead to the world as if he were buried in the cloister is already
a saint. But this is our ideal . . .

To Dixon

Roehampton. 29 Oct. 1881

. . . On the Sonnet and its history a learned book or two learned
books have been published of late and all is known about it – but
not by me. The reason why the sonnet has never been so effective
or successful in England as in Italy I believe to be this: it is not so
long as the Italian sonnet; it is not long enough, I will presently say
how. Now in the form of any work of art the intrinsic measure-
ments, the proportions, that is, of the parts to one another and to
the whole, are no doubt the principal point, but still the extrinsic
measurements, the absolute quantity or size goes for something.
Thus supposing in the Doric Order the Parthenon to be the
standard of perfection, then if the columns of the Parthenon have
so many semidiameters or modules to their height, the architrave
so many, and so on these will be the typical proportions. But if a
building is raised on a notably greater scale it will be found that
these proportions for the columns and the rest are no longer satis-
factory, so that one of two things – either the proportions must be
changed or the Order abandoned. Now if the Italian sonnet is one

of the most successful forms of composition known, as it is reck-
oned to be, its proportions, inward and outward, must be pretty
near perfection. The English sonnet has the same inward propor-
tions, 14 lines, 5 feet to the line, and the rhymes and so on may be
made as in the strictest Italian type. Nevertheless it is notably
shorter and would therefore appear likely to be unsuccessful, from
want not of comparative but of absolute length. For take any lines
from an Italian sonnet, as

> Non ha l'ottimo artista alcun concetto
> Che un marmor solo in se non circonscriva.

Each line has two elisions and a heavy ending or 13 syllables, though
only 10 or, if you like, 11 count in the scanning. An Italian heroic
line then and consequently a sonnet will be longer than an English
in the proportion 13:10, which is considerable. But this is not all:
the syllables themselves are longer. We have seldom such a delay
in the voice as is given to the syllable by doubled letters (as *ottimo*
and *concetto*) or even by two or more consonants (as *artista* and
circonscriva) of any sort, read as Italians read. Perhaps then the
proportions are nearer 4:3 or 3:2. The English sonnet is then in
comparison with the Italian short, light, tripping, and trifling.

This has been instinctively felt and the best sonnets shew various
devices successfully employed to make up for the short-coming. It
may be done by the mere gravity of the thought, which compels a
longer dwelling on the words, as in Wordsworth (who otherwise
is somewhat light in his versification), e.g.

> Earth has not anything to shew more fair – etc;

or by inversion and a periodic construction, which has something
the same effect: there is a good deal of this in Bridges' sonnets; or
by breaks and pauses, as

> Captain or colonel or knight-at-arms;

or by many monosyllables, as

> Both them I serve and of their train am I:

this is common with τοὺς περὶ Swinburne; or by the weight of the
syllables themselves, strong or circumflexed and so on, as may be
remarked in Gray's sonnet, an exquisite piece of art, whatever
Wordsworth may say,

> In vain to me the smiling mornings shine –

(this sonnet is remarkable for its falling or trochaic rhythm –

> In|vain to|me the|smiling|mornings|shine –

and not

      In vain|to me|the smil|ing morn|ings shine),

and it seems to me that for a mechanical difficulty the most mechan-
ical remedy is the best: none, I think, meet it so well as these 'out-
riding' feet I sometimes myself employ, for they more than equal
the Italian elisions and make the whole sonnet rather longer, if any-
thing, than the Italian is. Alexandrine lines (used throughout) have
the same effect: this of course is a departure from the Italian, but
French sonnets are usually in Alexandrines.

The above reasoning wd. shew that any metre (in the same
rhythm) will be longer in Italian than in English and this is in fact,
I believe, the case and is the reason perhaps why the *ottava rima* has
never had the success in England it has had in Italy and why
Spencer found it necessary to lengthen it in the ration from 20 to 23
(= 80 to 92).

Surrey's sonnets are fine, but so far as I remember them they are
strict in form. I look upon Surrey as a great writer and of the purest
style. But he was an experimentalist, as you say, and all his experi-
ments are not successful. I feel ashamed however to talk of English
or any literature, of which I was always very ignorant and which I
have ceased to read.

... This must be my last letter on literary matters while I stay
here, for they are quite out of keeping with my present duties. I am
very glad my criticism should be of any service to you: they have
involved a labour of love.

Nov. 2 – My sister is unwilling to send you the music, with which
she is not satisfied, till I have seen it. It must therefore wait awhile.

I am ashamed at the expression of high regard which your last
letter and others have contained, kind and touching as they are, and
do not know whether I ought to reply to them or not. This I say:
my vocation puts before me a standard so high that a higher can be
found nowhere else. The question then for me is not whether I am
willing (if I may guess what is in your mind) to make a sacrifice of
hopes of fame (let us suppose), but whether I am not to undergo a
severe judgment from God for the lothness I have shewn in making
it, for the reserves I may have in my heart made, for the backward
glances I have given with my hand upon the plough, for the waste of
time the very compositions you admire may have caused and their
preoccupation of the mind which belonged to more sacred or more

binding duties, for the disquiet and the thoughts of vainglory they have given rise to. A purpose may look smooth and perfect from without but be frayed and faltering from within. I have never wavered in my vocation, but I have not lived up to it. I destroyed the verse I had written when I entered the Society and meant to write no more; the *Deutschland* I began after a long interval at the chance suggestion of my superior, but that being done it is a question whether I did well to write anything else. However I shall, in my present mind, continue to compose, as occasion shall fairly allow, which I am afraid will be seldom and indeed for some years past has been scarcely ever, and let what I produce wait and take its chance; for a very spiritual man once told me that with things like composition the best sacrifice was not to destroy one's work but to leave it entirely to be disposed of by obedience. But I can scarcely fancy myself asking a superior to publish a volume of my verses and I own that humanly there is very little likelihood of that ever coming to pass. And to be sure if I chose to look at things on one side and not the other I could of course regret this bitterly. But there is more peace and it is the holier lot to be unknown than to be known . . .

TO DIXON

Roehampton. 1/16 Dec. 1881

(the very day 300 years ago of Father Campion's martyrdom).

MY DEAR FRIEND, – I am heartily glad you did not make away with, as you say you thought of doing, so warm and precious a letter as your last. It reached me on the first break or day of repose in our month's retreat; I began answering it on the second, but could not finish; and this is the third and last of them.

When a man has given himself to God's service, when he has denied himself and followed Christ, he has fitted himself to receive and does receive from God a special guidance, a more particular providence. This guidance is conveyed partly by the action of other men, as his appointed superiors, and partly by direct lights and inspirations. If I wait for such guidance, through whatever channel conveyed, about anything, about my poetry for instance, I do more wisely in every way than if I try to serve my own seeming interests in the matter. Now if you value what I write, if I do myself, much more does our Lord. And if he chooses to avail himself of what I leave at his disposal he can do so with a felicity and with a success which I could never command. And if he does not, then two things follow; one that the reward I shall nevertheless receive from him will be all the greater; the other that then I shall know how much a thing contrary to his will and even to my own best interests I should have done if I had taken things into my own hands and forced on publication. This is my principle and this in the main has been my practice: leading the sort of life I do here it seems easy, but when one mixes with the world and meets on every side its secret solicitations, to live by faith is harder, is very hard; nevertheless by God's help I shall always do so.

Our Society values, as you say, and has contributed to literature, to culture; but only as a means to an end. Its history and its experience shew that literature proper, as poetry, has seldom been found to be to that end a very serviceable means. We have had for three centuries often the flower of the youth of a country in numbers enter our body: among these how many poets, how many artists of all sorts, there must have been! But there have been very few Jesuit poets and, where they have been, I believe it would be found on examination that there was something exceptional in their circumstances or, so to say, counterbalancing in their career. For genius attracts fame and individual fame St. Ignatius looked on as the most dangerous and dazzling of all attractions. There was a certain Fr. Beschi who in Southern Hindustan composed an epic which has become one of the Tamul classics and is spoken of with unbounded admiration by those who can read it. But this was in India, far from home, and one can well understand that fame among Hindu pundits need not turn the head of an Italian. In England we had Fr. Southwell a poet, a minor poet but still a poet; but he wrote amidst a terrible persecution and died a martyr, with circumstances of horrible barbarity: that is the counterpoise in his career. Then what a genius was Campion himself! was not he a poet? perhaps a great one, if he had chosen. His History of Ireland, written in hiding and hurrying from place to place, Mr Simpson in his Life says, and the samples prove it, shews an eloquence like Shakspere's; and in fact Shakspere made use of the book. He had all and more than all the rhetoric of that golden age and was probably the most vigorous

mind and eloquent tongue engaged in theological strife then in
England, perhaps in Europe. It seems in time he might have done
anything. But his eloquence died on the air, his genius was quenched
in his blood after one year's employment in his country. Music is
more professional than poetry perhaps and Jesuits have com-
posed and well, but none has any fame to speak of. We had one
painter who reached excellence, I forget his name, he was a lay-
brother; but then he only painted flower pieces. You see then what
is against me, but since, as Solomon says, there is a time for every-
thing, there is nothing that does not some day come to be, it may
be that the time will come for my verses. I remember, by the by,
once taking up a little book of the life of St. Stanislaus told or com-
mented on under emblems; it was much in the style of Herbert and
his school and about that date; it was by some Polish Jesuit. I was
astonished at their beauty and brilliancy, but the author is quite
obscure. Brilliancy does not suit us. Bourdaloue is reckoned our
greatest orator: he is severe in style. Suarez is our most famous theo-
logian: he is a man of vast volume of mind, but without originality
or brilliancy; he treats everything satisfactorily, but you never
remember a phrase of his, the manner is nothing. Molina is the man
who *made* our theology: he was a genius and even in his driest
dialectic I have remarked a certain fervour like a poet's. But in the
great controversy on the Aids of Grace, the most dangerous crisis,
as I suppose, which our Society ever went through till its suppres-
sion, though it was from his book that it had arisen, he took, I think,
little part. The same sort of thing may be noticed in our saints.
St. Ignatius himself was certainly, every one who reads his life will
allow, one of the most extraordinary men that ever lived; but after
the establishment of the Order he lived in Rome so ordinary, so
hidden a life, that when after his death they began to move in the
process of his canonisation one of the Cardinals, who had known
him in his later life and in that way only, said that he had never re-
marked anything in him more than in any edifying priest. St.
Stanislaus Kostka's life and vocation is a bright romance – till he
entered the noviceship, where after 10 months he died, and at the
same time its interest ceases. Much the same may be said of St.
Aloysius Gonzaga. The Blessed John Berchmans was beatified for
his most exact observance of the rule; he said of himself and the text
is famous among us, Common life is the greatest of my mortifica-

tions; Gregory XVI (I think) when the first steps were to be taken
said of him too: At that rate you will have to canonize all the
Roman College. I quote these cases to prove that show and bril-
liancy do not suit us, that we cultivate the commonplace outwardly
and wish the beauty of the king's daughter the soul to be from
within.

I could say much more on all this, but it is enough and I must go
on to other things. Our retreat ended on the 8th. The 'hoity toity'
passage I have not seen; indeed I have never even had your book in
my hands except one day when waiting to see Bridges in his sick-
ness I found it on the table and was just going to open it – but to
the best of my remembrance I did not then open it either. I have for
some years past had to put aside serious study. It is true if I had
been where your book was easy of access I should have looked at it,
perhaps read it all, but in Liverpool I never once entered the public
library. However if, as I hope, the time for reading history should
ever come I shall try to read this one. You said once you did not
pretend not to have a side and that you must write as an Anglican:
this is of course and you could not honestly be an Anglican and not
write as one. Do you know Cobbett's *Reformation?* Cobbett was a
most honest man but not an honest Anglican; I shd. rather say that
he was an honest thinker and an honest speaker but not an honest
actor-out of his convictions but is a conspicuous 'bell in a bellcot'
and 'signpost on a road'. The book is written with the greatest vio-
lence of language; I must own that to me the strength seems not at
all too strong; but from the point of view of expediency it is far too
much so, it has overshot its mark, and those for whom it is meant
will not read it. I much wish some learned Catholic would reëdit it
and bring it up to date. The most valuable and striking part of it to
me is the doctrine about the origin of pauperism: I shd. much myself
like to follow this out. My Liverpool and Glasgow experience laid
upon my mind a conviction, a truly crushing conviction, of the
misery of town life to the poor and more than to the poor, of the
misery of the poor in general, of the degradation even of our race,
of the hollowness of this century's civilisation: it made even life a
burden to me to have daily thrust upon me the things I saw.

... About sonnet-writing I never meant to override your own
judgment. I have put the objections to licentious forms and I believe
they hold. But though many sonnets in English may in point of form

be great departures from and degenerations of the type, put aside
the reference to the type, and they may in themselves be fine poems
of 14 lines. Still that fact, that the poet has tied himself within 14
lines and calls the piece a sonnet, lays him open to objection.

I must hold that you and Morris belong to one school, and that
though you should neither of you have read a line of the other's. I
suppose the same models, the same masters, the same tastes, the
same keepings, above all, make the school. It will always be possible
to find differences, marked differences, between original minds; it
will be necessarily so. So the species in nature are essentially distinct,
nevertheless they are grouped into genera: they have one form in
common, mounted on that they have a form that differences them. I
used to call it the school of Rossetti: it is in literature the school of
the Prae-raphaelites. Of course that phase is in part past, neither do
these things admit of hard and fast lines; still consider yourself, that
you know Rossetti and Burne Jones, Rossetti through his sympathy
for you and Burne Jones – was it the same or your sympathy for
him? This modern medieval school is descended from the Romantic
school (Romantic is a bad word) of Keats, Leigh Hunt, Hood, in-
deed of Scott early in the century. That was one school; another was
that of the Lake poets and also of Shelley and Landor; the third was
the sentiment school, of Byron, Moore, Mrs Hemans, and Haynes
Bailey. Schools are very difficult to class: the best guide, I think, are
keepings. Keats' school chooses medieval keepings, not pure nor
drawn from the middle ages direct but as brought down through
that Elizabethan tradition of Shakspere and his contemporaries
which died out in such men as Herbert and Herrick. They were also
great realists and observers of nature. The Lake poets and all that
school represent, as it seems to me, the mean or standard of English
style and diction, which culminated in Milton but was never very
continuous or vigorously transmitted, and in fact none of these men
unless perhaps Landor were great masters of style, though their
diction is generally pure, lucid, and unarchaic. They were faithful
but not rich observers of nature. Their keepings are their weak
point, a sort of colourless classical keepings: when Wordsworth
wants to describe a city or a cloudscape which reminds him of a city
it is some ordinary rhetorical stage-effect of domes, palaces, and
temples. Byron's school had a deep feeling but the most untrust-
worthy and barbarous eye, for nature; a diction markedly modern;

and their keepings any gaud or a lot of Oriental rubbish. I suppose
Crabbe to have been in form a descendant of the school of Pope
with a strong and modern realistic eye; Rogers something between
Pope's school and that of Wordsworth and Landor; and Campbell
between this last and Byron's, with a good deal of Popery too, and a
perfect master of style. Now since this time Tennyson and his school
seem to me to have struck a mean or compromise between Keats
and the medievalists on the one hand and Wordsworth and the Lake
School on the other (Tennyson has some jarring notes of Byron in
Lady Clare Vere de Vere, *Locksley Hall* and elsewhere). The Lake
School expires in Keble and Faber and Cardinal Newman. The
Brownings may be reckoned to the Romantics. Swinburne is a
strange phenomenon: his poetry seems a powerful effort at estab-
lishing a new standard of poetical diction, of the rhetoric of poetry;
but to waive every other objection it is essentially archaic, biblical
a good deal, and so on: now that is a thing that can never last; a
perfect style must be of its age. In virtue of this archaism and on
other grounds he must rank with the medievalists . . .

On the Principle or Foundation

1881–2

. . . WHY DID GOD CREATE? – Not for sport, not for nothing.
Every sensible man has a purpose in all he does, every workman has
a use for every object he makes. Much more has God a purpose, an
end, a meaning in his work. He meant the world to give him praise,
reverence, and service; *to give him glory*. It is like a garden, a field he
sows: what should it bear him? praise, reverence, and service; it
should yield him glory. It is an estate he farms: what should it bring
him in? Praise, reverence, and service; it should repay him glory. It
is a leasehold he lets out: what should its rent be? Praise, reverence,
and service; its rent is his glory. It is a bird he teaches to sing, a pipe,
a harp he plays on: what should it sing to him? etc. It is a glass he
looks in: what should it shew him? With praise, reverence, and ser-
vice it should shew him his own glory. It is a book he has written, of
the riches of his knowledge, teaching endless truths, full lessons of
wisdom, a poem of beauty: what is it about? His praise, the rever-
ence due to him, the way to serve him; it tells him of his glory. It is a
censer fuming: what is the sweet incense? His praise, his reverence,

his service; it rises to his glory. It is an altar and a victim on it lying in his sight: why is it offered? To his praise, honour, and service: it is a sacrifice to his glory.

The creation does praise God, does reflect honour on him, is of service to him, and yet the praises fall short; the honour is like none, less than a buttercup to a king; the service is of no service to him. In other words *he does not need it*. He has infinite glory without it and what is infinite can be made no bigger. Nevertheless he takes it: he wishes it, asks it, he commands it, he enforces it, he gets it.

The sun and the stars shining glorify God. They stand where he placed them, they move where he bid them. 'The heavens declare the glory of God'. They glorify God, *but they do not know it*. The birds sing to him, the thunder speaks of his terror, the lion is like his strength, the sea is like his greatness, the honey like his sweetness; they are something like him, they make him known, they tell of him, they give him glory, but they do not know they do, they do not know him, they never can, they are brute things that only think of food or think of nothing. This then is poor praise, faint reverence, slight service, dull glory. Nevertheless what they can *they always do*.

But AMIDST THEM ALL IS MAN, man and the angels: we will speak of man. Man was created. Like the rest then to praise, reverence, and serve God; to give him glory . . .

I WAS MADE FOR THIS, each one of us was made for this . . .

Turn then, brethren, now and give God glory. You do say grace at meals and thank and praise God for your daily bread, so far so good, but thank and praise him now for everything. When a man is in God's grace and free from mortal sin, then everything that he does, so long as there is no sin in it, gives God glory and what does not give him glory has some, however little, sin in it. It is not only prayer that gives God glory but work. Smiting on an anvil, sawing a beam, whitewashing a wall, driving horses, sweeping, scouring, everything gives God some glory if being in his grace you do it as your duty. To go to communion worthily gives God great glory, but to take food in thankfulness and temperance gives him glory too. To lift up the hands in prayer gives God glory, but a man with a dungfork in his hand, a woman with a sloppail, gives him glory too. He is so great that all things give him glory if you mean they should. So then, my brethren, live.

A.M.D.G.

MEDITATION ON HELL

? 1881–2

Preparatory prayer.

1st. prelude – to see with the eyes of the imagination the length, breadth, and depth of Hell. Not known where Hell is; many say beneath our feet. It is at all events *a place of imprisonment*, a prison; *a place of darkness*; and *a place of torment* and that by fire (case of Dives). The devils wander, but bear their torment with them. There is such a place: shutting our eyes will not do away with a steeple or a sign-post nor will not thinking of or not believing in Hell put it out of being.

2nd. prelude – To ask for what we want, which here is such an inward feeling of the pain the damned suffer if we ever come to forget the love of the eternal Lord, through our faults (our venial sins, lukewarmness, worldliness, negligence), the fear of hell-pains at least may help us then and keep us from falling into mortal sin. The great evil of hell is the loss of God, but we think little enough of this: let us think then of what we dread even here, the pain of fire and others, that we understand.

1st point – *with the eyes of the imagination to see* those huge flames and the souls of the lost as if in bodies of fire. The lost now lying in hell are Devils without bodies and disembodied souls, they suffer nevertheless a torment as of bodily fire. Though burning and other pains afflict us through our bodies yet it is the soul that they afflict, the mind: if the mind can be deadened, as by chloroform no pain is felt at all: God can then if he chooses bodily afflict the mind that is out of or never had a body to suffer in. No one in the body can suffer fire for very long, the frame is destroyed and the pain comes to an end; not so, unhappily, the pain that afflicts the indestructible mind, nor after the Judgment day the incorruptible body. Christ speaks of the lost as being salted, that is preserved, with fire and some things, like asbestos-cloth or fireclay, burn but are unchanged. This fire afflicts the lost only so far as they have sinned: therefore the rich glutton asks for a drop of water for *his tongue*, for by the tongue he sinned on earth. Let all consider this: we are our own tormentors, for every sin we then shall have remorse and with remorse torment and the torment fire. The murderer suffers one way, the drunkard another, but all can say they are tormented in that flame. The glutton had there no tongue to torment and yet he was tormented in that flame, for God punishing him through his own guilty thoughts made him seem to suffer in the part that had offended. So of all. In that flame then see them now. They have no bodies there, flame is the body that they wear. You have seen a glassblower breathe on a flame; at once it darts out into a jet taper as a lance-head and as piercing too. The breath of God's anger first kindled the fire of hell; (Is. xxx 33.) it strikes with a distinct indignation still on each distinct unforgiven sin; the wretched soul starts into a flame that has some frightful and fantastic likeness to its sin; so sinners are themselves the flames of hell. O hideous and ungainly sight! which will cease only when at the day of Judgment the body and the soul are at one again and the sinful members themselves and in themselves receive their punishment, a punishment which lasts for ever. *Their worm*, our Lord says, *does not die and their fire is never quenched*.

2nd point – Hear with the ears the wailings (of despair), howls (of pain), cries (of self reproach), blasphemies against Christ our Lord and all his saints because they are in heaven and *they* lost in hell. They do not all blaspheme, there is a sullen dreadful silence of despair; but blaspheme or not, they know and are convinced their chastisement is just. They know that too well; their consciences, their own minds judge them and tell them so. They appeared before Christ at death, their mind's eye was opened, they saw themselves, condemned themselves, despaired, asked for no mercy, and turned from that sight to bury themselves anywhere, even in hell; as a frightened or shamed child buries its head in the pillow they bury theirs in the pit. Neither do they cry with throat and tongue, they have none, but their wailing is an utterance that passes in their woeful thoughts. Nevertheless spirits as they are, they hear and understand each other and add to each other's woe. And if it fears you, brethren, to think of it, but to imagine it, when your ears are open to other and to cheerful living sounds, believe that it is worse to them that have nothing else to do but wail or listen to but wailing.

3rd point – Smell with an imaginary smell the smoke, the brimstone, the dregs and bilgewater of that pit, all that is foul and loathsome. The same must be said of here as has been said of eyes and

ears. It is sin that makes them fuel to that fire: the blinding stifling
tear-drawing remembrance of a crowd of sins is to them like smoke;
stinging remorse is like the biting brimstone; their impurity comes
up before them, they loved it once and breathed it, now it revolts
them, it is to them like vomit and like dung, and they cannot quit
themselves of it: why not? because they are guilty of it; it is *their
own sin:* they wallowed in it willingly, now against their will they
must for ever wallow.

Sight does not shock like hearing, sounds cannot so disgust as
smell, smell is not so bitter as proper bitterness, which is in taste;
therefore for the

Fourth point – taste as with taste of tongue all that is bitter there,
the tears ceaselessly and fruitlessly flowing; the grief over their
hopeless loss; the worm of conscience, which is the mind gnawing
and feeding on its own most miserable self . . .

To Bridges

Roehampton. 10 June 1882

DEAREST BRIDGES, – It was a needless and tedious frenzy (no, the
phrase is *not* like Flatman's 'serene and rapturous joys' to which
poor Purcell had to drudge the music): another train came up on
that train's tail, and indeed it was a dull duncery that overhung us
both not to see that its being Ascot day ensured countless more
trains and not fewer. There was a lovely and passionate scene (for
about the space of the last trump) between me and a tallish gentle-
man (I daresay he was a cardsharper) in your carriage who was by
way of being you; I smiled, I murmured with my lips at him, I
waved farewells, but he would not give in, till with burning shame
(though the whole thing was, as I say, like the duels of archangels) I
saw suddenly what I was doing.

I wish our procession, since you were to see it, had been better:
I find it is agreed it was heavy and dead. Now a Corpus Christi
procession shd. be stately indeed, but it shd. be brisk and joyous.
But I grieve more, I am vexed, that you had not a book to follow
the words sung: the office is by St. Thomas and contains all his
hymns, I think. These hymns, though they have the imperfect rhe-
toric and weakness in idiom of all medieval Latin verse (except, say,

the Dies Irae: I do not mean weakness in classical idiom – that does not matter – but want of feeling for or command of *any* idiom), are nevertheless remarkable works of genius and would have given meaning to the whole, even to the music, much more to the rite.

It is long since such things had any significance for you. But what is strange and unpleasant is that you sometimes speak as if they had in reality none for me and you were only waiting with a certain disgust till I too should be disgusted with myself enough to throw off the mask. You said something of the sort walking on the Cowley Road when we were last at Oxford together – in '79 it must have been. Yet I can hardly think you do not think I am in earnest. And let me say, to take no higher ground, that without earnestness there is nothing sound or beautiful in character and that a cynical vein much indulged coarsens everything in us. Not that you do over-indulge this vein in other matters: why then does it bulk out in that diseased and varicose way in this?

Believe me your affectionate friend

GERARD M. HOPKINS S.J. ....

TO BRIDGES

Stonyhurst College, Blackburn, 26/27 Sept. 1882

MY DEAREST BRIDGES, – I *must* break this mournful silence. I began a letter yesterday, but am not pleased with it and now shall be brief.

I have been here since this month came in. My appointment is to teach our 'philosophers' (like undergraduate students) Latin, Greek, and perhaps hereafter English (when I know more about it) for the London B.A. degree. My pupils will be here with the next month. The Provincial further added that what time was left over I might employ in writing one or other of the books I had named to him. But very little time will be left over and I cd. never make time. Indeed now, with nothing to do but prepare, I cannot get forward with my ode. But one must hope against hope.

I did in my last week at Roehampton write 16 pages of a rough draft of a commentary on St. Ignatius' Spiritual Exercises. This work would interest none but a Jesuit, but to me it is interesting enough and, as you see, it is very professional.

I shall try and read the Greek tragic poets, but it is sad how slow I am. I am now in the *Agamemnon* and *Supplices* (Aeschylus's, I mean). How noble is the style! I have made some emendations which seem to be great improvements. But what I pay most attention to is the art of the choric parts, for this was one of the subjects on which I had proposed to write, the art of the Greek lyric poets, including of course the lyric parts of dramatic poets. I have not time at present to tell you what the leading idea or my leading discovery is. In part of course my work here may serve me for the books I should like to write.

The Provincial gave me leave to go to any one of our houses I liked till my term began. I did go for a week to Worcester, where there was, by the by, a very well worth seeing exhibition, but then I thought it better to come here at once. He said moreover that if I wanted to go elsewhere I was to apply to him. He would no doubt readily have given me leave to visit you and, had there been the possibility of saying mass, I might therefore have seen Yattenden. But it was not to be.

I wish I could show you this place. It is upon my word worth seeing. The new college, though there is no real beauty in the design, is nevertheless imposing and the furniture and fittings are a joy to see. There is always a stirring scene, contractors, builders, masons, bricklayers, carpenters, stonecutters and carvers, all on the spot; a traction engine twice a day fetches stone from a quarry on the fells; engines of all sorts send their gross and foulsmelling smoke all over us; cranes keep swinging; and so on. There are acres of flat roof which, when the air is not thick, as unhappily it mostly is, commands a noble view of this Lancashire landscape, Pendle Hill, Ribblesdale, the fells, and all round, bleakish but solemn and beautiful. There is a garden with a bowling green, walled in by massive yew hedges, a bowered yew-walk, two real Queen Anne summerhouses, observatories under government, orchards, vineries, greenhouses, workshops, a plungebath, fivescourts, a mill, a farm, a fine cricketfield besides a huge playground; then the old mansion, ponds, towers, quadrangles, fine cielings, chapels, a church, a fine library, museums, MSS illuminated and otherwise, coins, works of art; then two other dependent establishments, one a furlong, the other $\frac{3}{4}$ a mile off; the river Hodder with lovely fairyland views, especially at the bathingplace, the Ribble too, the Calder, Whalley with an abbey, Clitheroe with a castle, Ribchester with a strange old chapel and Roman remains; schoolboys and animation, philosophers and foppery (not to be taken too seriously) a jackdaw, a rookery, goldfish, a clough with waterfalls, fishing, grouse, an anemometer, a sunshine guage, a sundial, an icosihedron, statuary, magnetic instruments, a laboratory, gymnasium, ambulacrum, studio, fine engravings, Arundel chromos, Lancashire talked with *naïveté* on the premises (Hoo said this and hoo did that) – and, what caps all, if I were shewing it you, as I hope to do (I have to shew it too often: it takes from an hour and a half to three hours: I do it with more pride than pleasure) you could not make me wretched now by either stealing or buying fruit.

I want to hear about Yattenden (or Yattendon?). And when will *Prometheus* be out?

I should be sorry to think you did nothing down there but literary work: could you not be a magistrate? This would be honourable and valuable public duty. Consider it.

I am your affectionate friend

GERARD M. HOPKINS S.J.

TO BAILLIE

Stonyhurst College. 14 Jan. 1883

DEAREST BAILLIE, – I believe I am writing chiefly to withdraw something I said at our last meeting, though if there had been nothing to withdraw still I ought to write; but blackguardry stamps my whole behaviour to you from first to last.

Strong words are seldom much good and the more of heat the less of reason. The strong word I repent of using was that if ever there was a humbug it was Swedenborg. What I might reasonably have said (and what I really meant) was that Swedenborgianism (what a word!) is humbug. But I ought not to have seemed to imply that Swedenborg himself was an impostor or anything of the nature of Cagliostro, for so far as I know there is no ground for saying this. He had some very strange experiences: how he came by them no matter, but he may have related them faithfully. It is however a great folly of his followers to build on them. His first dealing with the other world took place at an eating-house in

London, where after a very heavy dinner (so he is quoted as saying in his journal) he saw the cieling (or the floor) covered with hideous reptiles. Then he was aware of a light in a corner of the room and of a luminous figure which sternly said to him 'Do not eat so much'. After that he began to receive communications. The circumstances suggest delirium tremens, as everyone must feel. Whatever the explanation, no sensible man would feel happy in a religion which began to to be revealed in that way.

I am here to coach classics for the London University Intermediate (say Moderations) and B.A. (say Greats) examinations. I like my pupils and do not wholly dislike the work, but I fall into or continue in a heavy weary state of body and mind in which my go is gone (the elegance of that phrase! as Thackeray says, it makes one think what vast sums must have been spent on my education!), I make no way with what I read, and seem but half a man. It is a sad thing to say. I try, and am even meant to try, in my spare time (and if I were fresher or if it were anyone but myself there would be a good deal of spare time taking short and long together) to write some books; but I find myself so tired or so harassed I fear they will never be written. The one that would interest you most is on the Greek Lyric Art or on, more narrowly, the art of the choric and lyric parts of the Gk. plays. I want it to be in two parts, one the metre, the other the style. It is, I am afraid, too ambitious of me, so little of a scholar as I am; only I think what I should say would throw a new light and that if I did not perhaps no one else would. But it is a laborious business and why shd. I undertake it? There are, I believe, learned books lately written in Germany on the choric metres and music, which if I could see and read them would either serve me or quench me; but on the other head I do not anticipate being anticipated – so to say. My thought is that in any lyric passage of the tragic poets (perhaps not so much in Euripides as the others) there are – usually; I will not say always, it is not likely – two strains of thought running together and like counterpointed; the overthought that which everybody, editors, see (when one does see anything – which in the great corruption of the text and original obscurity of the diction is not everywhere) and which might for instance be abridged or paraphrased in square marginal blocks as in some books carefully written; the other, the underthought, conveyed chiefly in the choice of metaphors etc used and often only half realised by the poet himself, not necessarily having any connection with the subject in hand but usually having a connection and suggested by some circumstance of the scene or of the story . . .

To Bridges

Stonyhurst College, 3/10 Feb. 1883

. . . I quite understand what you mean about gentlemen and 'damfools'; it is a very striking thing and I could say much on the subject. I shall not say that much, but I say this: if a gentleman feels that to be what we call a gentleman is a thing essentially higher than without being a gentleman to be ever so great an artist or thinker or if, to put it another way, an artist or thinker feels that were he to become in those ways ever so great he wd. still essentially be lower than a gentleman that was no artist and no thinker – and yet to be a gentleman is but on the brim of morals and rather a thing of manners than of morals properly – then how much more must art and philosophy and manners and breeding and everything else in the world be below the least degree of true virtue. This is that chastity of mind which seems to lie at the very heart and be the parent of all other good, the seeing at once what is best, the holding to that, and the not allowing anything else whatever to be even heard pleading to the contrary. Christ's life and character are such as appeal to all the world's admiration, but there is one insight St. Paul gives us of it which is the very secret and seems to me more touching and constraining than everything else is: This mind he says, was in Christ Jesus – he means as man: being in the form of God – that is, finding, as in the first instant of his incarnation he did, his human nature informed by the godhead – he thought it nevertheless no snatching matter for him to be equal with God, but annihilated himself, taking the form of servant; that is, he could not but see what he was, God, but he would see it as if he did not see it, and be it as if he were not and instead of snatching at once at what all the time was his, or was himself, he emptied or exhausted himself as far as that was possible, of godhead and behaved only as God's slave, as his creature, as man, which also he was, and then being in the guise of man humbled himself to death, the death of the cross. It is this holding of himself back, and not snatching at the truest and highest good, the good that was his right, nay his possession from a past eternity in his other nature, his own being and self, which seems to me the root of all his holiness and the imitation of this the root of all moral good in other men. I agree then, and vehemently, that a gentleman, if there is such a thing on earth, is in the position to despise the poet, were he Dante or Shakspere, and the painter, were he Angelo or Apelles, for anything in him that shewed him *not* to be a gentleman. He is in the position to do it, I say, but if he is a gentleman perhaps this is what he will not do. Which leads me to another remark.

The quality of a gentleman is so very fine a thing that it seems to me one should not be at all hasty in concluding that one possesses it. People assume that they have it, take it quite for granted, and claim the acknowledgment from others: now I should say that this also is 'no snatching-matter'. And the more a man feels what it means and is – and to feel this is certainly some part of it – the more backward he will be to think he can have realised in himself anything so perfect. It is true, there is nothing like the truth and 'the good that does itself not know scarce is'; so the perfect gentleman will know that he is the perfect gentleman. But few can be in the position to know this and, being imperfect gentlemen, it will perhaps be a point of their gentlemanliness, for a gentleman is modest, to feel that they are not perfect gentlemen.

By the by if the English race had done nothing else, yet if they left the world the notion of a gentleman, they would have done a great service to mankind.

As a fact poets and men of art are, I am sorry to say, by no means necessarily or commonly gentlemen. For gentlemen do not pander to lust or other basenesses nor, as you say, give themselves airs and affectations nor do other things to be found in modern works. And this adds a charm to everything Canon Dixon writes, that you feel he is a gentleman and thinks like one. But now I have prosed my prose and long enough.

Believe me your affectionate friend
GERARD M. HOPKINS S.J. ...

To Bridges

Stonyhurst College. 26 July 1883

... Our year begins with autumn and the appointments for this
college will be made public on the 1st of next month. It seems likely
that I shall be removed; where I have no notion. But I have long
been Fortune's football and am blowing up the bladder of resolu-
tion big and buxom for another kick of her foot. I shall be sorry to
leave Stonyhurst; but go or stay, there is no likelihood of my ever
doing anything to last. And I do not know how it is, I have no
disease, but I am always tired, always jaded, though work is not
heavy, and the impulse to do anything fails me or has in it no con-
tinuance.

Weather has been very wet and cold and has made me ill a little.
Believe me your affectionate friend

GERARD

To Dixon

The Holy Name, Oxford Road, Manchester. 15/16 Aug. 1883

... By 'unity of action' I understand (but I am not advised of the
subject) not simplicity of plot (in the ordinary sense of simple, that
is the opposite of complex) but connectedness of plot. There is
unity of action, as I understand, if the plot turns on one event,
incident, or, to speak more technically, motive and all its parts and
details bear on that and are relevant to that: if they are irrelevant or
disconnected or involve by-issues then the unity of action is
impaired. So I have been accustomed to understand the phrase. The
plot in some Greek plays is simple, slight, in the extreme: the
Agamemnon for instance is what we should call rather a scene than a
plot, a scene leading up to and then leading off from one incident,
the hero's murder; but the unity of action is also extreme, for almost
every word said and thing done leads up to, turns on, influences, or
is influenced by this. But in this play there is also the 'unity of
place' and, by a conventional abridgment, the semblance of 'unity
of time'. Where, as in the *Eumenides*, these two unities are not

observed the plot becomes more complicated. The plot, quite in our modern sense of plot, is well enough marked in the *Oedipus King* though the unities of time and place are there observed. In general I take it that other things being alike unity of action is higher the more complex the plot; it is the more difficult to effect and therefore the more valuable when effected. We judge so of everything. In practice something must be sacrificed, and on what shall be sacrificed temperaments differ and discover their differences. The incidents for instance of Goethe's *Faust* are fascinating, but the unity of action, the bearing of all these on one common lesson the play is to teach or effect it is to produce, is not telling at first sight and is perhaps – I have no opinion – really defective. The Gk. dramas are on the other hand well concentrated, but the play of incident and character is often slight: one does not quote from them either stage-effects or types of character. But my thoughts are unverified and undigested.

A friend recommended me if I met with them to read L. Stevenson's stories, the *New Arabian Nights* and others since. I read a story by him in *Longman's*, I think, and a paper by him on Romance. His doctrine, if I apprehend him, is something like this. The essence of Romance is incident and that only, the type of pure Romance the *Arabian Nights*: those stories have no moral, no character-drawing, they turn altogether on interesting incident. The incidents must of course have a connection, but it need be nothing more than that they happen to the same person, are aggravations and so on. As history consists essentially of events likely or unlikely, consequences of causes chronicled before or what may be called chance, just retributions or nothing of the sort, so Romance, which is fictitious history, consists of event, of incident. His own stories are written on this principle: they are very good and he has all the gifts a writer of fiction should have, including those he holds unessential, as characterisation, and at first you notice no more than an ordinary well told story, but on looking back in the light of this doctrine you see that the persons illustrate the incident or strain of incidents, the plot, *the story*, not the story and incidents the persons. There was a tale of his called the *Treasure of Fourvières* or something like that; it is the story of an old treasure found, lost, and found again. The finding of the treasure acts of course and rather for the worse upon the finder, a retired French doctor, and his wife; the loss cures them; you wait to see the effect of the refinding: but not at all, the story abruptly ends – because its hero was, so to say, this triplet of incidents. His own remarks on the strength and weakness of the Waverleys are excellent. But I have been giving my own version of the doctrine (which is, I think, clearly true) rather than his for I do not remember well enough what he says.

Now I think Shakspere's drama is more in this sense romantic than the Greek and that if the unity of action is not so marked (as it is not) the *interest of romance*, arising from a well calculated strain of incidents, is greater. You remember the scene or episode of the little Indian boy in the *Midsummer Night*: it is, I think, an allegory, to which, in writing once on the play, I believed I had found the clue, but whether I was right or wrong the meaning must have in any case been, and Shakespere must have known it wd. be, dark or invisible to most beholders or readers; yet he let it stand, just, as I suppose, because it is interesting as an incident in the story, not that it throws any light on the main plot or helps the unity of action, but rather, at all events superficially, hinders it. I could write much more but must stop. I am shortly starting for London, where my address is Oak Hill, Hampstead, N.W. I am going to let Mr Patmore know *Mano* is out: I heard from him this morning.

Believe me gratefully and affectionately your friend

GERARD HOPKINS S.J.

TO PATMORE

Stonyhurst. 24 Sept. 1883

... I am dissatisfied with 'Beauty' p. 159 sq. The text and principle stated is noble and deeply true, the development seems to me a decline and a surrender. It comes to this: beautiful evil is found, but it is nature's monstrosity. Then *is qui supplet locum idiotae*, the worldling, Philistine (or whatever he is to be called) answers: and all I have to add is that the monstrosity is very common, and so we are agreed. And so it wd. come to the same thing to say Beauty deludes or Ugliness does. This was not to be granted. It is certain that in nature outward beauty is the proof of inward beauty, outward good of inward good. Fineness, proportion, of feature comes from a moulding force which succeeds in asserting itself over the resistance of cumbersome or restraining matter; the bloom of health comes from the abundance of life, the great vitality within. The moulding force, the life, is the form in the philosophic sense, and in man this is the soul. But because its available activity is limited the matter it has to struggle with may be too much for it and the wax is either too cold and doughy (so to speak) and will not take or is too hot and boiling blots out the stamp of the seal – I speak under an old but a very apposite image not easily improved. This explains why 'ugly good' is found. But why do we find beautiful evil? Not by any freak of nature, nature is incapable of producing beautiful evil. The explanation is to be sought outside nature; it is old, simple, and the undeniable fact. It comes from wicked will, freedom of choice, abusing the beauty, the good of its nature. 'Thou wert' the Scripture says and great writers apply it to the Devil 'the seal of resemblance'. The instance is palmary and shews how far evil can be beautiful or beauty evil and what the phenomenon means when it occurs. – This at least is how the subject strikes me and I find it more interesting and pathetic so; it maybe however that you think no otherwise, and only that I have missed the turn of your thought.

Whether you agree with me or not about the above points they are all trifles and altered or let stand little affect the poem. The following is the matter where I have to make a serious objection.

P. 202 'Women *should* be vain,' p. 217 'The Koh-i-noor' no. 1, p. 251 'Because, although in act and word, ... unattain'd desert' – In the midst of a poem undertaken under a kind of inspiration from God and to express what, being most excellent, most precious, most central and important and even obvious in human life, nevertheless no one has ever yet, unless passingly thought of expressing, you introduce a vice, the germ of widespread evils, and make the highest relish of pure love come from the base 'smell of mortality'. Everyone has some one fault he is tender to and vice he tolerates. We do this ourselves, but when another does it towards another vice not our own favourite (of tolerance, I do not say of commission) we are disgusted. The *Saturday Review* contrasting the Catholic and Protestant ideal of a schoolboy came out with the frank truth, that it looked on chastity as a feminine virtue (= lewdness a masculine one: it was not quite so raw as I put it, but this was the meaning). Mommsen a brilliant historian I find thinks great nations should break treaties. Dr Ward (in his younger days) said candour was anything but a saintly virtue (perhaps he did not but is misquoted: let it at least serve as an illustration). Then violence is admired and, above all, insolence and pride. But it is our baseness to admire anything evil. It seems to me we shd. in everything side with virtue, even if we do not feel its charm, because good is good.

In particular how can anyone admire or (except in charity, as the greatest of sins, but in judgment and approval) tolerate vanity in women? Is it not the beginning of their saddest and most characteristic fall? What but vanity makes them first publish, then prostitute their charms? In Leonardo's famous picture 'Modesty and *Vanity*' is it not almost taken for granted that the one figure is that of a virgin, the other that of a courtezan? If modesty in women means two things at once, purity and humility, must not the pair of opposites be no great way apart, vanity from impurity? Who can think of the Blessed Virgin and of vanity? Then in one's experience, in my own, it seems to me that nothing in good women is more beautiful than just the absence of vanity and an earnestness of look and character which is better than beauty. It teaches me (if I may give such an instance – I cannot easily give others) in my own sisters that when they let me see their compositions in music or painting, which I, with a brother's biassed judgment but still sincerely, admire, they seem to be altogether without vanity – yet they might be with reason vainer of these than of their looks, and towards a brother not be ashamed to shew it (and I towards them can hardly conceal mine): they are glad when I admire nevertheless. It is the same in literature as in life: the vain women in Shakspere are the impure minded too, like Beatrice (I do not know that I may not call her a hideous character); those whose chastity one could have trusted, like Desdemona, are free from vanity too.

It is a lover who speaks in the 'Koh-i-noor', but that proves very little. He happens to be a good one, and therefore tolerates nothing worse than carelessness, talkativeness, and vanity; but take a bad one: he will want the smell of mortality stronger. What does the adulterer love in his neighbour's wife but her obligingness in committing adultery? Tennyson makes Guenevere say 'The low sun makes the colour': it is a happy touch and the whole passage is instructive. Those also who write of moral monsters born without a fault and 'Let other bards of angels sing [in the House or elsewhere] Bright suns without a spot; But thou art no such perfect thing:

Rejoice that thou art not', these people never saw and had lost the idea of holiness / and are no authority.

You will say that everything else, her own words and what others say of her, shew that in Honoria there was in reality no vanity and that your lines are not to be taken in such grim earnest. But the truth seems to me to be that in writing you were really in two inconsistent moods, a lower and a higher, and that the record of both is in your pages.

Naturally a lurking error appears in more places than one and a false principle gives rise to false consequences. An ideal becomes an idol and false worship sets in. So I call it at p. 251, where it is said that a wife calls her husband lord by courtesy, meaning, as I understand, only by courtesy and 'not with her least consent of will' to his being so. But he *is* her lord. If it is courtesy only and no consent then a wife's lowliness is hypocrisy and Christian marriage a comedy, a piece of pretence. How much more truly and touchingly did you make Mrs Graham speak! But if she was right then the contrary is wrong. Perhaps I misunderstand the passage: I hope I do, but then I hope you will prevent other people misunderstanding it. And now pernicious doctrines and practice are abroad and the other day the papers said a wretched being refused in church to say the words 'and obey': if it had been a Catholic wedding and I the priest I would have let the sacrilege go no further . . .

To Patmore

Stonyhurst. 6/7 Dec. 1883

. . . *1867* – 'Their Jew': this is a hard saying, all politics apart. Many people speak so, but I cannot see how they can be justified. For *Jew* must be a reproach either for religion or for race. It cannot be for religion here, for Disraeli was not by religion a Jew: he had been baptised young and had always professed Christianity. His Christianity was a shadowy thing, I know, but so is that of thousands. If he believed in anyone I suppose that was Christ and did not, as Jews do, 'look for another'. It must then be for race. But that is no reproach but a glory, for Christ was a Jew. You will I know say that this dilemma is as fallacious as most dilemmas are and that Jew is a reproach because the Jews have corrupted their race and nature, so that it is their vices and their free acts we stigmatise when we call cheating 'jewing' – and that you mean that Disraeli in 1871 over-reached and jewed his constituents. But what you say is wider than that and will be so taken and therefore it will sound unjust and passionate, the more as time goes on. For other things happened after 1867 and it is a very common feeling, even among those who in his lifetime opposed or detracted from Lord Beaconsfield, that he, of all eminent statesmen, was truly devoted to and truly promoted the honour of England; that he, a Jew born, was above all things a British patriot. This is the meaning of the primrose worship that goes on . . .

A LETTER TO 'NATURE'

Stonyhurst. 21 Dec. 1883

The body of evidence now brought in from all parts of the world must, I think, by this time have convinced Mr Piazzi Smyth that the late sunrises and sunsets do need some explanation, more particular than he was willing to give them. With your leave I should like to point out from my own observations and those of others that, 'given a clear sky' and the other conditions put by Mr Smyth, the sun-rises and sunsets of other days, however bright and beautiful, have *not* given any such effects as were witnessed, to take an instance, here on Sunday night, December 16th. I shall speak chiefly of the sunsets.

(1) *These sunsets differ from others, first in their time and their place or quarter* . . .

(2) *They differ in their periodic action or behaviour* . . .

(3) *They differ in the nature of the glow, which is both intense and lustreless,* and that both in the sky and in the earth. The glow is intense, this is what strikes everyone; it has prolonged the daylight, and optically changed the season; it bathes the whole sky, it is mis-taken for the reflection of a great fire; at the sundown itself and southwards from that on December 4, I took a note of it as more like inflamed flesh than the lucid reds of ordinary sunsets. On the same evening the fields facing west glowed as if overlaid with yellow wax.

But it is also lustreless. A bright sunset lines the clouds so that their brims look like gold, brass, bronze, or steel. It fetches out those dazzling flecks and spangles which people call fish-scales. It gives to a mackerel or dappled cloudrack the appearance of quilted crimson silk, or a ploughed field glazed with crimson ice. These effects may have been seen in the late sunsets, but they are not the specific after-glow; that is, without gloss or lustre.

The two things together, that is intensity of light and want of lustre, give to objects on the earth and peculiar illumination which may be seen in studios and other well-like rooms, and which itself affects the practice of painters and may be seen in their works, notably Rembrandt's, disguising or feebly showing the outlines and distinctions of things, but fetching out white surfaces and coloured stuffs with a rich and inward and seemingly self-luminous glow.

(4) *They differ in the regularity of their colouring.* Four colours in particular have been noticeable in these after-glows, and in a fixed order of time and place – orange, lowest and nearest the sundown; above this, and broader, green; above this, broader still, a variable red, ending in being crimson; above this a faint lilac. The lilac disappears; the green deepens, spreads and encroaches on the orange; and the red deepens, spreads, and encroaches on the green, till at last one red, varying downwards from crimson to scarlet or orange fills the west and south. The four colours I have named are mentioned in Lieut. G. N. Bittleson's letter from Umballa: 'The sun goes down as usual and it gets nearly dark, and then a bright red and yellow and green and purple blaze comes in the sky and makes it lighter again'. I suppose the yellow here spoken of to be an orange yellow, and the purple to be what I have above called lilac.

Ordinary sunsets have not this order; this, so to say, fixed and limited palette. The green in particular, is low down when it appears. There is often a trace of olive between the sundown and the higher blue sky, but it never developes, that I remember, into a fresh green.

(5) *They differ in the colours themselves, which are impure and not of the spectrum.* The first orange and the last crimson flush are perhaps pure, or nearly so, but the two most remarkable glows, the green and the red, are not. The green is between an apple-green or pea-green (which are pure greens) and an olive (which is tertiary colour): it is vivid and beautiful, but not pure. The red is very

impure, and not evenly laid on. On the 4th it appeared brown, like a strong light behind tortoiseshell, or Derbyshire alabaster. It has been well compared to the colour of incandescent iron. Sometimes it appears like a mixture of chalk with sand and muddy earths. The pigments for it would be ochre and Indian red.

Now the yellows, oranges, crimsons, purples, and greens of bright sunsets are beautifully pure. Tertiary colours may of course also be found in certain cases and places.

(6) *They differ in the texture of the coloured surfaces,* which are neither distinct cloud of recognised make nor yet translucent mediums. Mr Russell's observations should here be read. I have further noticed streamers, fine ribbing or mackerelling, and other more curious textures, the colour varying with the texture.

In ordinary sunsets the yellows and greens and the lower reds look like glass, or coloured liquids, as pure as the blue. Other colours, or these in other parts, are distinct flushes or illuminations of cloud or landscape.

I subjoin an account of the sunset of the 16th, which was here very remarkable, from my own observations and those of one of the observatory staff.

A bright glow had been round the sun all day and became more remarkable towards sunset. It then had a silvery or steely look, with soft radiating streamers and little colour; its shape was mainly elliptical, the slightly longer axis being vertical; the size about 20° from the sun each way. There was a pale gold colour, brightening and fading by turns for ten minutes as the sun went down. After the sunset the horizon was, by 4.10, lined a long way by a glowing tawny light, not very pure in colour and distinctly textured in hummocks, bodies like a shoal of dolphins, or in what are called gadroons, or as the Japanese conventionally represent waves. The glowing vapour above this was as yet colourless; then this took a beautiful olive or celadon green, not so vivid as the previous day's, and delicately fluted; the green belt was broader than the orange, and pressed down on and contracted it. Above the green in turn appeared a red glow, broader and burlier in make; it was softly brindled, and in the ribs or bars the colour was rosier, in the channels where the blue of the sky shone through it was a mallow colour. Above this was a vague lilac. The red was first noticed 45° above the horizon, and spokes or beams could be seen in it, compared by one beholder to a man's open hand. By 4.45 the red had driven out the green, and, fusing with the remains of the orange, reached the horizon. By that time the east, which had a rose tinge, became of a duller red, compared to sand; according to my observation, the ground of the sky in the east was green or else tawny, and the crimson only in the clouds. A great sheet of heavy dark cloud, with a reefed or puckered make, drew off the west in the course of the pageant: the edge of this and the smaller pellets of cloud that filed across the bright field of the sundown caught a livid green. At 5 the red in the west was fainter, at 5.20 it became notably rosier and livelier; but it was never of a pure rose. A faint dusky blush was left as late as 5.30, or later. While these changes were going on in the sky, the landscape of Ribblesdale glowed with a frowning brown.

The two following observations seem to have to do with the same phenomena and their causes. For some weeks past on fine bright days, when the sun has been behind a big cloud and has sent up (perspectively speaking) the dark crown or paling of beams of shadow in such cases commonly to be seen, I have remarked, upon the ground of the sky, sometimes an amber, sometimes a soft rose colour, instead of the usual darkening of the blue. Also on moonlight nights, and particularly on December 14, a sort of brown or muddy cast, never before witnessed, has been seen by more than one observer, in the sky.

GERARD HOPKINS

TO BRIDGES

University College, 85 and 86, Stephens Green, Dublin. 7 March 1884
MY DEAREST BRIDGES, – Remark the above address: it is a new departure or a new arrival and at all events a new abode. I dare say you know nothing of it, but the fact is that, though unworthy of and unfit for the post, I have been elected Fellow of the Royal University of Ireland in the department of classics. I have a salary of £400 a year, but when I first contemplated the six examinations I have yearly to conduct, five of them running, and to the Matriculation there came up last year 750 candidates, I thought that Stephen's Green (the biggest square in Europe) paved with gold would not

pay for it. It is an honour and an opening and has many bright sides, but at present it has also some dark ones and this in particular that I am not at all strong, not strong enough for the requirements, and do not see at all how I am to become so. But to talk of weather or health and especially to complain of them is poor work.

The house we are in, the College, is a sort of ruin and for purposes of study very nearly naked. And I have more money to buy books than room to put them in.

I have been warmly welcomed and most kindly treated. But Dublin itself is a joyless place and I think in my heart as smoky as London is: I had fancied it quite different. The Phoenix Park is fine, but inconveniently far off. There are a few fine buildings . . .

To Bridges

Furbough House, near Galway. 18 July 1884

DEAREST BRIDGES, – I must let you have a line now, I see, and write more hereafter. I ought to have answered you before, but indeed I hardly thought you were in earnest in proposing I should be your best man, pleasant and honourable as the position would be. But to show no other reasons why not, at the time you name I should be about beginning my examination work and it would be altogether impossible for me to be out of Ireland. However you do not want for friends better fitted to do the work than I.

I am here on holiday. I have been through Connemara, the fine scenery of which is less known than it should be. Yesterday I went to see the cliffs of Moher on the coast of Clare, which to describe would be long and difficult. In returning across the Bay we were in some considerable danger of our lives. Furbough House stands amidst beautiful woods, an Eden in a wilderness of rocks and treeless waste. The whole neighbourhood is most singular.

The weakness I am suffering from – it is that only, nervous weakness (or perhaps I ought not to say nervous at all, for I am not in any unusual way nervous in the common understanding of the word) – continues and I see no ground for thinking I can, for a long time to come, get notably better of it, but I may reasonably hope that this pleasant holiday may set me up a little for a while. Your enquiries are very kind: there is no reason to be disquieted about me, though weakness is a very painful trial in itself. If I could have regular hard exercise it would be better for me.

The reason of course why I like men to marry is that a single life is a difficult, not altogether a natural life; to make it easily manageable special provision, such as we have, is needed, and most people cannot have this . . .

To Bridges

University College, Dublin. 21/24 Aug. 1884

. . . Our society cannot be blamed for not valuing what it never knew of. The following are all the people I have let see my poems (not counting occasional pieces): some of them however, as you did, have shewn them to others. (1) The editor and sub-editor of our *Month* had the *Deutschland* and later the *Eurydice* offered them – (2) my father and mother and two sisters saw these, one or both of them, and I have sent them a few things besides in letters – (3) You – (4) Canon Dixon – (5) Mr Patmore – (6) Something got out about the *Deutschland* and Fr. Cyprian Splaine, now of Stonyhurst, wrote to me to send it him and perhaps other poems of mine: I did so and he shewed it to others. They perhaps read it, but he afterwards acknowledged to me that in my handwriting he found it unreadable; I do not think he meant illegible – (7) On the other hand Fr. Francis Bacon, a fellownovice of mine, and an admirer of my sermons saw all and expressed a strong admiration for them which was certainly sincere. They are therefore, one may say, unknown. It always seems to me that poetry is unprofessional, but that is what I have said to myself, not others to me. No doubt if I kept producing I should have to ask myself what I meant to do with it all; but I have long been at a standstill, and so the things lie. It would be less tedious talking than writing: now at all events I must stop.

I must tell you a humorous touch of Irish Malvolio or Bully Bottom, so distinctively Irish that I cannot rank it: it amuses me in bed. A Tipperary lad, one of our people, lately from his noviceship, was at the wicket and another bowling to him. He thought there was no one within hearing, but from behind the wicket he was overheard after a good stroke to cry out 'Arrah, sweet myself!'

I must write once more against the 3rd.
Believe me always your affectionate friend
                                    GERARD M. HOPKINS S.J.

TO HIS SISTER KATE

University College, Dublin. 9 Dec. 1884

ME DEAR MISS HOPKINS, – Im intoirely ashamed o meself. Sure its
a wonder I could lave you iligant corspondance so long onans-
wered. But now Im just afther conthroiving a jewl of a convan-
iance be way of a standhen desk and tis a moighty incurgement
towards the writin of letters intoirelee. Tis whoy ye hear from me
this evenin.

It bates me where to commince, the way Id say anything yed be
interistud to hear of. More be token yell be plased tintimate to me
mother Im intirely obleeged to her for her genteel offers. But as
titchin warm clothen tis undher a misapprehinsion shes labourin.
Sure twas not the inclimunsee of the saysons I was complainin of at
all at all. Twas the povertee of books and such like educational
convaniences.

And now, Miss Hopkins darlin, yell chartably exkees me writin
more in the rale Irish be raison I was never rared to ut and thats why
I do be so slow with my pinmanship, bad luck to ut (savin your
respects), but for ivery word I delineate I disremember two, and
thats how ut is with me . . .

TO HIS MOTHER

University College, Dublin. 2 March 1885

MY DEAREST MOTHER, – I wish you many very happy returns of
tomorrow and time scarcely allows of my saying more than that.

Yesterday Mr O'Brien M.P. held his monster meeting in the
Phoenix Park to protest against his suspension. It was not so very
monster, neither were the people excited. Boys on the skirt of the
crowd made such a whistling and noise for their own amusement as
must have much interfered with the hearing of the speeches. Fr
Mallac and I went: I fancy it was rather compromising. There were

bands – it gave them an outing – and banners, including the stars
and stripes and the tricolour. The people going were in Sunday
clothes when they had got any, otherwise in their only suit, which
with some was rags. They were quiet, well behaved, and not jocular
(which the Irish in public are not, that I see) – 'neither sad nor glad
like a dog at his father's funeral'. Mr O'Brien spoke bareheaded
from a drag, the wind was (alas, it long will be) in the east, and
today he must have a terrible cold. I looked at him through opera
glasses and got near enough to hear hoarseness, but no words.
Excitable as the Irish are they are far less so than from some things
you would think and ever so much froths off in words. Fr Mallac,
who in Paris witnessed the revolution of '48, said that there the
motions of the crowd were themselves majestic and that they
organized themselves as with a military instinct.

Though this particular matter did not disturb me, yet the grief of
mind I go through over politics, over what I read and hear and see
in Ireland about Ireland and about England, is such that I can
neither express it nor bear to speak of it.

I should correct what I said above about the crowd, that it was
neither sad nor glad: it was, I should say, cheerful but not merry
(except some drunken fellows).

They are crying some bad news in the streets. All news is bad.

I have no more time.

I should like you to see Mr Curtis some day – to see him (or
know him) is to love him – but hitherto he has never been out of
Ireland.

Believe me your loving son

GERARD

I enclose a programme for Grace. I have another somewhere
mislaid for her.

Did I tell you of our German count? He is a splendid sample of a
young nobleman, especially on horseback.

To Baillie

University College, Dublin. 24 April 1885

MY DEAREST BAILLIE, – I will this evening begin writing to you
and God grant it may not be with this as it was with the last

letter I wrote to an Oxford friend, that the should-be receiver
was dead before it was ended. (There is no bad omen in this, as
you will on reflexion – REMARK: *REFLEXION:* I USED TO WRITE
REFLECTION TILL YOU POINTED OUT THE MISTAKE; YOU DID SO
TWICE, FOR I HAD, THROUGH HUMAN FRAILTY AND INADVERTENCE,
LAPSED – see.) I mean poor Geldart, whose death, as it was in
Monday last's *Pall Mall,* you must have heard of. I suppose it was
suicide, his mind, for he was a selftormentor, having been un-
hinged, as it had been once or twice before, by a struggle he had
gone through. Poor Nash's death, not long before, was certainly
suicide and certainly too done in insanity, for he had been sleepless
for ten nights: of this too you will have heard. It much comforts me
and seems providential that I had renewed my friendship with Gel-
dart some weeks before it was too late. I yesterday wrote to his
widow. Three of my intimate friends at Oxford have thus drowned
themselves, a good many more of my acquaintances and con-
temporaries have died by their own hands in other ways: it must
be, and the fact brings it home to me, a dreadful feature of our
days. I should say that Geldart had lent me his autobiography called
(I wish it had another name) *A Son of Belial.* It is an amusing
and a sad book – but perhaps you have seen it. I am in it and
Addis, Coles, Jeune, MacInnon, Nash, Jowett, Liddon, and lots
more thinly disguised, though some I do not recognize. You are
not there.

May 8 – For one thing I was sorry when I got your late delightful
letter. Since my sister told me of her meeting you I had been mean-
ing to write and be first with you – but now I am slow even in
answering. Some time since, I began to overhaul my old letters,
accumulations of actually ever since I was at school, destroying all
but a very few, and growing ever lother to destroy, but also to read,
so that at last I left off reading; and there they lie and my old note-
books and beginnings of things, ever so many, which it seems to me
might well have been done, ruins and wrecks; but on this theme I
will not enlarge by pen and ink. However there were many of your
letters among them and overflowing with kindness (but not
towards Hannah and MacFarlane; however you need not distress
yourself so much about them; I agree with you in the main, and
believe I used to remonstrate sometimes of old on their behalf,
because they were good fellows and the persistency of their atten-

tions was a most real compliment – a sort of compliment that as one gets older and writes the senile parenthetic style I am maundering in now one values a great deal higher – but still I can distinctly remember, though I shall not recall, real provocation they gave you; and you never did more than have a humorous fling at them; but to return) and for those letters I was deeply grateful and keep it constantly before me that I was undeserving of them; but still it was a cruel thing of you now to tell me that my own very first letter to you begins with 'Yes, you are a fool'. The context, I suppose, the sequel, I mean, does something to mitigate, but mitigate as you may I wish it were not said. But I have to regret so much! and what is it to withdraw a thing long after the event? Almost meaningless.

As I told you before, the first thing not that you said to me but that I can remember your saying was some joke about a watering hose which lay on the grass plot in the Outer Quad: a small spray was scattering from it. I stood watching it and you, coming in from a walk, waving your stick at it quoted or parodied either 'Busy curious thirsting fly' or the Dying Christian to his Soul. You never could remember this after and IN FINE (an expression which, it has always appeared to me, could never take root in our garden and yet we could never make up our minds to throw back again over the wall into the French one where it came from) I am more sure that it was said than that you said it.

I think this is from a literary point of view (not from a moral) the worst letter I ever wrote to you, and it shall not run much longer. You will wonder I have been so long over it. This is part of my disease, so to call it. The melancholy I have all my life been subject to has become of late years not indeed more intense in its fits but rather more distributed, constant, and crippling. One, the lightest but a very inconvenient form of it, is daily anxiety about work to be done, which makes me break off or never finish all that lies outside that work. It is useless to write more on this: when I am at the worst, though my judgment is never affected, my state is much like madness. I see no ground for thinking I shall ever get over it or ever succeed in doing anything that is not forced on me to do of any consequence.

I forget what the verses were I shewed you and you 'did not criticise'. It is putting friendship unwisely to a strain to shew verses, neither did I do it much. Those verses were afterwards burnt and I wrote no more for seven years; then, it being suggested to write something I did so and have at intervals since, but the intervals are now long ones and the whole amount produced is small. And I make no attempt to publish.

You said, and it was profoundly true then, that Mr Gladstone ought to be beheaded on Tower Hill and buried in Westminster Abbey. Ought he now to be buried in Westminster Abbey? As I am accustomed to speak too strongly of him I will not further commit myself in writing.

Much could be said about Ireland and my work and all, but it would be tedious; especially as I hope we may meet soon. I seem glad you keep up your Oriental studies. Believe me always your affectionate friend

GERARD M. HOPKINS S.J.

May 17 '85 and still winter.

To Bridges

University College, Dublin. 17 May 1885

DEAREST BRIDGES, – I must write something, though not so much as I have to say. The long delay was due to work, worry, and languishment of body and mind – which must be and will be; and indeed to diagnose my own case (for every man by forty is his own physician or a fool, they say; and yet again he who is his own physician has a fool for his patient – a form of epigram, by the bye, which, if you examine it, has a bad flaw), well then to judge of my case, I think that my fits of sadness, though they do not affect my judgment, resemble madness. Change is the only relief, and that I can seldom get.

I saw that *Ulysses* was a fine play, the action and interest well centred, the characters finely drawn and especially Penelope, the dialogue throughout good; nevertheless, perhaps from my mood of mind, I could not take to it, did not like it, beyond a dry admiration. Not however to remain in a bare Doctor Felldom on the matter, I did find one fault in it which seems indeed to me to be the worst fault a thing can have, unreality. I hope other people will think otherwise, but the introduction in earnest of Athene gave me a distaste I could not recover from. With *Prometheus* it was not the same. Three kinds of departure from truth I understand and agree to in a play – first in a History those changes and conventions without which, as in other works of art, the facts could not be presented at all; secondly a plot of fiction: though the facts never actually happened they are a picture of life and a sample of the sort of facts that do – those also subject to their own changes and conventions; lastly an allegory, where things that neither do nor could be mask and mean something that is. To this last class *Prometheus*, as I take it, belongs; moreover it was modelled on the Greek and scarcely meant for acting. But *Ulysses* is to act; and in earnest, not allegorically, you bring in a goddess among the characters: it revolts me. Then, not unnaturally, as it seemed to me, her speech is the worst in the play: being an unreality she must talk unreal. Believe me, the Greek gods are a totally unworkable material; the merest frigidity, which must chill and kill every living work of art they are brought into. Even if we put aside the hideous and, taken as they stand, unspeakable stories told of them, which stories nevertheless are as authentic as their names and personalities – both are equally imaginary; if you do not like that, both equally symbolical –, putting these out of sight and looking only at their respectable side, they are poor ignoble conceptions ennobled bodily only (as if they had bodies) by the artists, but once in motion and action worthless – not gentlemen or ladies, cowards, loungers, without majesty, without awe, antiquity, foresight, character; old bucks, young bucks, and Biddy Buckskins. What did Athene do after leaving Ulysses? Lounged back to Olympus to afternoon nectar. Nothing can be made of it . . .

To Bridges

University College, Dublin. 1 Sept. 1885

. . . Mr Patmore lent me Barnes' poems – 3 volumes, not all, for indeed he is prolific. I hold your contemptuous opinion an unhappy mistake: he is a perfect artist and of a most spontaneous inspiration; it is as if Dorset life and Dorset landscape had taken flesh and tongue in the man. I feel the defect or limitation or whatever we are to call it that offended you: he lacks fire; but who is perfect all round? If one defect is fatal what writer could we read?

An old question of yours I have hitherto neglected to answer, am I thinking of writing on metre? I suppose thinking too much and doing too little. I do greatly desire to treat that subject; might perhaps get something together this year; but I can scarcely believe that on that or on anything else anything of mine will ever see the light – of publicity nor even of day. For it is widely true, the fine pleasure is not to do a thing but to feel that you could and the mortification that goes to the heart is to feel it is the power that fails you; *qui occidere nolunt Posse volunt*; it is the refusal of a thing that we like to have. So with me, if I could but get on, if I could but produce work I should not mind its being buried, silenced, and going no further; but it kills me to be time's eunuch and never to beget. After all I do not despair, things might change, anything may be; only there is no great appearance of it. Now because I have had a holiday though not strong I have some buoyancy; soon I am afraid I shall be ground down to a state like this last spring's and summer's, when my spirits were so crushed that madness seemed to be making approaches – and nobody was to blame, except myself partly for not managing myself better and contriving a change.

Believe me, with kind wishes to Mrs Bridges, your affectionate friend

GERARD M. HOPKINS S.J. . . .

To Everard Hopkins

Clongowes Wood College, Naas. 5/8 Nov. 1885

. . . I am sweetly soothed by your saying that you cd. make any one understand my poem by reciting it well. That is what I always hoped, thought, and said; it is my precise aim. And thereby hangs so considerable a tale, in fact the very thing I was going to write about Sprung Rhythm in general (by the bye rhythm, not metre: metre is a matter of arranging lines, rhythm is one of arranging feet; anapaests are a rhythm, the sonnet is a metre; and so you can write any metre in any rhythm and any rhythm to any metre – supposing of course that usage has not tied the rhythm to the metre, as often or mostly it has), that I must for the present leave off, give o'ër, as they say in Lancashire.

Every art then and every work of art has its own play or performance. The play or performance of a stageplay is the playing it on the boards, the stage: reading it, much more writing it, is not its performance. The performance of a symphony is not the scoring it however elaborately; it is in the concert room, by the orchestra, and then and there only. A picture is performed, or performs, when anyone looks at it in the proper and intended light. A house performs when it is now built and lived in. To come nearer: books play, perform, or are played and performed when they are read; and ordinarily by one reader, alone, to himself, with the eyes only. Now we are getting to it, George. Poetry was originally meant for either singing or reciting; a record was kept of it; the record could be, was, read, and that in time by one reader, alone, to himself, with the eyes only. This reacted on the art: what was to be performed under these conditions, for these conditions ought to be and was composed and calculated. Sound-effects were intended, wonderful combinations even; but they bear the marks of having been meant for the whispered, not even whispered, merely mental performance of the closet, the study, and so on. You follow, Edward Joseph? You do: then we are there. This is not the true nature of poetry, the darling child of speech, of lips and spoken utterance: it must be spoken; *till it is spoken it is not performed*, it does not perform, it is not itself. Sprung rhythm gives back to poetry its true soul and self. As poetry is emphatically speech, speech purged of dross like gold in the furnace, so it must have emphatically the essential elements of speech. Now emphasis itself, stress, is one of these: sprung rhythm makes verse stressy; it purges it to an emphasis as much brighter, livelier, more lustrous than the regular but commonplace emphasis of common rhythm as poetry in general is brighter than common speech. But this it does by a return from that regular emphasis towards, not up to the more picturesque irregular emphasis of talk – without however becoming itself lawlessly irregular; then it would not be art; but making up by regularity, equality, of a larger unit (the foot merely) for inequality in the less, the syllable. There it wd. be necessary to come down to mathematics and technicalities which times does not allow of, so I forbear. For I believe you now understand. Perform the *Eurydice*, then see. I must however add that to perform it quite satisfactorily is not at all easy, I do not say I could do it; but this is nothing against the truth of the principle maintained. A composer need not be able to play his violin music or sing his songs. Indeed the higher wrought the art, clearly the wider severance between the parts of the author and the performer.

Neither of course do I mean my verse to be recited only. True poetry must be studied. As Shakespere and all great dramatists have their maximum effect on the stage but bear to be or must be studied at home before or after or both, so I shd. wish it to be with my lyric poetry...

By the bye, as prose, though commonly less beautiful than verse and debarred from its symmetrical beauties, has, at least possible to it, effects more beautiful than any verse can attain, so perhaps the inflections and intonations of the speaking voice may give effects more beautiful than any attainable by the fixed pitches of music. I look on this as an infinite field and very little worked. It has this great difficulty, that the art depends entirely on living tradition. The phonograph may give us one, but hitherto there could be no record of fine spoken utterance.

In drama the fine spoken utterance has been cultivated and a tradition established, but everything is most highly wrought and furthest developed where it is cultivated by itself; fine utterance then will not be best developed in the drama, where gesture and action generally are to play a great part too; it must be developed in recited lyric. Now hitherto this has not been done. The Greeks carried lyric to its highest perfection in Pindar and the tragic choruses, but what was this lyric? not a spoken lyric at all, but song; poetry written neither to be recited nor chanted even nor even sung to a transferable tune but each piece of itself a song. The same remark then as above recurs: the natural performance and delivery belonging properly to lyric poetry, which is speech, has not been enough cultivated, and should be. When performers were trained to do it (it needs the rarest gifts) and audiences to appreciate it it would be, I am persuaded, a lovely art. Incalculable effect could be produced by the delivery of Wordsworth's *Margaret* ('Where art thou, my beloved son?' – do you know it?). With the aid of the phonograph each phrase could be fixed and learnt by heart like a song...

To Patmore

University College, Dublin. 4/6 June 1886

MY DEAR MR PATMORE, – I have been meaning and meaning to write to you, to return the volumes of Barnes' poems you lent me and for other reasons, and partly my approaching examination work restrained me, when last night there reached me from Bell's the beautiful new edition of your works. I call it beautiful and think it is the best form upon the whole for poetry and works of pure literature that I know of and I thank you for your kindness in sending it. And I hope the bush or the bottle may do what little in a bush or bottle lies to recommend the liquor to the born and the unborn. But how slowly does the fame of excellence spread! And crooked eclipses and other obscure causes fight against its rise and progress.

Your poems are a good deed done for the Catholic Church and another for England, for the British Empire, which now trembles in the balance held in the hand of unwisdom. I remark that those Englishmen who wish prosperity to the Empire (which is not all Englishmen or Britons, strange to say) speak of the Empire's mission to extend freedom and civilisation in India and elsewhere. The greater the scale of politics the weightier the influence of a great name and a high ideal. It is a terrible element of weakness that now we are not well provided with the name and ideal which would recommend and justify our Empire. 'Freedom': it is perfectly true that British freedom is the best, the only successful freedom, but that is because, with whatever drawbacks, those who have developed that freedom have done so with the aid of law and obedience to law. The cry then shd. be Law and Freedom, Freedom and Law. But that does not please: it must be Freedom only. And to that cry there is the telling answer: No freedom you can give us is equal to the freedom of letting us alone: take yourselves out of India, let us first be free of you. Then there is civilisation. It shd. have been Catholic truth. That is the great end of Empires before God, to be Catholic and draw nations into their Catholicism. But our Empire is less and less Christian as it grows. There remains that part of civilisation which is outside Christianity or which is not essentially Christian. The best is gone, still something worth having is left.

How far can the civilisation England offers be attractive and valuable and be offered and insisted on as an attraction and a thing of value to India for instance? Of course those who live in our civilisation and belong to it praise it: it is not hard, as Socrates said, among the Athenians to praise the Athenians; but how will it be represented by critics bent on making the worst of it or even not bent on making the best of it? It is good to be in Ireland to hear how enemies, and those rhetoricians, can treat the things that are unquestioned at home. I know that to mere injustice and slander innocence and excellence themselves stand condemned, but since there is always in mankind some love of truth and admiration for good (only that the truth must be striking and the good on a great scale) what marked and striking excellence has England to shew to make her civilisation attractive? Her literature is one of her excellences and attractions and I believe that criticism will tend to make this more and more felt; but there must be more of that literature, a continued supply and in quality excellent. This is why I hold that fine works of art, and especially if, like yours, that are not only ideal in form but deal with high matter as well, are really a great power in the world, an element of strength even to an empire. But now time and tediousness forbid me to write more on this . . .

To Bridges

11 Church Street, Tremadoc, North Wales. 2 Oct. 1886

DEAREST BRIDGES, – Your letter, you see, written from South Wales reaches me in Gwynedd after making a long elbow at Dublin. A delightful holiday comes to an end to-day, but I am going to take duty at Pwllheli tomorrow and start for Holyhead in the evening.

I will back Tremadoc for beauty against Fishguard. There are no myrtles, at least I have seen none, but right over the village (clean, modern, solidly built, spacious, and somewhat picturesque) rises a cliff of massive selfhewn rock, all overrun with a riot of vegetation which the rainy season seems to breathe here. Tremadoc is said to take its name from some Mr Madox and is in the parish of Ynys Cynhaiarn. Portmadoc half a mile off is still more modern: my landlord remembers when there were only three houses there.

It is rising, but fashion has not found it. Bretons come here in jerseys, earrings, and wooden shoes to sell vegetables, and Portmadoc and all N. Wales seem to live upon slate, to get which they are quarrying away great mountains: nowhere I suppose in Europe is such a subjection of nature to man to be witnessed. The end is that the mountains vanish, but in the process they take a certain beauty midway between wildness and art. Mountains are all round. The feature of the coast are the great traethau or tracts of sand – sea-sand, links, and reclaimed land; two estuaries, at the meeting point of which Penrhyn Deudraeth (two tracts) stands, reach the sea hereabouts; they are commanded by Moelwyn and other mountains and by Criccieth and Harlech Castles. A long walk skirting one of these and discovering Snowdon and other grand mountain views leads to Pont Aberglaslyn and into the Pass which from that leads to the valley where Beddgelert is. The beauty of this Pass is extreme. The Glaslyn, a torrent of notably green water, runs through it and thereby hangs a sad tale. I made a drawing (its ruins enclosed) of one fall of it over a rock, not at all so good as I could have wished, for water in motion, highly difficult at best (I need not say) needs the most sympathetic pencils, and this was done with an unsatisfactory HB and touched, not for the better, with a better at home; but however I thought well enough of it to mean to 'set' it and send it to you. I used milk in a saucer and put the saucer by the fire, where the gluey milk stuck it so fast to the earthenware that it could not be got off without grievous tearing . . .

To Patmore

University College, Dublin. 6 Oct. 1886

MY DEAR MR PATMORE, – I have just returned from a very reviving fortnight or so of North Wales, the true Arcadia of wild beauty.

I have a long letter somewhere to you, but shall never send it. I read with pleasure the account of you in the *World*, but you have not sent the papers from the *St. James's*.

You are not to think I now begin to admire Barnes: I always did so, but it was long since I had read him. (Bridges is quite wrong about him and off his orthodoxy.) I scarcely understand you about reflected light: every true poet, I thought, must be original and originality a condition of poetic genius; so that each poet is like a species in nature (*not* an *individuum genericum* or *specificum*) and can never recur. That nothing shd. be old or borrowed however cannot be, and that I am sure you never meant.

Still I grant in Barnes an unusual independence and originality, due partly to his circumstances. It is his naturalness that strikes me most; he is like an embodiment or incarnation or manmuse of the country, of Dorset, of rustic life and humanity. He comes, like Homer and all poets of native epic, provided with epithets, images, and so on which seem to have been tested and digested for a long age in their native air and circumstances and to have a *keeping* which nothing else could give; but in fact they are rather all of his own finding and first throwing off. This seems to me very high praise. It is true they are not far-fetched or exquisite (I mean for instance his mentions of rooks or of brooks) but they are straight from nature and quite fresh. His rhythms are charming and most characteristic: these too smack of the soil. However his employment of the Welsh *cynghanedd* or chime I do not look on as quite successful. To tell the truth, I think I could do that better, and it is an artificial thing and not much in his line. (I mean like *Paladore* and *Polly dear*, which is in my judgment more of a miss than a hit.) I have set tunes to two of them which appear to me very suitable to the words and as if drawn out of them, and one I have harmonised and got today played; but I can never succeed with piano music, for the piano cannot really execute independent parts, as I make mine; indeed my pianist said to me, Your music dates from a time before the piano was invented. However two schoolboys sang the air; which went well. But now no more of Barnes or of music, for I have overhanging me 500 examination papers and that only one batch out of three.

With the kindest remembrances to Mrs Patmore and the Miss Patmores, I am your sincere friend

GERARD M. HOPKINS S.J.

Before I went to Wales I was much pulled down: that was why I did not sooner write. Bridges says Barnes has no fire, and this I think we must grant.

To Bridges

University College, Dublin. 13 Oct. 1886

... By the bye, I say it deliberately and before God, I would have you and Canon Dixon and all true poets remember that fame, the being known, though in itself one of the most dangerous things to man, is nevertheless the true and appointed air, element, and setting of genius and its works. What are works of art for? to educate, to be standards. Education is meant for the many, standards are for public use. To produce then is of little use unless what we produce is known, if known widely known, the wider known the better, for it is by being known it works, it influences, it does its duty, it does good. We must then try to be known, aim at it, take means to it. And this without puffing in the process or pride in the success. But still. Besides, we are Englishmen. A great work by an Englishman is like a great battle won by England. It is an unfading bay tree. It will even be admired by and praised by and do good to those who hate England (as England is most perilously hated), who do not wish even to be benefited by her. It is then even a patriotic duty τῇ ποιήσει ἐνεργεῖν and to secure the fame and permanence of the work. Art and its fame do not really matter, spiritually they are nothing, virtue is the only good; but it is only by bringing in the infinite that to a just judgment they can be made to look infinitesimal or small or less than vastly great; and in this ordinary view of them I apply to them, and it is the true rule for dealing with them, what Christ our Lord said of virtue, Let your light shine before men that they may see your good works (say, of art) and glorify yr. Father in heaven (that is, acknowledge that they have an absolute excellence in them and are steps in a scale of infinite and inexhaustible excellence) ...

To Dixon

University College, Dublin. 23 Oct. 1886

MY DEAR FRIEND. – There are some points in your letter I have to reply to. First of the Greek mythology. Of course I agree with the rest of the world in admiring its beauty. Above everything else the Greeks excelled in art: now their mythology was the earliest of their arts that have in any way survived, older in the main than Homer's poems, and is I daresay as much more beautiful than other mythologies as Homer's epic is than other epics; speaking of epic proper. It is free from that cumber of meaningless and childish rubbish which interrupts and annoys one even in the midst of fine invention in for instance the Irish legends.

This however is to speak of it as stories, as fairytales, well invented well told fairytales. But mythology is something else besides fairytale: it is religion, the historical part of religion. It must have been this side of the Greek mythology I was speaking of in that letter; and could I speak too severely of it? First it is as history untrue. What is untrue history? Nothing and worse than nothing. And that history religion? Still worse. I cannot enter on this consideration without being brought face to face with the great fact of heathenism. Now we mostly pass heathenism by as a thing utterly departed, which indeed it is not but in India rank and flourishing; but if for once we face it what are we to say of it? For myself literally words would fail me to express the loathing and horror with which I think of it and of man setting up the work of his own hands, of that hand within the mind the imagination, for God Almighty who made heaven and earth. Still he might set up beings perfect in their kind. But the Greek gods are rakes, and unnatural rakes. Put that aside too; put yourself in the position of a man who like Homer first believes in them, next forgets or passes over their wickedness: even so are the Greek gods majestic, awe inspiring, as Homer that great Greek genius represents them? They are not. The Indian gods are imposing, the Greek are not. Indeed they are not brave, not self controlled, they have no manners, they are not gentlemen and ladies. They clout one another's ears and blubber and bellow. You will say this is Homer's fun, like the miracle-plays of Christendom. Then where is his earnest about them? At their best they remind me of some company of beaux and fashionable world at Bath in its palmy days or Tunbridge Wells or what not. Zeus is like the Major in *Pendennis* handsomer and better preserved sitting on Olympus as behind a club-window and watching Danae and other pretty seamstresses cross the street – not to go farther. You will think this is very Philistine and vulgar and be pained. But I am pained: this is the light in which the matter strikes me, the only one in which it will; and I do think it is the true light.

But I grant that the Greek mythology is very susceptible of fine treatment, allegorical treatment for instance, and so treated gives rise to the most beautiful results. No wonder: the moral evil is got rid of and the pure art, morally neutral and artistically so rich, remains and can be even turned to moral uses.

The letter you saw must have been in criticism of Bridges' *Ulysses*. I was set against that play by the appearance of Athene in the prologue or opening. Bridges took her almost seriously: so then did I, and was disgusted. But I hold it was a false step of his: the heathen gods cannot be taken seriously on our stage; nowadays they cannot even be taken humorously; and it would tell against the play's success. I know that was a noble play; but I had another objection besides to it, the great severity, the aridity even and joylessness of the lyrics. So I damped and damned and must have hurt Bridges.

I feel now I am warm and my hand is in for my greater task, Wordsworth's ode; and here, my dear friend, I must earnestly remonstrate with you; must have it out with you. Is it possible that – but it is in black and white: you say the ode is not, for Wordsworth, good; and much less great.

To say it was the second ode in the language was after all only a comparative remark: one might maintain, though I daresay you will not, that English is not rich in odes. The remark therefore is not of itself extravagant. But if the speaker had said that it was one of the dozen or of the half dozen finest odes of the world I must own that to me there would have seemed no extravagance. There have been in all history a few, a very few men, whom common repute, even where it did not trust them, has treated as having had something happen to them that does not happen to other men, as having *seen something*, whatever that really was. Plato is the most famous of these. Or to put it as it seems to me I must somewhere have written to you or to somebody, human nature in these men saw something, got a shock; wavers in opinion, looking back, whether there was anything in it or no; but is in a tremble ever since. Now what Wordsworthians mean is, what would seem to be the growing mind of the English speaking world and may perhaps come to be that of the world at large / is that in Wordsworth when he wrote that ode human nature got another of those shocks, and the tremble from it is spreading. This opinion I do strongly share; I am, ever since I knew the ode, in that tremble. You know what happened to crazy Blake, himself a most poetically electrical subject both active and passive, at his first hearing: when the reader came to 'The pansy at my feet' he fell into a hysterical excitement. Now commonsense forbid we should take on like these unstrung hysterical creatures: still it was a proof of the power of the shock.

The ode itself seems to me better than anything else I know of Wordsworth's, so much as to equal or outweight everything else he wrote: to me it appears so. For Wordsworth was an imperfect artist, as you say: as his matter varied in importance and as he varied in insight (for he had a profound insight of some things and little of others) so does the value of his work vary. Now the interest and importance of the matter were here of the highest, his insight was at its very deepest, and hence to my mind the extreme value of the poem.

His powers rose, I hold, with the subject: the execution is so fine. The rhymes are so musically interlaced, the rhythms so happily succeed (surely it is a magical change 'O joy that in our embers'), the diction throughout is so charged and steeped in beauty and yearning (what a stroke 'The moon doth with delight'!). It is not a bit of good my going on if, which is to me so strange in you and disconcerting, you do not feel anything of this. But I hope you will reconsider it. For my part I shd. think St. George and St. Thomas of Canterbury wore roses in heaven for England's sake on the day that ode, not without their intercession, was penned; for, to better a little the good humoured old cynical proverb, 'When grace of God is gone and spent Then learning is most excellent' and goes to make the greatness of a nation – which is what I urge on Bridges and now on you, to get yourselves known and be up betimes on our Parnassus . . .

To Bridges

University College, Dublin. 28 Oct. 1886

DEAREST BRIDGES, – To't again; for though my last was long and tedious and the one before that, if I remember, a literary budget, I have not yet dealt with your last.

My examinations are over till the next attack of the plague. My

lectures, to call them by that grand name, are begun: vae unum abiit
et vae alterum venit. I was I cannot tell when in such health and
spirits as on my return from Cadwalader and all his goats but 331
accounts of the First Punic War with trimmings, have sweated me
down to nearer my lees and usual alluvial low water mudflats,
groans, despair, and yearnings.

Now I have at much length remonstrated with Canon Dixon for
slighting Wordsworth's Ode on the Intimations, at which he might
have taken offence but on the contrary he took it with his usual
sweetness; and I beg you will my remonstrances with you about
Barnes and Stevenson; of both of whom, but especially S., you
speak with a sourness which tinges your judgment.

It is commonly thought of Barnes that 'local colour' is just what
he excells in and this is my own opinion. A fine and remarkable
instance (a case of colour proper) was quoted by the *Saturday* in
the article on him which followed the news of his death. But of him
another time or never; no more now. (The expression 'the sup-
posed emotions of peasants' grates on me, but let it pass.)

I have not read *Treasure Island*. When I do, as I hope to, I will
bear your criticisms in mind. (By the bye, I am sorry those poor
boys lost the book because you found consecutive fifths some-
where. However give 'em Rider Haggard's *King Solomon's Mines*.
They certainly will enjoy it; anyone would; and the author is not a
highflier.) Nevertheless I mean to deal with two of these criticisms
now, for it is easy to do so on the face of them.

One is that a boy capable of a brave deed would be incapable of
writing it down – well *that* boy. Granting this, still to make him tell
it is no fault or a trifling one. And the criticism, which ignores a
common convention of romance or literature in general, is surely
then some ἀγροικία on your part. Autobiography in fiction is com-
monly held a hazardous thing and few are thought to have suc-
ceeded in it on any great scale: Thackeray in *Esmond* is I believe
held for one of the exceptions. It is one of the things which 'O
Lord, sir, we must connive at'. The reader is somehow to be in-
formed of the facts. And in any case the fault is removeable without
convulsing the structure of the whole: like a bellglass or glass frame
over cucumbers or flowers it may be taken off, cleansed, and re-
placed without touching them. So this criticism I look on as trifling.

The other criticism is the discovery of a fault of plot about the whereabouts of some schooner: I take your word for it. One blot is no great matter, I mean not a damning matter. One blot may be found in the works of very learned clerks indeed. *Measure for Measure* is a lovely piece of work, but it was a blot, as Swinburne raving was overheard for hours to say, to make Isabella marry the old Duke. *Volpone* is one of the richest and most powerful plays ever written, but a writer in a late *Academy* points out a fault of construction (want of motive, I think, for Bonario's being at Volpone's house when Celia was brought there): it will stand that one fault. True you say that in Stevenson's book there are many such: but I do not altogether believe there are.

This sour severity blinds you to his great genius. *Jekyll and Hyde* I have read. You speak of 'the gross absurdity' of the interchange. Enough that it is impossible and might perhaps have been a little better masked: it must be connived at, and it gives rise to a fine situation. It is not more impossible than fairies, giants, heathen gods, and lots of things that literature teems with – and none more than yours. You are certainly wrong about Hyde being overdrawn: my Hyde is worse. The trampling scene is perhaps a convention: he was thinking of something unsuitable for fiction.

I can by no means grant that the characters are not characterised, though how deep the springs of their surface action are I am not yet clear. But the superficial touches of character are admirable: how can you be so blind as not to see them? e.g. Utterson frowning, biting the end of his finger, and saying to the butler 'This is a strange tale you tell me, my man, a very strange tale'. And Dr Lanyon: 'I used to like it, sir [life]; yes, sir, I liked it. Sometimes I think if we knew all' etc. These are worthy of Shakespeare. Have you read the *Pavilion on the Links* in the volume of *Arabian Nights* (not one of them)? The absconding banker is admirably characterised, the horror is nature itself, and the whole piece is genius from beginning to end.

In my judgment the amount of gift and genius which goes into novels in the English literature of this generation is perhaps not much inferior to what made the Elizabethan drama, and unhappily it is in great part wasted. How admirable are Blackmore and Hardy! Their merits are much eclipsed by the overdone reputation of the Evans—Eliot—Lewis—Cross woman (poor creature! one ought not to speak slightingly, I know), half real power, half imposition.

Do you know the bonfire scenes in the *Return of the Native* and still better the sword-exercise scene in the *Madding Crowd*, breathing epic? or the wife-sale in the *Mayor of Casterbridge* (read by chance)? But these writers only rise to their great strokes; they do not write continuously well: now Stevenson is master of a consummate style and each phrase is finished as in poetry. It will not do at all, your treatment of him ...

To Bridges

University College, Dublin. 17 Feb. 1887

... Tomorrow morning I shall have been three years in Ireland, three hard wearying wasting wasted years. (I met the blooming Miss Tynan again this afternoon. She told me that when she first saw me she took me for 20 and some friend of hers for 15; but it won't do: they should see my heart and vitals, all shaggy with the whitest hair.) In those I have done God's will (in the main) and many many examination papers. I am in a position which makes it befitting and almost a duty to write anything (bearing on classical study) which I may feel that I could treat well and advance learning by: there is such a subject; I do try to write at it; but I see that I cannot get on, that I shall be even less able hereafter than now. And of course if I cannot do what even my appliances make best and easiest, far less can I anything else. Still I could throw myself cheerfully into my day's work? I cannot, I am in a prostration. Wales set me up for a while, but the effect is now past. But out of Ireland I shd. be no better, rather worse probably. I only need one thing – a working health, a working strength: with that, any employment is tolerable or pleasant, enough for human nature; without it, things are liable to go very hardly with it.

Now come on Mrs Gaskell. What ails poor Mrs Gaskell? One book of hers I have read through, *Wives and Daughters*: if that is not a good book I do not know what a good book is. Perhaps you are so barbarous as not to admire Thomas Hardy – as you do not Stevenson; both, I must maintain, men of pure and direct genius.

Have you followed the course of late Homeric criticism? The pendulum is swinging heavily towards the old view of a whole original Iliad. In the track of the recent dialectic investigations I have made out, I think, a small but (as a style-test) important point; but my induction is not yet complete.

I will bear in mind to send for the *Feast of Bacchus* at an early opportunity, if (but that is not certain) one should occur.

I am almost afraid I have offended, not offended but not pleased, Mr Patmore by a late letter: I hope it is not so bad. I hope you will enjoy yourselves there: let me see, do you know Mrs Patmore? If you do you cannot help liking her. With best love to Mrs Bridges I am your affectionate friend

GERARD

Yesterday Archbishop Walsh had a letter in the *Freeman* enclosing a subscription to the defence of Dillon and the other traversers on trial for preaching the Plan of Campaign and saying that the jury was packed and a fair trial impossible. The latter was his contribution to the cause of concord and civil order. Today Archbp. Croke has one proposing to pay no taxes. One archbishop backs robbery, the other rebellion; the people in good faith believe and will follow them. You will see, it is the beginning of the end: Home Rule or separation is near. Let them come: anything is better than the attempt to rule a people who own no principle of civil obedience at all, not only to the existing government but to none at all. I shd. be glad to see Ireland happy, even though it involved the fall of England, if that could come about without shame and guilt. But Ireland will not be happy: a people without a principle of allegiance cannot be; moreover this movement has throughout been promoted by crime. Something like what happened in the last century between '82 and 1800 will happen in this: now as then one class has passed off its class-interests as the interests of the nation and so got itself upheld by the support of the nation; now as then it will legislate in its own interest and the rest will languish; distress will bring on some fresh convulsion; beyond that I cannot guess.

The ship I am sailing in may perhaps go down in the approaching gale: if so I shall probably be cast up on the English coast.

After all I have written above my trouble is not the not being able to write a book; it is the not being fit for my work and the struggling vainly to make myself fitter.

18 Feb. 1887

To Bridges

University College, Dublin. 30 July 1887

... On Irish politics I had something to say, but there is little time. 'It only needs the will', you say: it is an unwise word. It is true, it (that is, to govern Ireland) does 'only need the will'; but Douglas Jerrold's joke is in place, about Wordsworth (or whoever it was) that could write plays as good as Shakespeare's 'if he had the mind', and 'only needed the mind'. It is a just reproach to any man not to do what lies in his own power and he could do if he would: to such a man you may well say that the task in question only needs the will. But where a decision does *not* depend on us and we cannot even influence it, then it is only wisdom to recognize the facts – the will or want of will in those, not us, who have control of the question; and that is the case now. The will of the nation is divided and distracted. Its judgment is uninformed and misinformed, divided and distracted, and its action must be corresponding to its knowledge. It has always been the fault of the mass of Englishmen to know and care nothing about Ireland, to let be what would there (which, as it happened, was persecution, avarice, and oppression): and now, as fast as these people wake up and hear what wrong England has done (and has long ceased doing) to Ireland, they, like that woman in Mark Twain, 'burst into tears and rushing upstairs send a pink silk parasol and a box of hairpins to the seat of war'. If you in your limited but appreciable sphere of influence can bring people to a just mind and a proper resolution about Ireland (as you did, you told me, take part in your local elections) do so: you will then be contributing to that will which 'only is wanting'; but do not reproach me, who on this matter have perhaps both more knowledge and more will than most men. If however you think you could do but little and are unwilling even to do that (for I suppose while you are writing plays you cannot be canvassing electors), then recognise with me that with an unwavering will, or at least a flood of passion, on one, the Irish, side and a wavering one or indifference on the other, the English, and the Grand Old Mischief-maker loose, like the Devil, for a little while and meddling and marring all the fiercer for his hurry, Home Rule is in fact likely to come and

even, in spite of the crime, slander, and folly with which its advance
is attended, may perhaps in itself be a measure of a sort of equity
and, considering that worse might be, of a kind of prudence . . .

To Patmore

University College, Dublin. 20/24 Oct. 1887

My Dear Mr Patmore, – I find I began writing to you a fortnight
since. I was then examining: I am still, but am nearly at an end. I
enclose the Paper you sent, supposing that you could not wait for it
longer. I had meant to write some remarks on it, but I cannot delay
the Paper for them. I may send them afterwards.

But I make one now which will amaze you and, except that you
are very patient of my criticisms, may incense you. It is that when I
read yr. prose and when I read Newman's and some other modern
writers' the same impression is borne in on me: no matter how
beautiful the thought, nor, taken singly, with what happiness
expressed, you do not know what *writing prose* is. At bottom what
you do and what Cardinal Newman does is to think aloud, to think
with pen to paper. In this process there are certain advantages; they
may outweigh those of a perfect technic; but at any rate they ex-
clude that; they exclude the belonging technic, the belonging rhetoric
the own proper eloquence of written prose. Each thought is told off
singly and there follows a pause and this breaks the continuity, the
contentio, the strain of address, which writing should usually have.

The beauty, the eloquence, of good prose cannot come wholly
from the thought. With Burke it does and varies with the thought;
when therefore the thought is sublime so does the style appear to be.
But in fact Burke had no style properly so called: his style was
colourlessly to transmit his thought. Still he was an orator in form
and followed the common oratorical tradition, so that his writing
has the strain of address I speak of above.

But Newman does not follow the common tradition – of writing.
His tradition is that of cultured, the most highly educated, conver-
sation; it is the flower of the best Oxford life. Perhaps this gives it
a charm of unaffected and personal sincerity that nothing else could.
Still he shirks the technic of written prose and shuns the tradition
of written English. He seems to be thinking 'Gibbon is the last great

master of traditional English prose; he is its perfection: I do not propose to emulate him; I begin all over again from the language of conversation, of common life.'

You too seem to me to be saying to yourself 'I am writing prose, not poetry; it is bad taste and a confusion of kinds to employ the style of poetry in prose: the style of prose is to shun the style of poetry and to express one's thoughts with point'. But the style of prose is a positive thing and not the absence of verse-forms and pointedly expressed thoughts are single hits and give no continuity of style.

After all the very Paper which leads me to make these remarks is entitled 'Thoughts on Knowledge' etc, so that I am blaming you for not doing what you do not attempt to do. Perhaps then I ought to blame you for not attempting and doing. However I have said my say and feel inclined to burn it.

In the Paper itself there are some things I feel hard but do not speak of now. The parable of the carcase is in the highest degree illustrative and ghastly-vivid: it ought to be everywhere known.

During the summer examinations one of my colleagues brought in one day a *St. James's Gazette* with a piece of criticism he said it was a rare pleasure to read. It proved to be a review by you of Colvin's book on Keats. Still, enlightening as the review was, I did not think it really just. You classed Keats with the feminine geniuses among men and you would have it that he was not the likest but rather the unlikest of our poets to Shakspere. His poems, I know, are very sensuous and indeed they are sensual. This sensuality is their fault, but I do not see that it makes them feminine. But at any rate (and the second point includes the first) in this fault he resembles, not differs from Shakspere. For Keats died very young and we have only the work of his first youth. Now if we compare that with Shakspere's early work, written at an age considerably more than Keats's, was it not? such as *Venus and Adonis* and *Lucrece*, it is, as far as the work of two very original minds ever can be, greatly like in its virtues and its vices; more like, I do think, than that of any writer you could quote after the Elizabethan age; which is what the common opinion asserts. It may be that Keats was no dramatist (his *Otho* I have not seen); but it is not for that, I think, that people have made the comparison. The *Cap and Bells* is an unhappy performance, so bad that I could not get through it; senselessly planned to have no plan and doomed to fail: but Keats would have found out that. He was young; his genius intense in its quality; his feeling for beauty, for perfection intense; he had found his way right in his Odes; he would find his way right at last to the true functions of his mind. And he was at a great disadvantage in point of education compared with Shakspere. Their classical attainments may have been much of a muchness, but Shakespere had the school of his age. It was the Renaissance: the ancient Classics were deeply and enthusiastically studied and influenced directly or indirectly all, and the new learning had entered into a fleeting but brilliant combination with the medieval tradition. All then used the same forms and keepings. But in Keats's time, and worst in England, there was no one school; but experiment, division, and uncertainty. He was one of the beginners of the Romantic movement, with the extravagance and ignorance of his youth. After all is there anything in *Endymion* worse than the passage in *Romeo and Juliet* about the County Paris as a book of love that must be bound and I can't tell what? It has some kind of fantastic beauty, like an arabesque; but in the main it is nonsense. And about the true masculine fibre in Keats's mind Matthew Arnold has written something good lately ...

To Bridges

University College, Dublin. 6 Nov. 1887

DEAREST BRIDGES, – I must write at once, to save you the trouble of copying that music: I reproduced it by a jelly-process at Stonyhurst on purpose and only wanted the copy back in case you had one already. I do not remember anything about the harmony: it is the tune I think so good, and this I revived my memory of before I sent it you. I cannot at all make out the meaning of 'If your sister has learnt harmony I can't understand what the moderns mean'. Grace did learn harmony, but girls are apt not to study things thoroughly and perhaps she has not kept it up as she should. I remember years ago that the organist at Liverpool found fault with a hymn of hers, in four parts, very regular, for hidden fifths in the inner parts. But he was an ignoramus: I did not know then but I know now that hidden fifths must be and are freely used in the inner parts and are only faintly kept out of the outer ones. And see what became of him: he got drunk at the organ (I have now twice had this experience: it is distressing, alarming, agitating, but above all delicately comic; it brings together the bestial and the angelic elements in such a quaint entanglement as nothing else can; for musicians never play such clever descants as under those circumstances and in an instant everybody is thrilled with the insight of the situation) and was dismissed. He was a clever young fellow and thoroughly understood the properties of narrow-necked tubes.

I am thankful to you for the account of the Coda, over which you gave yourself even unnecessary trouble. You say the subject is treated in many books. That was just it. I had not got those books and the readiest source of information was you. It seems they are formed on an invariable plan and that Milton's sonnet gives an example. Of course one example was enough if there is but one type; but you should have said so.

I want Harry Ploughman to be a vivid figure before the mind's eye; if he is not that the sonnet fails. The difficulties are of syntax no doubt. Dividing a compound word by a clause sandwiched into it was a desperate deed, I feel, and I do not feel that it was an unquestionable success. But which is the line you do not understand? I do myself think, I may say, that it would be an immense advance in notation (so to call it) in writing as the record of speech, to distinguish the subject, verb, object, and in general to express the construction to the eye; as is done already partly in punctuation by everybody, partly in capitals by the Germans, more fully in accentuation by the Hebrews. And I daresay it will come. But it would, I think, not do for me: it seems a confession of unintelligibility. And yet I don't know. At all events there is a difference. My meaning surely *ought* to appear of itself; but in a language like English, and in an age of it like the present, written words are really matter open and indifferent to the receiving of different and alternative verse-forms, some of which the reader cannot possibly be sure are meant unless they are marked for him. Besides metrical marks are for the performer and such marks are proper in every art. Though indeed one might say syntactical marks are for the performer too. But however that reminds me that one thing I am now resolved on, it is to prefix short prose *arguments* to some of my pieces. These too will expose me to carping, but I do not mind. Epic and drama and ballad and many, most, things should be at once intelligible;

but everything need not and cannot be. Plainly if it is possible to express a subtle and recondite thought on a subtle and recondite subject in a subtle and recondite way and with great felicity and perfection, in the end, something must be sacrificed, with so trying a task, in the process, and this may be the being at once, nay perhaps even the being without explanation at all, intelligible. Neither, in the same light, does it seem to be to me a real objection (though this one I hope not to lay myself open to) that the argument should be even longer than the piece; for the merit of the work may lie for one thing in its terseness. It is like a mate which may be given one way only, in three moves; otherwise, various ways, in many . . .

No, I do not ask 'enthusiastic praise'. But is it not the case that the day when you could give enthusiastic praise to anything is passing or past? As for modern novels I will only say one thing now. It is in modern novels that wordpainting most abounds and now the fashion is to be so very subtle and advanced as to despise wordpainting and to say that old masters were not wordpainters. Just so. Wordpainting is, in the verbal arts, the great success of our day. Every age in art has its secret and its success, where even second rate men are masters. Second rate, third rate men are fine designers in Japan; second rate men were masters of painting in Raphael's time; second rate men were masters of sculpture in Phidias' time; second rate men of oratory in Cicero's; and so of many things. These successes are due to steady practice, to the continued action of a school: one man cannot compass them. And wordpainting is in our age a real mastery and the second rate men of this age often beat at it the first rate of past ages. And this I shall not be bullied out of.

For my case I shd. also remark that we turned up a difference of taste and judgment, if you remember, about Dryden. I can scarcely think of you not admiring Dryden without, I may say, exasperation. And my style tends always more towards Dryden. What is there in Dryden? Much, but above all this: he is the most masculine of our poets; his style and his rhythms lay the strongest stress of all our literature on the naked thew and sinew of the English language, the praise that with certain qualifications one would give in Greek to Demosthenes, to be the greatest master of bare Greek . . .

To Baillie

University College, Dublin. 1 May 1888

... The Pope has just dealt us a stunning blow. We attribute it to
the unscrupulous wirepulling of English intriguers: this or nearly
this is the idom, but I do not understand it. The Pope condemns
certain practices as sinful: he is right or wrong. We do not say he is
wrong, it seems we allow he is right. If so, the practices *are* sinful,
and they have been and are widely practised; they must then need
to be forbidden. If then the Pope ought to forbid them it is not un-
scrupulous for those concerned to ask him to do so. What is un-
scrupulous is to practise them, defend, support, or conceal them.
It would be unscrupulous of the Pope not to condemn them.

However this action of his is no doubt taken upon his own visi-
tor's report.

Whirligig of time! The body by which the Pope acts so much to
the advantage (in effect) of British government is the Holy Office of
the Inquisition.

On the whole I believe the decision will be obeyed and things
pass off quietly, here in Ireland.

I have just reread your last but one letter. It has nearly the same
matter as this morning's. This for instance is in both, that life in
London is intolerable. I find this difficult to follow. Like you I love
country life and dislike any town and that especially for its bad and
smokefoul air. Still I prefer London to any large town in these
islands (as for little ones they are for many purposes merely a block
of houses in the fields, combining country air with certain postal
conveniences and so on). In fog it is dreadful, but it has many fine
days, and in summer – now I see you will scout this and fling your-
self about, but I know it to be true – in summer its air is a balmy air,
certainly in the West End. Then it – well the West End – is cheerful
and quietly handsome, with many fine trees, and then there are so
many resources, things to go to and hear and see and do. Every-
thing is there. No, I think that very much may be said for life in
London; though my dream is a farm in the Western counties, glow-
worms, new milk . . . but in fact I live in Dublin.

What I most dislike in towns and in London in particular is the misery of the poor; the dirt, squalor, and the illshapen degraded physical (putting aside moral) type of so many of the people, with the deeply dejecting, unbearable thought that by degrees almost all our population will become a town population and a puny unhealthy and cowardly one. Yes, cowardly. Do you know and realise what happened at Majuba Hill? 500 British troops after 8 hours' firing, on the Dutch reaching the top, ran without offering hand to hand resistance before, it is said, 80 men. Such a thing was never heard in history. The disgrace in itself is unspeakable. Still it might have been slurred over by pushing on the campaign. But Gladstone was equal to himself and the occasion. He professed that the Queen's honour was by this dishonour vindicated, made the convention, and stamped the memory of Majuba in the minds of all African colonists for ever. What one man could do to throw away a continent and weaken the bonds of a world wide empire he did. He may do more in that kind yet. I therefore agree with you that the duty of keeping this fatal and baleful influence, spirit, or personality or whatever word one is to use out of political power is a duty paramount to that of forwarding any particular measure of Irish or other politics that he can, for whatever reason, espouse and advance. Strange being! He is, without foresight, insight, or resolution himself, the bright form of the thoughts and wishes of the Liberal masses. Their views supply him with his, but he defines their uncertainty into one doctrine at a time; their wishes inspire his, but he concentrates their fluctuation first on one attainable object, then on another.

Believe me you affectionate friend

GERARD M. HOPKINS

TO PATMORE

Milltown Park, Milltown, Dublin. 6 May 1888

... Since I last wrote I have reread Keats a little and the force of your criticism on him has struck me more than it did. It is impossible not to feel with weariness how his verse is at every turn abandoning itself to an unmanly and enervating luxury. It appears too that he said something like 'O for a life of impressions instead of thoughts!' It was, I suppose, the life he tried to lead. The impressions are not likely to have been all innocent and they soon ceased in death. His contemporaries, as Wordsworth, Byron, Shelley, and even Leigh Hunt, right or wrong, still concerned themselves with great causes, as liberty and religion; but he lived in mythology and fairyland the life of a dreamer. Nevertheless I feel and see in him the beginnings of something opposite to this, of an interest in higher things and of powerful and active thought. On this point you shd. if possible read what Matthew Arnold wrote. His mind had, as it seems to me, the distinctively masculine powers in abundance, his character the manly virtues, but while he gave himself up to dreaming and self indulgence of course they were in abeyance. Nor do I mean that he wd. have turned to a life of virtue – only God can know that –, but that his genius wd. have taken to an austerer utterance in art. Reason, thought, what he did not want to live by, would have asserted itself presently and perhaps have been as much more powerful than that of his contemporaries as his sensibility or impressionableness, by which he did want to live, was keener and richer than theirs. His defects were due to youth – the self indulgence of his youth; its ill-education; and also, as it seems to me, to its breadth and pregnancy, which, by virtue of a fine judgment already able to restrain but unable to direct, kept him from flinging himself blindly on the specious Liberal stuff that crazed Shelley and indeed, in their youth, Wordsworth and Coleridge. His mind played over life as a whole, so far as he a boy, without (seemingly) a dramatic but still with a deeply observant turn and also without any noble motive, felt at first hand, impelling him to look below its surface, cd. at that time see it. He was, in my opinion, made to be a thinker, a critic, as much as a singer or artist of words. This can be seen in certain reflective passages, as the opening to *Endymion* and others in his poems. These passages are the thoughts of a mind very ill instructed and in opposition; keenly sensible of wrongness in things established but unprovided with the principles to correct that by. Both his principles of art and his practice were in many things vicious, but he was correcting them, even eagerly; for *Lamia* one of his last works shews a deliberate change in manner from the style of *Endymion* and in fact goes too far in change and sacrifices things that had better have been kept. Of construction he knew nothing to the last: in this same *Lamia* he has a long introduction about Mercury, who is only brought in to disenchant Lamia and ought not to have been employed or else ought to be employed again. The story has a moral element or interest; Keats was aware of this and touches on it at times, but could make nothing of it; in fact the situation at the end is that the sage Apollonius does more harm than the witch herself had done – kills the hero; and Keats does not see that this implies one of two things, either some lesson of the terrible malice of evil which when it is checked drags down innocence in its own ruin or else the exposure of Pharisaic pretence in the wouldbe moralist. But then if I could have said this to Keats I feel sure he wd. have seen it. In due time he wd. have seen these things himself. Even when he is misconstructing one can remark certain instinctive turns of construction in his style, shewing his latent power – for instance the way the vision is introduced in *Isabella* . . .

To his Mother

University College, Dublin. 5 July 1888

MY DEAREST MOTHER, – I am now working at examination-papers all day and this work began last month and will outlast this one. It is great, very great drudgery. I can not of course say it is wholly useless, but I believe that most of it is and that I bear a burden which crushes me and does little to help any good end. It is impossible to say what a mess Ireland is and how everything enters into that mess. The Royal University is in the main, like the London University, an examining board. It does the work of examining well; but the work is not worth much. This is the first end I labour for and see little good in. Next my salary helps to support this college. The college is very moderately successful, rather a failure than a success, and there is less prospect of success now than before. Here too, unless things are to change, I labour for what is worth little. And in doing this almost fruitless work I use up all opportunity of doing any other.

About my holiday I have no plan and know nothing.

We no longer take the *Times* now, so whenever you like to post a number it will be welcome.

The weather has been wet and cold, so that yesterday, after leaving off winter clothing for less than a week, I returned to it again.

I spent a few days lately at Judge O'Hagan's at Howth – the kindest people; and their house is beautifully but somewhat bleakly situated, overlooking the Bay of Dublin southwards.

I owe my father a letter, but it is no time to write now. I am your loving son

GERARD

To Bridges

University College, Dublin. 7 Sept. 1888

DEAREST BRIDGES, – I believe I wrote to you last from Fort William. I went thence to Whitby, to be with my brothers, and returned here after being 3 weeks away. Since, I have been trying to set a discursive MA. Examination Paper, in a distress of mind difficult both to understand and to explain. It seems to me I can not always last like this: in mind or body or both I shall give way – and all I really need is a certain degree of relief and change; but I do not think that what I need I shall get in time to save me. This reminds me of a shocking thing that has just happened to a young man well known to some of our community. He put his eyes out. He was a medical student and probably understood how to proceed, which was nevertheless barbarously done with a stick and some wire. The eyes were found among nettles in a field. After the deed he made his way to a cottage and said 'I am blind: please let me rest for an hour.' He was taken to hospital and lay in some danger – from shock, I suppose, or inflammation –, but is recovering. He will not say what was the reason, and this and other circumstances wear the look of sanity; but it is said he was lately subject to delusions. I mention the case because it is extraordinary: suicide is common.

It is not good to be a medical man in the making. It is a fire in which clay splits. There was a young man in this house in my first year, an Englishman, manly and winning too, the sweetest mannered boy. After he left us he went astray. I tried to call on him, but after many trials, finding he shunned me, I gave up trying. I hear he has made a mess of it and is going to make a new beginning in Australia.

There are as many doctors as patients at Dublin, a'most.

Feeling the need of something I spent the afternoon in the Phoenix Park, which is large, beautiful, and lonely. It did me good, but my eyes are very, very sore. Also there goes ten. Goodnight. Sept. 8 (it is now 20 years to a day since I began my noviceship). Well and I had a great light. I had in my mind the first verse of a patriotic song for soldiers, the words I mean: heaven knows it is needed. I hope to make some 5 verses, but 3 would do for singing: perhaps you will contribute a verse. In the Park I hit on a tune, very flowing and spirited. I enclose the present form of this, just the tune, for I cannot set a bass till I have an instrument. I believe however that you can make nothing of a bare tune; at which I am surprised. – I find I have made 4 verses, rough at present, but I send them: do you like them and could you add one? I hope you may approve what I have done, for it is worth doing and yet is a task of great delicacy and hazard to write a patriotic song that shall breathe true feeling without spoon or brag. How I hate both! and yet feel myself half blundering or sinking into them in several of my pieces, a thought that makes me not greatly regret their likelihood of perishing . . .

Can there be gout or rheumatism in the eyes? If there can I have it. I am a gouty piece now.

Gouty rhymes to Doughty. Since you speak so highly of his book I must try to see it: to read 1200 pages I do not promise. But I have read several reviews of it, with extracts. You say it is free from the taint of Victorian English. H'm. Is it free from the taint of Elizabethan English? Does it not stink of that? for the sweetest flesh turns to corruption. Is not Elizabethan English a corpse these centuries? No one admires, regrets, despairs over the death of the style, the living masculine native rhetoric of that age, more than I do; but ' 'tis gone, 'tis gone, 'tis gone'. He writes in it, I understand, because it is manly. At any rate affectation is not manly, and to write in an obsolete style is affectation. As for the extracts I saw they were not good even as that – wrong as English, for instance calling a *man* a jade; and crammed with Latin words, a fault, let do it who will . . .

To Bridges

University College, Dublin. 19/20 Oct. 1888

. . . I am warming myself at the flame of a little exploit of my own done last night. I could not have believed in such a success nor that life had this pleasure to bestow. Somebody had tried to take me in and I warned him I wd. take him in at our next meeting. Accordingly I wrote him a letter from 'the son of a respected livery and bait stables in Parteen [suburb of Limerick] oftentimes employed by your Honoured Father' asking for an introduction to one of the Dublin newspapers 'as Reporter, occasional paregraphs or sporting inteligence'. The sentence I think best of was one in which I said I (or he) could 'give any color which may be desired to reports of speeches or Proceedings subject to the Interests of truth which must always be the paremount consideration'. It succeeded beyond my wildest hopes and action is going to be taken. The letter is even to be printed in the *Nation* as a warning to those who are continually applying in the like strain; but before this takes place I must step in.

It is as you say about Addis. But why should you be glad? Why at any rate should you burst upon me that you are glad, when you know that I cannot be glad?

It seems there is something in you interposed between what shall we say? the Christian and the man of the world which hurts, which is to me like biting on a cinder in bread. Take the simplest view of this matter: he has made shipwreck, I am afraid he must even be in straits: he cannot support himself by his learned writings; I suppose he will have to teach. But this is the least. I hope at all events he will not pretend to marry, and especially no one he has known in his priestly life. Marriage is honourable and so is the courtship that leads to marriage, but the philanderings of men vowed to God are not honourable nor the marriages they end in. I feel the same deep affection for him as ever, but the respect is gone. I would write to him if I had his address, which, I am sorry to say, is still or was lately somewhere at Sydenham; for after bidding farewell to his flock he had not the grace to go away . . .

RETREAT NOTES

St. Stanislaus' College, Tullabeg. 1 Jan. 1889

Principium seu Fundamentum: 'Homo creatus est ut laudet' etc – All moral good, all man's being good, lies in two things – in being right, being in the right, and in doing right; in being on the right side, on the side of good, and on that side of doing good. Neither of these will do by itself. Doing good but on the wrong side, promoting a bad cause, is rather doing wrong. Doing good but in no good cause is no merit: of whom or what does the doer deserve well? Not at any rate of God. Nor plainly is it enough to be on the right side and not promote it.

But men are variously constituted to make much of one of these things and neglect the other. The Irish think it enough to be Catholics or on the right side and that it is no matter what they say and do to advance it; practically so, but what they think is that all they and their leaders do to advance the right side is and must be right. The English think, as Pope says for them, he can't be wrong whose life is in the right. Marcus Aurelius seems in his Meditations to be leading the purest and most unselfish life of virtue; he thinks, though with hesitation, that Reason governs the Universe and that by this life he ranks himself on the side of that Reason; and indeed, if this was all he had the means of doing, it was enough; but he does not know of any particular standard the rallying to which is the appointed signal of, taking God the sovereign Reason's, God the Word's, side; and yet that standard was then raised in the world and the Word and sovereign Reason was then made flesh and he persecuted it. And in any case his principles are principles of despair and, again, philosophy is not religion.

But how is it with me? I was a Christian from birth or baptism, later I was converted to the Catholic faith, and am enlisted 20 years in the Society of Jesus. I am now 44. I do not waver in my allegiance, I never have since my conversion to the Church. The question is how I advance the side I serve on. This may be inwardly or outwardly. Outwardly I often think I am employed to do what is of little or no use. Something else which I can conceive myself doing might indeed be more useful, but still it is an advantage for there to be a course of higher studies for Catholics in Ireland and that that should be partly in Jesuit hands; and my work and my salary keep that up. Meantime the Catholic Church in Ireland and the Irish Province in it and our College in that are greatly given over to a partly unlawful cause, promoted by partly unlawful means, and against my will my pains, laborious and distasteful, like prisoners made to serve the enemies' gunners, go to help on this cause. I do not feel then that outwardly I do much good, much that I care to do or can much wish to prosper; and this is a mournful life to lead. In thought I can of course divide the good from the evil and live for the one, not the other: this justifies me but it does not alter the facts. Yet it seems to me that I could lead this life well enough if I had bodily energy and cheerful spirits. However these God will not give me. The other part, the more important, remains, my inward service.

I was continuing this train of thought this evening when I began to enter on that course of loathing and hopelessness which I have so often felt before, which made me fear madness and led me to give up the practice of meditation except, as now, in retreat and here it is again. I could therefore do no more than repeat *Justus es, Domine, et rectum judicium tuum* and the like, and then being tired I nodded and woke with a start. What is my wretched life? Five wasted years almost have passed in Ireland. I am ashamed of the little I have done, of my waste of time, although my helplessness and weakness is such that I could scarcely do otherwise. And yet the Wise Man warns us against excusing ourselves in that fashion. I cannot then be excused; but what is life without aim, without spur, without help? All my undertakings miscarry: I am like a straining eunuch. I wish then for death: yet if I died now I should die imperfect, no master of myself, and that is the worst failure of all. O my God, look down on me.

Jan. 2 – This morning I made the meditation on the Three Sins, with nothing to enter but loathing of my life and a barren submission to God's will. The body cannot rest when it is in pain nor the mind be at peace as long as something bitter distills in it and it aches. This may be at any time and is at many: how then can it be pretended there is for those who feel this anything worth calling happiness in this world? There is a happiness, hope, the anticipation of happiness hereafter: it is better than happiness, but it is not happiness now. It is as if one were dazzled by a spark or star in the dark, seeing it but not seeing by it: we want a light shed on our way and a happiness spread over our life.

Afternoon: on the same – more loathing and only this thought, that I can do my spiritual and other duties better with God's help. In particular I think it may be well to resolve to make the examen every day at 1.15 and then say vespers and compline if not said before. I will consider what next.

Jan. 3 – Repetition of 1st and 2nd exercise – Helpless loathing.

Then I went out and I said the Te Deum and yet I thought what was needed was not praise of God but amendment of life.

Jan. 5th. – Repetition of meditations on Incarnation and Nativity – All that happens in Christendom and so in the whole world affected, marked, as a great seal, and like any other historical event, and in fact more than any other event, by the Incarnation; at any rate by Christ's life and death, whom we by faith hold to be God made man. Our lives are affected by the events of Roman history, by Caesar's victory and murder for instance. Yet one might perhaps maintain that at this distance of time individuals could not find a difference in their lives, except in what was set down in books of history and works of art, if Pompey instead of Caesar had founded the Empire or Caesar had lived 20 years longer.

But our lives and in particular those of religious, as mine, are in their whole direction, not only inwardly but most visibly and outwardly, shaped by Christ's. Without that even outwardly the world could be so different that we cannot even guess it. And my life is determined by the Incarnation down to most of the details of the day. Now this being so that I cannot even stop it, why should I not make the cause that determines my life, both as a whole and in much detail, determine it in greater detail still and to the greater efficiency of what I in any case should do, and to my greater happiness in doing it?

It is for this that St. Ignatius speaks of the angel *discharging his mission*, it being question of action leading up to, as now my action leads from, the Incarnation. The Incarnation was for my salvation and that of the world: the work goes on in a great system and machinery which even drags me on with the collar round my neck though I could and do neglect my duty in it. But I say to myself that I am only too willing to do God's work and help on the knowledge of the Incarnation. But this is not really true: I am not willing enough for the piece of work assigned me, the only work I am given to do, though I could do others if they were given. This is my work at Stephen's Green. And I thought that the Royal University was to me what Augustus's enrolment was to St. Joseph: *exiit sermo a Caesare Augusto* etc; so resolution of the senate of the R.U. came to me, inconvenient and painful, but the journey to Bethlehem was inconvenient and painful; and then I am bound in justice, and paid. I hope to bear this in mind . . .

To Bridges

University College, Dublin. 23 Feb. 1889

... The Italian tour must have been very nice and I am very glad
you took Mary Plow. I am sorry the monks were dirty and the ex-
treme poverty they have been reduced to does not excuse them; but
I offer the following remarks. Shaving is conventional cleanliness:
if it were otherwise, the longer the beard the dirtier wd. the wearer
be, 'which' (in the language of St. Thomas) 'is inconvenient'. Next
your countrymen at Cambridge keep their rooms, you told me,
'dirty, yea filthy', and they are not poor. Next spitting in the North
of England is very, very common with the lower classes: as I went
up Brunswick Road (or any street) at Liverpool on a frosty morn-
ing it used to disgust me to see the pavement regularly starred with
the spit of the workmen going to their work; and they do not turn
aside, but spit straight before them as you approach, as a French-
man remarked to me with abhorrence and I cd. only blush. And in
general we cannot call ours a cleanly or a clean people: they are not
at all the dirtiest and they know what cleanliness means, as they
know the moral virtues, but they do not always practise it. We
deceive ourselves if we think otherwise. And our whole civilisation
is dirty, yea filthy, and especially in the north; for is it not dirty,
yea filthy, to pollute the air as Blackburn and Widnes and St. Helen's
are polluted and the water as the Thames and the Clyde and the
Irwell are polluted? The ancients with their immense public baths
would have thought even our cleanest towns dirty.

About singing out of tune, I am not altogether displeased to hear
the Italians do it, as the Germans do. Carl Rosa in an article on
English Opera (=opera by anybody you like with the words in
English, translated of course; *not* opera by English composers)
remarks on the good ear of English audiences and amateur perform-
ers and says that he has witnessed Germans at a concert listen undis-
concerted to a singer out of tune where in England half the audience
would manifest signs of distress; and to the same effect of per-
formers.

Also a good musical shrill bell at mass is pleasing and effective
enough.

'The first touch of decadence destroys all merit whatever': this is a hard saying. What, all technical merit – as chiaroscuro, anatomical knowledge, expression, feeling, colouring, drama? It is plainly not true. And, come to that, the age of Raphael and Michelangelo was in a decadence and its excellence is technical. Everything after Giotto is decadent in form, though advancing in execution. Go to.

You return home to see your country in a pretty mess – to speak jokingly of matter for tears. And the grand old traitor must have come home almost or quite in the same boat with you. And what boobies your countrymen are! They sit in court at the Commission giggling, yea guffawing at the wretched Pigot's mess; making merry because a traitor to government and then a traitor to rebellion, both in a small way, has not succeeded in injuring an enemy of their own who is a traitor to government in a great way and a danger on an imperial scale; and that after a trail which has at least shewn the greatness and the blackness of the crime lawful government and the welfare of the empire have to contend with. And this I say as if Pigot were or employed the forger of those letters. For in my judgment, unless further evidence is forthcoming, those letters are genuine. But no more of this misery. With kindest remembrances to Mrs Bridges and Mrs Molesworth I am your affectionate friend

GERARD M. HOPKINS

To his Mother

University College, Dublin. 5 May 1889

MY DEAREST MOTHER, – I am grieved that you should be in such anxiety about me and I am afraid my letter to my father, which you must now have seen and ought, it seems to me, to have had before this morning's letter was sent, can not much have relieved you. I am now in careful hands. The doctor thoroughly examined me yesterday. I have some fever; what, has not declared itself. I am to have perfect rest and to take only liquid food. My pains and sleeplessness were due to suspended digestion, which has now been almost cured, but with much distress. There is no hesitation or difficulty about the nurses, with which Dublin is provided, I dare say, better than any place, but Dr Redmond this morning said he must wait further to see the need; for today there is no real difference; only that I feel better.

You do not mention how Mary is.

I am and I long have been sad about Lionel, feeling that his visits must be few and far between and that I had so little good of this one, though he and I have so many interests in common and shd. find many more in company. I cd. not send him my Paper, for it had to be put aside.

It is an ill wind that blows nobody good. My sickness falling at the most pressing time of the University work, there will be the devil to pay. Only there is no harm in saying, that gives *me* no trouble but an unlooked for relief. At many such a time I have been in a sort of extremity of mind, now I am the placidest soul in the world. And you will see, when I come round, I shall be the better for this.

I am writing uncomfortably and this is enough for a sick man. I am your loving son

Best love to all.

GERARD

BIOGRAPHICAL APPENDIX

ALEXANDER BAILLIE (1843–1921)

Alexander Baillie, who was a close friend of Hopkins at Oxford and a regular correspondent in later life, was born in Edinburgh in 1843. The son of a doctor, he was a pupil at Edinburgh Academy, and won an exhibition to Balliol in 1862. He took a double First in Classics (1866). Although a Presbyterian by upbringing, he seems for a time to have been sympathetic towards the High Church Movement, but in later years had no fixed religious beliefs.

He failed to win a fellowship and began to study law at the Temple; he was called to the Bar in 1871. During these years correspondence between himself and Hopkins was infrequent. Having private means, he was not dependent on the law for his livelihood, but he had in any case to suspend work at the end of 1874 when he fell ill from consumption. Like his contemporary Stevenson, he was 'ordered south' (*Journal*, p.262) and visited Egypt and Algeria.

Correspondence was renewed in January 1877, but continued at irregular intervals until Hopkins went to Dublin in 1884. Throughout his life Baillie took a strong interest in Egyptology and related subjects, and during Hopkins's last years letters were often concerned with obscure points of ancient scholarship, uninteresting to the general reader but fulfilling a need for Hopkins: 'It is a great help to me to have someone interested in something . . . and it supplies some sort of intellectual stimulus' (*FL*, p.263).

Their political attitudes were similar, although Baillie was the more conservative. He opposed any relaxation of English rule in Ireland, and his dislike for Gladstone seems to have been no less than Hopkins's.

A few days after his friend's death, he wrote to Mrs Hopkins: 'Apart from my own nearest relations, I never had so strong an affection for anyone' (*FL*, p.449). Baillie was unmarried and lived by himself in London. He was remembered by one of his nieces as enjoying the company of children and content with an unambitious existence. He died in 1921.

ROBERT BRIDGES (1844–1930)

Robert Bridges went up to Corpus Christi, Oxford, in October 1863, six months after Hopkins came into residence at Balliol. The first surviving letter between them is dated August 1865, the beginning of a correspondence that was to last nearly 25 years.

Born in 1844 – the same year as Hopkins – at Walmer in Kent, Bridges's family were prosperous country gentry whose name went back to the 16th century. The children, nine in all, never needed to work for a living, and although Bridges lost his father when he was only ten, his mother remarried the Reverend John Molesworth, Vicar of Rochdale, which then became Bridges's home.

In 1854 he went to Eton, where he had a happy boyhood, and enjoyed some distinction both as a cricketer and a rower. He became a great friend of a younger boy, Digby Dolben, who was later to meet a tragic early death at the age of nineteen: both claimed to be Puseyites, both assumed they were destined to take holy orders. But Bridges's sense of vocation vanished rapidly and it is as a sceptical Anglican, unsympathetic to doctrine and ritual, that he figures in most of the correspondence with Hopkins.

As Hopkins had forecast, he took a second in classics in 1867, and after a foreign tour which included the Middle East, he began his medical studies at Barts (November 1869). His intention was to practise until he was forty, and then retire and devote his life to the poetry which he was already writing. Hopkins only seems to have known of his ambitions as a poet in 1874 when his first collection appeared. The same year he gained his MB and then went to work in London hospitals. He was casualty physician at Barts and wrote an *Account of the Casualty Department at St. Bartholomew's Hospital* (1878) which showed he had seen 30,000 patients in one year. He was always sensitive to the spectacle of physical suffering.

On his stepfather's death he set up house with his mother in 1877 in Bedford Square. In 1881, when a number of his books began to appear from the private press of C. H. Daniel, later Provost of Worcester, he fell ill from pneumonia and spent a long holiday in Italy. He now retired from medicine and moved house to Yattendon on the Berkshire Downs, where he married Monica Waterhouse, daughter of the architect, with whom and their family of three he lived happily to the end of a long life.

Throughout the 1880s and after Hopkins's death, the regular publication of his plays, poems, and essays – including two on Milton's prosody, an interest he shared with Hopkins – slowly brought him fame. He was appointed Poet Laureate 1913, and in 1929, the year before his death, there appeared *The Testament of Beauty*, perhaps his most considerable achievement. His edition of Hopkins's verse in 1918 is his great tribute to his friend's memory.

He was not interested in self-revelation: his poetry is usually impersonal, he asked that no biography should be written of him, and he kept no copies of his letters – which have, in any case, been described as 'not usually very interesting' (Edward Thompson, *Robert Bridges*, p.88). Both men were conservative in their basic attitudes and genuinely patriotic, but Hopkins had a capacity for an individual point of view on many questions which Bridges lacked.

Until a biography is attempted, it will remain difficult to give a fair estimate of a man whose friendship Hopkins valued so deeply and whose loyalty was eventually to bring him fame.

R. W. DIXON (1833–1900)

Richard Watson Dixon, one of Hopkins's closest correspondents during the last ten years of his life, was born in Islington on 5 May 1833. His father was a Wesleyan minister and his mother also came from a Nonconformist background. He was educated at King Edward's School, Birmingham, where Edward Burne-Jones was a close friend, and went in 1851 to Pembroke College, Oxford. Here he became part of a circle that included William Morris, and wrote poetry and painted in the Pre-Raphaelite manner.

Without the parental opposition that Hopkins experienced at his conversion, he was ordained into the Anglican Church in 1858, the year of his BA. He was married in 1861, when his book of poems *Christ's Company* was published and when, as a master at Highgate, he saw Hopkins for the first time. It was the memory of this fleeting acquaintance that led Hopkins to write praising him for his poetry nearly twenty years later.

A further volume, *Historical Odes*, appeared in 1863 when he became 2nd Master at Carlisle High School. From 1868–75 he was a Minor Canon and Honorary Librarian of Carlisle Cathedral and began research for the great historical work that was to play such a large part in the rest of his life. The first of the six volumes of the *History of the Church of England from the Abolition of the Roman Jurisdiction* was actually begun while he held the living of Hayton 1875–83, a parish ten miles east of Carlisle. It was an attempt to write an original work on the English Reformation, to acknowledge its faults as well as its achievements, and not to deal 'dishonestly with materials' (*LD*, p. 34).

The value of the *History*, which took some thirty years to complete, was only slowly recognized, while his poetry, although admired by Hopkins and D. G. Rossetti, was never popular. It was in June 1878, just after the first volume of the *History* was published, that Hopkins wrote to Dixon regretting that Dixon's poetry was not better known. The correspondence continued for the next eleven years, often on the subject of each other's verse and reflecting faithfully Dixon's modest and attractive character. Their only meeting seems to have been briefly at Carlisle while Hopkins was travelling between Maryport and Preston in March 1882. But their friendship led to one between Dixon and Bridges, and Dixon's admiration for Hopkins resulted in one of his poems being printed in an anthology and his help being acknowledged in a footnote in the *History* (vol. iii, pp. 418–19).

More of Dixon's poetry was published in the 1880s, and for a time he was a candidate for the Professorship of Poetry at Oxford. In 1885 the third volume of the *History* met with warm approval from its reviewer in the *Academy*, the future Bishop of London, but the most pleasing recognition came just before his death when he was made an honorary Fellow of Pembroke College.

He died on 23 January 1900 at Warkworth in Northumberland where he had been a conscientious and respected priest since moving from Hayton in 1883. The last volumes of his life's work appeared posthumously, fulfilling his ambition of 'writing a work of importance: not ... adding to the pestering swarm of little books with which we are afflicted' (*LD*, p. 34).

KATE HOPKINS (1821–1920)

Kate Hopkins, the mother of Gerard Manley Hopkins, was born at Tower Hill, London on 3 March 1821. She was the eldest child of John Simm Smith, a successful doctor, and Maria Hodges, whose father was an underwriter. There were seven other brothers and sisters and the family was a cultured one, with music and reading popular occupations (Kate later wrote a private memoir of her family life). Before her marriage she lived for a time with a family in Hamburg, learning German. The books in her personal library included Dante, Chateaubriand, and Schiller, in the original language.

She married Manley Hopkins, who was soon to establish his own firm of average adjusters, on 8 August 1843, and they went to live at Stratford in Essex. Gerard, their first child, was born in July the following year. Eight years later the family moved to Hampstead.

Kate was a pious woman, deeply attached to her own and her husband's Anglicanism. When Gerard was at Highgate, he regularly read a portion of the New Testament in fulfilment of a promise to her. The shock of both his parents at his conversion to Catholicism in October 1866 can be judged from the letters in this Selection.

But this painful period seems to have lasted only a short time. Once he became a Jesuit, he wrote to her freely about religious matters and about his poetry in which she took a proud interest. Throughout his life as a religious he remembered her birthday with some personal token of his affection, while she used to send him practical gifts like shirts, jerseys, medicine, and cuttings to help with the composition of *The Wreck of the Deutschland*.

In 1881 she was very ill from gastric fever, but she long outlived both her husband and her son. She died on 30 September 1920 – only six months short of her hundredth birthday – at Haslemere in Surrey where the family had moved in 1886. One sonnet Gerard had sent her she kept framed on the walls of her home, and she and Bridges corresponded at length over her son's poems, the publication of which she lived to see in 1918.

COVENTRY PATMORE (1823–96)

Coventry Patmore was already well known as a man of letters when Hopkins first made his acquaintance at the Stonyhurst Great Academies in August 1883. Hopkins had been an admirer of his verse since his Balliol days and in a letter to Dixon in June 1878 described him as a poet 'whose fame . . . is very deeply below his great merit' (*LD*, p. 6).

The son of a literary father, his first poems had been published in 1844, but it was not until his name became associated with the Pre-Raphaelite movement and the appearance of the first part of *Angel in the House* (1854) that he achieved some measure of fame. In 1864 he was received into the Catholic Church, demonstrating thereafter a personal and mystical faith that was as individual as his extreme right-wing politics. Hopkins protested about an anti-semitic reference to Disraeli in one of Patmore's poems, but the author was unrepentant and added: 'The political action and inaction of England . . . fill me with an actual thirst for vengeance – such vengeance as I have felt towards myself in former times, when I have asked with ardour that I might not go unpunished' (*FL*, p. 344).

Patmore was married three times. One of his daughters became a nun and died in 1882 at the age of twenty-six; his son Henry, a promising poet, was only twenty-two when he died the following year. Patmore deeply appreciated the frank but sympathetic assessment that Hopkins gave of his son's verse.

During their six years of correspondence the two men met only twice, at Stonyhurst and at Patmore's home in Hastings in 1884. They wrote much about poetry, including their own – Bridges sent Patmore his manuscript book of Hopkins's verse – and that of Bridges and Dixon, to whose work Hopkins introduced him. Compared with the letters to Bridges and Dixon, those to Patmore are both less varied in subject-matter and less relaxed in manner, but neither man was afraid to speak his mind about the other's work. 'You do not know', wrote Hopkins of a Patmore essay in the *Fortnightly*, 'what *writing prose* is' (*FL*, p. 380), and Patmore in turn complained of his friend's poetry, 'I often find it as hard to follow you as I have found it to follow the darkest parts of Browning' (ibid. 353).

Both shared a strong interest in the work of Barnes and in the theory of prosody, but a projected work on the latter by themselves and Bridges did not materialize. *The Unknown Eros* (1878) was Patmore's last important volume of verse, although he continued to write for the periodical press on literary and political subjects until his death. The appeal of Hopkins's character exerted its influence on him as it had on so many, and when he heard the sad news from Dublin he wrote to Bridges, 'Gerard Hopkins was the only orthodox, and as far as I could see, saintly man in whom religion had absolutely no narrowing effect upon his general opinions and sympathies' (Derek Patmore, *The Life and Times of Coventry Patmore*, p. 189).

NOTES

13 *C. N. Luxmoore.* Charles Luxmoore was a contemporary of Hopkins at Highgate School. He later became a close friend of his brother Arthur, to whom he sent a long letter about Gerard after the latter's death: 'Once roused by a sense of undeserved injustice he usually so quiet and docile was furiously keen for the fray' (*FL*, p. 395).

Oak Hill. The Hopkins family home 1852–86.

Elgin. Elgin and Grove Bank were two boarders' houses in Highgate village, both the personal property of Dr Dyne.

the Exhibition. The award which Hopkins won to Balliol.

Dyne. The Reverend John Dyne (1809–98), Headmaster of Highgate 1838–74, formerly Dean and Divinity Lecturer at Wadham College, Oxford.

Nesfield. John Nesfield taught at Highgate 1859–64 and was in charge of Elgin House.

Bord. Richard Bord was a pupil at Highgate 1858–62.

with the chill off. A slang expression, emphasizing here the triviality of the incident referred to.

Clarke. Marcus Clarke (1846–81) was at Highgate 1858–62, emigrated to Australia, and became a well-known writer: his most famous work is *For the Term of His Natural Life*. Hopkins appears as a fictional character in some of his stories.

14 *scout's hole.* Pantry would be the modern expression.

no oak to sport. No outer door to close to signify that the occupant is 'not at home'.

Strachan-Davidson. James Strachan-Davidson (1843–1916) was at Balliol 1862–6, became a Fellow and eventually Master of the College. 'Man in a punt' is a drawing by Hopkins, *Journal*, plate 21.

15 *Palmer.* Reverend Edwin Palmer, Fellow of Balliol 1845–67.

Papa. Manley Hopkins (1818–97) came from a commercial, middle-class background and had worked in insurance since the age of fifteen. He became a successful average adjuster, founded his own firm, and was Consul-General for Hawaii in London for forty years. He was a committed and active Anglican, and published a number of books and articles, including volumes of verse.

Bond. Edward Bond (1844–1920), one of Hopkins's closest friends at Oxford. He took a First in Greats at St. John's in 1866, was one of the few people told beforehand of Hopkins's conversion, and accompanied him on the Swiss holiday. In later life he was a barrister and a Conservative MP, but the friendship with Hopkins lapsed. On the latter's death, he

wrote to his mother: 'I shall never lose the memory of our early friend-
ship nor my sense of that fine spirituality which distinguished him from
his fellows' (*Journal*, p. 303).

Jowett. Benjamin Jowett (1817–93), Fellow and tutor at Balliol, Regius
Professor of Greek, and (1870) Master of the College. One of the most
celebrated figures of Victorian Oxford, his contribution to the liberal
Essays and Reviews (1860) resulted in a charge of heresy which had still
to be settled at this date. His silences in conversation were notorious: 'In
private the Greek Professor was not a communicative man' (*A Son of
Belial*, p. 156: see note to p. 132, 'poor Geldart').

Addis. William Addis (1844–1917), another close Balliol friend, took a
First in Greats (1865). He became a Catholic at the same time as Hop-
kins, joined the London Oratory, and was ordained in 1872. A Fellow of
the Royal University of Ireland for a short time, he was parish priest of
Sydenham 1878–88 and then, to Hopkins's sorrow, left the Church: see
p. 163 and note.

Littlemore Church which Newman's mother built. Littlemore, three miles
from Oxford, was part of Newman's parish when he was Vicar of St.
Mary's. His mother was active in good works in the village and laid the
foundation stone of the new church. His last sermon as an Anglican, *The
Parting of Friends*, was preached in September 1843 and is one of the
best-known episodes in his break with the Anglican Church.

Margaret St. Church, now All Saints, Margaret Street, off Cavendish
Square, was well known for its High Church ritual. Ruskin praised it as a
successful building in the Gothic style (Butterfield was the architect), but
Hopkins was still doubtful about its merit when he visited it in June 1874
(*Journal*, p. 248). His sister Milicent later joined the High Anglican com-
munity of nuns attached to the church.

Baillie. See Biographical Appendix. Manor Farm, Shanklin, was where
the Hopkinses were enjoying a family holiday.

Millais' Eve of S. Agnes. John Millais (1829–96), one of the founders of
the Pre-Raphaelite school of painting, whose picture inspired by Keats's
poem was exhibited at the Royal Academy 1863. The two other pictures
were *The Wolf's Den* and *My First Sermon*. Hopkins remained an
admirer for most of his life (cf. *LB*, p. 32), but critics seem to disagree
with his insistence here that Millais was still a Pre-Raphaelite (cf.
Hopkins Quarterly, II, no. 1, pp. 5 ff.).

Eddis. Eden Upton Eddis (1812–1901), who lived in Harley Street, was
well known as a portrait-painter and exhibited at the Royal Academy,
1834–81.

16 *Ruskinese point of view.* Examples of Hopkins's sketches in the Ruskin
style may be seen in the Plates in the *Journal*, Appendix 1. Ruskin insisted
on the importance of detail: 'Every landscape painter should know the
specific characters of every object he has to represent, rock, flower, or
cloud' (*Modern Painters*, I, xxv, 7th edn., 1867), and he gives an example

of an 'Ancient, or Giottesque' aspen which shows 'varied symmetry [and] a perfect definiteness' (ibid. IV, 77, 2nd edn., 1868). The leaf of the ash is illustrated, V, 25 (1860). Giotto was one of Ruskin's most admired painters.

turpid. i.e. turbid, confused.

confusion . . . worse confounded. Milton, *Paradise Lost*, II, 996.

17 *It is the exact complement of carnation.* 'Carnation is flesh colour 'Complementary colours are those which are the greatest distance apart when the hues are arranged in their natural order around the circumference of a circle' (*Oxford Companion to Art*, p. 258).

chrysoprase. Golden green.

There was neither rain, etc. An experiment in the novel-style?

Berlin wool. 'A fine dyed wool used for knitting, tapestry, and the like' (*NED*).

walked to Edgware. This walk is more fully described in a letter to Baillie, *FL*, pp. 207–8.

no royal road to poetry. The expression, applied to learning, was proverbial.

excelsior. Cf. Longfellow's anthology-piece of this name, and Patmore: 'Thousands and thousands climb, with praiseworthy struggles and integrity of purpose and with shouts of "Excelsior!" the minor peaks of life' (*Possibilities and Performances* in *Principle in Art*, p. 27).

E. H. Coleridge. Ernest Hartley Coleridge, grandson of the poet, was at Highgate with Hopkins, and at Balliol 1866–70. Later, private tutor and literary editor.

18 *the head and fount of Catholicism.* In the sense of Anglo-Catholicism, Oxford being the home of the High Church movement.

Blunt House, Croydon. The home of the Simm Smiths, Hopkins's grandparents on his mother's side.

Wharton. Perhaps the Edward Wharton who took a double First at Trinity in 1867, and who visited Hopkins in his first year at Oxford and left his card (*FL*, p. 43, Abbott's note, and p. 83).

Baillejus ap. Hopk. 'Baillie as quoted by Hopkins', a mock classical annotation.

19 Enoch Arden *and the other new poems.* Published August 1864.

I was shaken too you know by Addis. Presumably Addis had offered some unconventional opinion on Tennyson.

the Hexameron. A short-lived, mainly undergraduate society of High Church sympathies, which included many of Hopkins's friends, so-called because it met six times a term. In the diaries for 1864 (*Journal*, p. 38) appear what are presumably notes for the 'essay'.

Parnassian. Hopkins repeats the same idea in 1881 when he defines the term as 'the language and style of poetry mastered and at command but employed without any fresh inspiration' (*LD*, p. 72).

20 *a passage much quoted*. Lines 573–81.

21 *no author palls so much as Wordsworth*. Wordsworth, 'great sonneteer as he was ... wrote in "Parnassian"' (*LD*, p. 72). But compare Hopkins's high praise of the *Immortality Ode*, p. 145.

'*intolerable deal*'. 'This intolerable deal of sack', I *Hen. IV* II. iv. 598.

the stanza of In Memoriam. No. CXX, which begins '*Sad* Hesper ...'

22 *which I call* Castalian. Castalia was the spring of the Muses on Parnassus

Yet despair, etc. The last lines of Wordsworth's sonnet, *Composed near Calais ... Aug. 7, 1802.*

Delphic, the tongue of the Sacred Plain. Delphi was on a mountainside; the the image does not seem very appropriate.

Milman's poetry. Henry Milman (1791–1868), Dean of St. Paul's, minor poet and dramatist during the Romantic period, later a religious historian.

unusual poetry has a tendency to seem so at first. Cf. his advice to Bridges for reading the *Wreck of the Deutschland*, pp. 69–70.

Chagford. Hopkins was there for a month in July–August, walking and visiting relatives.

23 *electrum*. Pale yellow colour.

the manufactory. Under Chagford, Lewis's *Topographical Dictionary of England*, 1831, notes: 'On the banks of the Teign a large woollen manufactory has been established'.

Mallowy. Reddish purple.

For Lent. Acts of penance such as these were very common with followers of the Tractarian movement. Newman's fasting was extreme.

Journal. Editors have conventionally distinguished between the earlier, more fragmentary notes made by Hopkins, and the later and fuller entries, by calling the former manuscript books 'Early Diaries' and the latter the 'Journal'.

St. Philip's. St. Philip and St. James, a church on the northern side of Oxford, well known for its High Anglican ritual, where Hopkins's friend, Edward Urquhart, was curate (see note to p. 27).

24 *Newman*. Since his reception into the Catholic Church, Newman had established the Oratory community and school in Birmingham. The *Apologia Pro Vita Sua* (1864) continued to keep him in the public eye.

when I pass through Birmingham in a few days. He was going to spend a holiday with Bridges in Rochdale: cf. the next letter.

25 *what Mr. Oakley calls a minimizing Catholicism*. Frederick Oakeley (1802–80) was one of the prominent figures of the Tractarian movement. Formerly chaplain and Fellow of Balliol, he became minister of Margaret

Street Church 1839–45 (see note to p. 15), and was received into the Catholic Church in 1845. In *Leading Topics of Dr Pusey's Recent Work Reviewed*, published early in 1866, he rejected Pusey's suggestion of finding a union between the churches based on a 'Catholic minimum and Anglican maximum' (p. 54). The term 'minimiser' was in current use in the sense of a Catholic who refrained from taking up a dogmatic position.

Dr Molesworth. John Molesworth, Vicar of Rochdale, became Bridges's stepfather when he married the latter's mother, a widow, in 1854. He was not a Tractarian, and, as the next letter indicates, Hopkins was careful not to reveal his impending reception into the Church while staying with the Molesworths.

26 *Fili hominis*, etc. 'Son of man, dost thou think these bones shall live? [And I answered:] O Lord God, thou knowest.' Ezek. 37:3.

John Walford (1834–94) had been educated at Eton several years before Bridges, went to King's, Cambridge, where he was appointed a Fellow, then returned to Eton as an asistant master. He became a Catholic (March 1866), was a master at the Oratory for a short time, and entered the Jesuit novitiate in September 1867. He looked after Hopkins when he was a newcomer at Roehampton the following year. He was ordained in 1883.

27 *E. W. Urquhart.* Edward William Urquhart (1839–1916), who took a First at Balliol in 1861, was Anglican curate at St. Philip and St. James, Oxford 1864–6, and became a close friend of Hopkins. He was one of those whom Hopkins told beforehand of his reception into the Church, and was clearly considering a similar step. Despite Hopkins's exhortations, however, he remained an Anglican: cf. the letters on pp. 34 and 37.

Macfarlane and Garrett. William Macfarlane and Alfred Garrett were both friends of Hopkins at Balliol. During July, when Hopkins was on holiday with them in Sussex, Macfarlane wrote in his diary: 'Walked out with Hopkins and he confided to me his fixed intention of going over to Rome' (*FL*, p. 397). Garrett joined the Catholic Church just before Hopkins; Macfarlane became ordained in the Anglican Church.

Birchington. A village in 'dull flat corn country between Margate and Ramsgate . . . and yet inland' (*FL*, p. 20).

28 *Magnificavit Dominus*, etc. 'The Lord hath done great things for us; we are become joyful', Ps. 125:3.

Challis or Gurney. Henry Challis was at Merton 1859–63, became a Catholic in July 1866, and taught for a time at the Oratory. He later left the Church. Frederick Gurney was at Balliol 1860–4, and took Anglican orders in 1868.

my actual conversion was two months ago. Cf. *Journal*, 17 July, p. 146: 'It was this night I believe but possibly the next that I saw clearly the impossibility of staying in the Church of England, but resolved to say nothing to anyone till three months are over.'

18 New Inn Hall Street. From May 1866 Hopkins (and Addis) had been lodging at this address. He was to move again in October. The feast-day of St. Teresa of Avila is 15 Oct.

to come to Birmingham. He went on Sunday 21 October, and was received into the Church on that day: see p. 33.

communicatio in sacris. Hopkins explains the rule at the beginning of the next letter.

29 *Alexander Wood,* originally a Presbyterian, was at Oxford 1863–70. He and Hopkins were still in touch in 1883.

Dr Pusey. Edward Pusey (1800–82), Professor of Hebrew, canon of Christ Church, was a leading figure of the High Church movement, but discouraged conversion to Rome. He had some correspondence with Hopkins before his final step.

Chale. A village on the S. coast of the Isle of Wight.

F. William Neville. Newman's constant companion and secretary from 1851 until the Cardinal's death.

Monsignor Eyre. (?) Charles Eyre (1817–1902) who worked as a priest mainly in the North-East of England until 1868, when he moved to Glasgow and became archbishop.

I must begin with a practical immediate point. Attendance at College chapel was compulsory, unless the parents or guardians made a written request for exemption. A similar statement was required by the University Statutes to excuse examination candidates 'from examination in the XXXIX Articles, or in the Rudiments of Faith and Religion' (*Statuta Universitatis Oxoniensis,* 1876, V.C. 10). Although the Catholic authorities forbade Catholics to go up to Oxford and Cambridge, in practice many went.

the Master. The Reverend Robert Scott (1811–87), Master of Balliol 1854–70, and with Henry Liddell author of the famous Greek lexicon.

30 *if I were to delay and die in the meantime.* It was said of Addis that he 'trembled lest, if attacked by cholera, he sd. die out of the church' (*FL,* p. 436).

31 *which only wants to be known in order to be loved.* Cf. Dryden, *Hind and the Panther,* i, 34.

Mr Liddon. Henry Liddon (1829–90), Pusey's great friend who exercised considerable influence over religious life at Oxford, especially in the 1860s. In October 1866, at the appeal of Hopkins's father, he wrote four letters in five days to try to restrain Hopkins from becoming a Catholic.

the Bp. of Oxford. Samuel Wilberforce (1805–73), son of the abolitionist, and Bishop 1845–69, who had the difficult task of mediating between the Tractarian and Evangelical factions in his diocese. Contemporaries differ in their estimate of his character, but he was fond of riding (and in fact died as the result of a riding accident). He wrote a preface to Manley Hopkins's history of Hawaii (1862).

32 *Mr Lane Fox.* George Lane-Fox (1838–1918), son and heir to a Yorkshire landed family, educated Eton and Christ Church, who became a convert in 1866 and was disinherited by his father.

Our Lord's last care. See John 19:26–7.

the Mother of sorrows. Hopkins refers to a popular Catholic devotion known as the Seven Dolours of Mary. The whole passage reflects a convert's recent experience of the language of Catholic prayer.

33 *the time that I was with Bridges.* See p. 24 and note.

Arthur. Arthur Hopkins (1847–1930), one of Gerard's three brothers, who was then working in the family firm of average adjusters, but eventually became a successful professional artist.

34 διὰ τὸ πεφυκέναι. 'From their very nature'.

Urquhart. See notes to p. 27. Hopkins had just spent a fortnight's holiday in August–September with Urquhart at Bovey Tracy, where he was curate.

The Oratory. Newman had established the Oratory School for some fifty pupils, mainly sons of Catholic convert gentlemen, in 1859. He took a considerable interest in and had final control over the school, but many of the duties of headmaster were carried out by Fr Ambrose St. John (see below). Hopkins arrived at the Oratory on 10 September.

35 *Tracy.* Alfred Hanbury-Tracy, educated at Eton, who took his B.A in 1867, and became vicar of a Bristol parish.

Mr Oxenham. Henry Oxenham had been at Balliol and taken Anglican orders in 1854. He became a convert in 1857, and taught for a time at the Oratory. He kept strong links with Oxford and wrote in favour of the idea of Church unity.

bucculae. The part of a helmet which covers the cheeks and mouth.

Wharton. See note to p. 18.

their field, which they call Bosco. John Bosco (1815–88), later canonized, was an Italian priest and founder of a community devoted to teaching poor children, which later became the Salesian teaching order.

looking over exercises (which takes a long time). This and the following letter are the first evidence of distaste for certain aspects of teaching which was to assume obsessive proportions in later years.

Mr Disraeli. A controversial and sweeping electoral reform bill had been passed through Parliament by the Disraeli government in August. Jokes about what title Disraeli would take were frequent. Mt. Horeb was where God spoke to Moses. Bashan was a kingdom to the east of Jordan that was conquered by the Israelites.

F. Ambrose. Ambrose St John (1815–75), Headmaster in effect of the Oratory, and companion of Newman since the Littlemore days.

36 *p.p.s.* Private puils.

Dr. Newman. He was an accomplished violinist.

Thomas Pope. A convert in his late forties who eventually became a priest.

You know what my specific is. It is not clear what Hopkins meant: his letters to Urquhart over conversion to the Catholic faith covered many topics.

Challis. See note to p. 28.

'damned, shepherd'. As You Like It, III. ii. 30 ff.

37   *minor orders.* Hopkins describes their significance, p. 61.

the Jesuit noviciate. He had been accepted on 30 May.

in a passage of the Anglican Difficulties. In *Difficulties Felt by Anglicans in Catholic Teaching* (1850), Newman criticized Anglican priests who refused to listen to their Catholic consciences: 'There is the same round of parochial duties and charities; sick people to be visited, the school to be inspected. The sun shines, and the rain falls, the garden smiles, as it used to do; and can some one definite, external event have changed the position of this happy scene of which I am the centre?' (Lecture IV, section 7, 4th edn., pp. 108–9) There is no further correspondence with Urquhart after this letter: no doubt its tone offended him.

38   *Domine, quid vis ut faciam?* 'Lord, what do you wish me to do?'

Journal. The following pages are a selection from the Journal kept by Hopkins during his month's holiday with Edward Bond in Switzerland. The interests of art and scenery – Turner and Ruskin had been earlier distinguished tourists of the Alps – and the Swiss law against the entry of Jesuits must have been among the reasons for his choice of this country for his last holiday as a layman. Switzerland's attraction for the English is reflected by the appearance of the 13th edition of Murray's *Handbook for Travellers* in 1868 and the similar popularity of Baedeker's *Switzerland* a copy of which Hopkins used.

39   *meridians.* Elongated semicircles.

coigns. Angles.

'blue bow'. See *The Tempest*, IV. i. 80. 'The reason Shakspere calls it "the blue bow" . . . is because the blue band edged by and ending in violet, though not the broadest, is the deepest expression of colour in the bow' (*Journal*, p. 148).

Brill. A village near Thame in Buckinghamshire on a 600 ft. hill overlooking the surrounding countryside.

Charlotte Bronte's school in Brussels. The Pensionnat Heget where Charlotte was both teacher and student 1842–4.

the bridge. The wooden Alte Brücke which spanned the Rhine.

We got up to a height. '. . . The Pfalz, a terrace behind the Munster, 65 ft. above the Rhine, planted with chestnuts, and affording a pleasing survey of the green river and the hills of the Black Forest' (Baedeker's *Switzerland*, p. 5, 16th edn., 1895).

40 *the Munster*. Baedeker's English term for the Protestant cathedral.

scape. See note on *well inscaped* below.

I do not know the technical name. This was presumably a chalk drawing.

shell-rayed. Marked by, formed of similar curving lines to a shell.

Thorvaldsen's monument. This was the 'Lion of Lucerne', a carving out of the natural rock based on a model by the Danish sculptor, Thorwaldsen, commemorating the Swiss Guards who fell defending the Bourbons at the Tuileries in 1792. 'The rock . . . is overhung with trees and creepers. A spring at the top flows on one side and forms a dark pool at the base' (Baedeker, p. 84).

well-inscaped. 'Scape' and 'inscape' are both words developed by Hopkins to convey his perception of and personal response to the external world, and are used in a sometimes bewildering variety of contexts. 'Scape' often describes the special physical impression given by an object, scene, etc., often with the suggestion of a particular harmonious pattern. 'Inscape' tends to emphasize an inner, distinctive quality or characteristic of an object, etc. See Weyand, *Immortal Diamond*, pp. 216 ff. and Peters, *Gerard Manley Hopkins*, p. 1 ff. and notes.

quains. A variant of 'coigns'. Cf. p. 39 and note.

the Rigi. A mountain reaching nearly 6,000 ft., described by Ruskin in 1867 as 'the travelling public's . . . favourite mountain' (*Time and Tide*, xix, 116). There were several hotels on the summit from which the recommended time for seeing the view was either sunrise or sunset. Of special interest to the Catholic traveller were the thirteen oratories or 'stations' which marked the path to the church of Our Lady of the Snows near the top.

the purple expressing the rose of the chord to the eye. Chord: a harmonious combination of colours. The term was much used by Ruskin. Hopkins's meaning is best understood by studying a colour circle, – see p. 17 and note. He is discussing how far a colour suggests a colour that comes 'before' or 'after' it.

41 *the Rossberg*. A range rising over 5,000 ft., a few miles to the east of the Rigi.

Shanklin. Cf. p. 15 and note.

Cassiopeïa. Hopkins would have seen this group of stars like a rough W on its side, the two base angles pointing to the right.

Pilatus. A range rising nearly 7,000 ft., some 10 miles SE of the Rigi.

purpurea candidior nive. 'Whiter than shining snow', l. 62 of the first of two elegies on Maecenas, written about 8 BC. The authorship is uncertain (*Minor Latin Poets*, ed. J. and A. Duff, Loeb, 1934, p. 126).

strombus shell. Which is spiral-shaped.

42 *Solomon's seal.* A plant with green and white flowers.

43 *the Matterhorn.* Or Mont Cervin, 14,705 ft., as it was also known, had
    only recently been climbed (by Whymper, 1865). Its picturesqueness
    inspired Ruskin in *Modern Painters* and *Stones of Venice.* 'No mountain
    in the Alps produces a more vigorous impression of peakedness,' he
    wrote (*Modern Painters*, IV, 184), and seeing it, like Hopkins, from the
    Riffel, he used similar exotic imagery: 'the seams of canvass in a Vene-
    tian felucca's sail', 'an Egyptian temple' (ibid. 243, 245). In *Stones of
    Venice* the mountain lifts itself 'like a rearing horse' (2nd edn., 1858, I,
    57).

    rostrum. The ramming device on the bows of a Roman galley.

    cutwater. The prow.

    the Riffel. A mountain plateau, some 8,000 ft. high, of which the Gorner
    Grat (10,290 ft.) is an extension. The vast views are illustrated in Baed-
    eker by a 'Panorama' which shows all the peaks mentioned by Hopkins.

    hooded-snake frontal. A mask which projects over the upper part of the
    face.

44 *cusped.* Smoothly pointed like arcs in Gothic tracery.

    Weisshorn. Described by Ruskin as 'ascertainably peaked in the true
    sense of the word, – pointed at the top, and sloping steeply on all sides'
    (*Modern Painters*, IV, 182).

    George Simcox (1841–1905), Fellow of Queen's 1863, poet and classical
    scholar, whose poetry and character were both admired by Hopkins.

    porter. The duty of porter was to assist the novice-master in day-to-day
    matters and to keep a regular journal of the day's events. Hopkins held
    the post December 1869–February 1870.

    Father Rector. Peter Gallwey (1820–1906), an Irishman, educated at
    Stonyhurst, who joined the Jesuits in 1836, and held several important
    positions, including that of Provincial. He was Rector and Master of
    Novices at Roehampton 1869–73.

45 *'A Secretis'.* A Manresa euphemism for cleaning the lavatories. The
    novices did most of the community's housework.

    the Long Retreat. For the first-year novices, which Hopkins had experi-
    enced the previous year.

    Sister Emmerich. Anne Emmerich (1774–1824), a German Augustinian
    nun, whose visions were recorded in *The Dolorous Passion of Our Lord
    Jesus Christ according to the Meditations of Anne Catherine Emmerich*
    (1833).

46 *The Seminary.* St. Mary's Hall. See Introduction.

    my vows. The three simple vows of poverty, chastity, and obedience,
    when the Jesuit moves from the noviceship and becomes a scholastic.

our new church which is building. The Church of the Holy Name, designed by Joseph Hansom and completed 1871, opposite the present University of Manchester.

a Scotchman. See note on 'a young Campbell', p. 50.

Fr. Gallwey. See notes to p. 44.

47 *warp.* Curve.

Laus Deo. Praise be to God.

Hodder Roughs. A stretch of the river about half a mile from St. Mary's Hall, full of rocks and pools.

its seizure by the Italian government. 'Sept. 20 [1870] – Storming of Porta Pia and capture of Rome' (*Journal*, p. 203). There were refectory readings on the subject of the Pope's defeat by Victor Emmanuel.

48 *Pendle.* A prominent hill on the opposite side of the Ribble Valley from Stonyhurst.

knoppled. Not listed in *NED*: (?) 'knobbed'.

water-runs were then mulled. Streams were dirtied with particles of stone and earth.

forepitch. Hopkins's coinage: 'projection'.

or | best of all. This sign is informally used by Hopkins, often to indicate a pause or parenthesis, as here.

49 *I will tell you something about this place.* Cf. the account of Stonyhurst and its surroundings, p. 113.

we have the highest rain-guage in England. Hopkins means highest rainfall, but Stonyhurst's 50 inches a year is by no means the highest in England. For a number of years the College observatory had been recognized as one of the principal meteorological stations in the British Isles.

50 *a young Campbell.* Donald Campbell (b. 1849), who was at Roehampton 1869–73.

three beautiful rivers. The Hodder, Ribble, and Calder.

a big library. The Arundell Library, which contains many old books and manuscripts bequeathed to the College in 1837 by the 10th Lord Arundell.

which is more than violets knee-deep. i.e. and this is no mere platitude. Hopkins's personal religious experience is brought out vividly in the opening stanzas of *The Wreck of the Deutschland*.

instress. 'Vital energy' (?). Cf. Hopkins's notes on the Greek philosopher Parmenides: 'All things are upheld by instress and are meaningless without it' (*Journal*, p. 127). But the term also means in Hopkins a person's experience of a thing's distinctiveness or inscape.

The young lambs bound. Wordsworth, *Ode, Intimations of Immortality*, ll. 20–1.

warp. Cf. note to p. 47.

51 *diapered.* A kind of diamond pattern.

rosette. The cluster of organs in a leaf.

'*wracking*' *install.* Not an easy phrase to understand: 'install', an aspect of nature with its own specific inscape.

'*wagon*'. (?) Heavy, slow-moving cloud.

ravelling. Frayed, loose ends.

Sauley Abbey. A ruin 4 miles NE of Clitheroe.

the abiding offscape. The duck 'remembers' and is controlled by what no longer physically affects her.

52 *Kate Hopkins* (1856–1933), his second sister, whom he described as 'a sort of humourist' (*FL*, p. 240).

53 *Arthur ... the American yacht Sappho.* For Arthur Hopkins, whose paintings reflect an interest in sea-subjects, see note to p. 33. In May 1870 a series of international yacht races had taken place between an English boat, the *Cambria*, and the *Sappho*, and Hopkins had noted 'three successes of the American yacht Sappho' (*Journal*, p. 202).

It has not come here yet. Four days later he wrote: 'I first heard the cuckoo' (*Journal*, p. 208).

Hurst Green cloughs. Hurst Green is a village half a mile from Stonyhurst. 'Clough' is a Lancashire word for valley.

slacks. Dips in the ground (another northern term).

54 '*knoop*'. A protuberance like a stud or button.

the siding of the axes. The tending to one side of the stems.

55 *To Bridges.* This 'red letter', as Hopkins was to describe it (*LB*, p. 29), so offended Bridges that correspondence ceased for the next two and a half years. But its radical point of view, although surprising in a Jesuit scholastic of his background, was essentially the same as Ruskin and Carlyle had been expressing over the past quarter of a century. Fears of a coming violent upheaval were common in many areas of society. About 1870 Fr Edmund Purbrick, Rector of Stonyhurst, gloomily reflected that

> many currents ... are quietly sapping the foundations of our English Constitution, infidelity, liberal notions, or that worst form of unbelief, indifferentism, trades-unions, peace fallacies, commercial dishonesty, scraps of godless legislation, divorce courts, educational movements ... One day will come from without a war which will come in aid of their work, and seem to accomplish what has in fact been their doing. When will that day come? Perhaps not in '70 or '71, but sooner or later come it must.

(*Month*, Sept. 1926, p. 207)

Only four days following this letter, Hopkins wrote: 'The fear of the Revolution makes me sad now' (*Journal*, p. 213).

Karl Marx's International Working Men's Association had been established in London in 1864. On 1 Aug. 1871 it met in Brussels, and throughout July and August the *Tablet* carried a series of leading articles attacking Communism, but agreeing, like Hopkins, that 'We are bound to do our very utmost for the alleviation of those hapless toilers who are the builders and the victims of our vaunted civilisation' (12 Aug., p. 197). Thus echoing Carlyle's dictum, 'In the midst of plethoric plenty, the people perish' (*Selected Writings*, ed. Shelston, p. 263), and Ruskin's criticisms of the ugliness and materialism of modern civilization.

Shooting Niagara. First published *Macmillan's Magazine*, August 1867, *Shooting Niagara: And After?* is a characteristic attack upon modern English society and especially democracy, which is the 'Niagara leap' into the abyss. Republished in pamphlet form, it sold 7,000 copies in three months.

bating. Leaving out of account.

56 *the copy of Scotus . . . in the Baddely library.* Edward Baddely (d. 1868) was an ecclesiastical lawyer who left St. Mary's Hall a valuable collection of books on canon law. The work *Scriptum Oxoniense super Sententiis* was a commentary by the medieval philosopher Duns Scotus on Peter Lombard and began a far-reaching influence on Hopkins.

mouldboards. The curved board of a plough which turns over the furrow.

gnarls. Things which are twisted and knotted.

law out. (Not in *NED*) Give a pattern, order to.

Whitewell. A tiny hamlet and beauty-spot on the River Hodder 6 miles north of Stonyhurst.

Mr Clarke. Charles Clarke entered the Society in 1869, and in 1873 was in his first year at St. Mary's Hall. He eventually left the Jesuits.

57 *Mr Strappini.* Walter Strappini, of Italian descent, entered the Society in 1868 and did his first two years of Philosophy at St. Mary's Hall at the same time as Hopkins.

melled. (?) of mixed colours.

the lilies of Eton College. Three lily-flowers argent appear on the Eton coat of arms.

Parlick . . . Kemble End. Kemple End (as it is now spelt) is at the eastern end of Longridge Fell, a mile from the College. Parlick is another hill, 7 miles away to the north-west.

John Myerscough. One of the workers on the Stonyhurst estate, probably the John Myerscough whose death at the age of 58 on 15 March 1877 is recorded in the register of St. Peter's Church, Stonyhurst.

white pieings. The streaks of whiteness which give variety.

the shot of the neck. (?) The neck when it is outstretched.

Saddle Hill. A fell just to the east of Parlick.

58 *as at Aosta*. The beautiful valley in N. Italy which Hopkins visited on his Swiss tour and noted: 'The thunder musical and like gongs and rolling in great floors (?) of sound' (*Journal*, p. 183).

A Blandyke. Stonyhurst name for a holiday, called after the village near St. Omers where pupils used to go for holidays when Stonyhurst was a school on the Continent.

Mr Colley. Reginald Colley entered the Society in 1870, later becoming Rector of Stonyhurst and Provincial.

Hacking. This and the other places mentioned are all within 4 or 5 miles of the College on the Whalley side.

the Oratory. The London Oratory, founded 1849, had moved from the Strand to Brompton in 1854. *Addis* (see note to p. 15) joined the Oratory in 1868. Thomas *Law* (1836–1904) was a convert who had studied at Stonyhurst and became a priest in the Oratory in 1860. He later left the Church and became known as a religious historian.

David Lewis ... Brande Morris. Both formerly Oxford Fellows, who had become Catholics at the time of Newman's conversion. Morris was ordained in 1848.

59 *Mr Knowles ... Fr Johnson*. Thomas Knowles entered the Society in 1866, but after completing part of his training and teaching for a short time in Jesuit schools, left in 1874. Fr Joseph Johnson (1810–93) was formerly Provincial, and from 1873–81 was socius (or secretary) to the Provincial.

the Schools Endowment bill. This was the second reading of a bill regarded by the Liberal opposition as likely to discriminate against non-Anglican schools. The *Tablet* saw it as another stage in the denominationalism and secularism conflict, but Catholic MPs were divided in their opinion. Viscount *Sandon* was the government education spokesman; W. E. *Forster* had held the same post in Gladstone's lately defeated administration. Charles *Newdigate* was a Conservative MP well known for his anti-Catholic views. Robert *Lowe* had been Chancellor of the Exchequer in the previous Liberal government and had the reputation of being a forceful speaker.

Beaumont. The Jesuit boarding-school near Windsor, founded 1862. Rector's day was a holiday.

the Provincial. Fr Gallwey. See note to p. 44.

Teignmouth. Where Hopkins went on holiday with the Beaumont community.

St. Beuno's. The College, 6 miles SE of Rhyl, designed by Hansom, which was opened as the Jesuit theologate in 1849. See Introduction.

60 *like Lancing*. Arthur Hopkins had been a pupil at Lancing.

bopeeps. (?) Nooks and corners. Not in *NED* in this sense.

Excelsiors. Hills. Cf. note to p. 17.

Wm. Kerr. A convert, partly educated at Stonyhurst, who joined the Society in 1867. From 1872–5 he did his theology at Beuno's, where he was ordained.

I felt an instress and charm of Wales. He discusses his Carmarthenshire ancestry, *FL* p. 109. Within two years from this entry he was writing Welsh poetry.

61   *the Rector.* Fr James Jones (1828–93), who was Rector and Professor of Moral Philosophy at St. Beuno's. He wrote shortly before his death: 'I have loved St. Beuno's as I never loved any other place' (*Letters and Notices*, April 1893, pp. 144–5).

St. Ignatius' rules of election. The making of an election, or decision regarding one's way of life, is one of the main themes of the *Exercises:* 'In every good Election, so far as it rests with us, the eye of our intention ought to be simple, solely regarding the end for which I am created, that is, to the praise of God our Lord and the salvation of my soul' (*The Spiritual Exercises of St. Ignatius*, ed. Rickaby, p. 149).

62   *Barraud.* Charles Barraud (1843–1926) became a convert at Lancing and entered the Society in 1862. He went to St. Beuno's in 1874 and was ordained two years later. He contributed some not very interesting reminiscences of Hopkins to the *Month*, Aug. 1919: see p. 57, note.

Holywell. Where there has been a pilgrim's well since early times. It was associated with St. Winefred who was said to have been killed at the spot and then miraculously brought back to life by her uncle St. Beuno. Hopkins related the 7th century story to Bridges (*LB*, p. 40) and made several attempts to treat the subject in verse.

foils. Leaf-shaped areas radiating around the centre.

Fr di Pietro. A Sicilian attached to the English province, in charge of the Jesuit mission at Holywell 1870–6. He sent two letters from people who had experienced 'wonderful cures' to the Jesuit journal, *Letters and Notices*, June 1872, p. 97. The case of 'Arthur Kent' (not mentioned in the letters) Hopkins attempted to verify for the benefit of his father, but without success: 'The case therefore was not satisfactory' (*FL*, p. 132).

Rickaby. Joseph Rickaby (1845–1932), a brilliant scholar at Stonyhurst, entered the Society 1862, and was at St. Beuno's 1874–7, where he was ordained. Apart from his writing, which included an English edition of *The Spiritual Exercises*, he later became well known for his work at Campion Hall, Oxford.

63   *Purbrick.* James Purbrick, brother of the more famous Edward (see note to p. 112), who was ordained 1875, when he was in his late forties.

Wm. Splaine, who was educated at Stonyhurst, joined the Society in 1866, and did his theology at St. Beuno's 1874–8. His brother Cyprian taught at Stonyhurst while Hopkins was there (see p. 129 and note).

Mr Hughes. John Hughes entered the Society in 1860 and studied at St. Beuno's 1873–5. He then appears to have left the Society.

Moel y Parch. A part of the Clwydian Hills which rises over 1,000 ft. 6 miles SE of St. Beuno's.

'canting'. A nautical term: 'To take ... an oblique position in reference to any defined course' (*NED*).

(Soon after this, the Journal comes to an end.)

64 *Lionel* Hopkins (1854–1952), Gerard's brother, who was educated at Winchester, where he showed exceptional ability in modern languages. He joined the British Consular Service and sailed for Peking in March 1874. He became a distinguished Chinese scholar.

my poem on the Deutschland. The German steamer *Deutschland* sank off the Thames, 7 December 1875. Hopkins was encouraged to write on the subject by his Rector, Fr Jones, and was soon in correspondence with his Mother for newspaper cuttings on the subject. As is now well known, the poem was submitted to the Jesuit periodical, the *Month*, and eventually rejected.

Fr Coleridge. Henry Coleridge (1822–93), a distant relative of the poet, entered the Catholic Church in 1852, after a brilliant career at Oxford. He joined the Society in 1857 and was editor of the *Month* 1865–81. Hopkins seems to have first met him when he came to give a retreat at the Oratory, Easter 1868 (*Journal*, p. 163). His literary tastes were traditional; the 'new sort of poetry' in America is presumably a reference to Walt Whitman, whose *Leaves of Grass* had reached a 6th edition by 1876. On the rejection of Hopkins's poem, see p. 129 and note.

Ernest Coleridge. See p. 17 and note.

a lamentable account in the Graphic. An article regretting the changes in Japanese society due to Western manners: 'Every step forward seems made at the cost of something which never can be recovered' (24 June 1877, p. 619).

he is on the unfathering deeps outward bound. These are phrases from stanzas 12 and 13 of *The Wreck of the Deutschland.* The *Tablet*, 25 Aug. 1877, announced: 'The Provincial, F. Jones, is going out to the West Indies on business connected with the Society' (p. 249).

65 *Wooldridge.* Harry Wooldridge (1845–1917), painter and musician, a close friend of Bridges. He was to see some of Hopkins's music and to correspond with him. In 1887 he was painting his portrait from a photograph.

the Bremen *stanza.* That is, stanza 12. Later (p. 72), he spoke of a silence of 'seven years', which corresponds more precisely with the date of 11 May 1868 given in the Journal for the destruction of his poems.

Fifty-two Bedford Square. Bridges's London address.

molossic. Having a metrical foot of 3 long syllabuses. But the illustration given is amphibrachic. Hopkins was more accurate when he described both metres in his Lecture Notes for the Roehampton Juniors (*Journal*, p. 272).

sprung rhythm. In which feet are made up of from one to four syllables, of which only one is a heavy stress. Hopkins's 'Preface' to the 1918 edition of his poem explains his metrical ideas. See also pp. 72–4.

I have pointed them out in lecturing. When Professor of Rhetoric at Roehampton. In both this letter and on pp. 72–3 he uses the same example from his Lecture Notes.

'why should this : desert be?' This line, from *As You like It*, III. ii. 115, is usually printed '*a* desert', after Rowe's emendation.

'There to meet with Macbeth'. Macbeth, I. i. 7.

Battle of the Baltic. The line should read, 'And her arms along …' (l. 5). The line from *Ye Mariners of England* is as quoted (l. 17).

Grongar Hill. By the 18th-century poet, John Dyer.

66 *lashed : rod.* Stanza 2 of *Wreck of the Deutschland.*

My verse is less to be read than heard. Cf. his remarks to Bridges, p. 70, and to Everard Hopkins, pp. 136–8.

presumptious. The spelling is listed as obsolete by the *NED.*

67 *my dear grandfather.* John Simm Smith, his mother's father, who lived in Croydon.

the Feast of the Holy Rosary. Pius V commemorated the Christian victory over the Turks at Lepanto, 7 Oct. 1571, by instituting this Feast on the first Sunday in October.

the seventh time. One was an occasion six years after the death of Digby Dolben, a young man who had made a deep impression on Hopkins: 'I received as I think a great mercy about Dolben' (*Journal*, p. 236). What form these spiritual experiences took he never explained.

68 *Mount St. Mary's College.* The Jesuit boarding-school, established 1842 6 miles NE of Chesterfield. See the Introduction for Hopkins's life there.

Berkeley. Herbert Berkeley was a senior boy who won several academic prizes while at the Mount.

Lady Macbeth, in spite of being turned into 'Fergus'. By a rule of the Order, which did not fall into disuse until the beginning of the 20th century, Jesuit schools were forbidden to impersonate female characters on the stage. Hopkins saw another *Macbeth* at Stonyhurst, in which Lady Macbeth became 'Uncle Donald' — 'incredible as it may seem … the effect is not so disastrous as you might think it must be' (*FL*, p. 237).

69 *the Earthquake of Lisbon.* The great disaster of 1755 in which over 30,000 people were killed.

the Earl of Nithsdale's escape. A Jacobite in the 1715 Rebellion who made a dramatic escape from the Tower the day before he was to be executed.

my Eurydice, which the Month *refused.* He wrote *The Loss of the Eurydice* in April 1878, a month after the disaster in which the training-ship sank off the South Coast with the loss of 300 men. The same subject had been set in a verse competition between Jesuit schools in which Berkeley had entered in 1878.

'*If it were done when 'tis done*'. *Macbeth*, I. vii. 1.

70   '*Fame is the spur* . . .' Milton, *Lycidas*, l.70.

Coventry Patmore. See the Biographical Appendix. Patmore's *The Unknown Eros* (not 'Hidden') was published in two parts 1877–8.

go unwitnessed. Cf. p. 55, the Journal entry for 19 July 1872.

71   *you say, I remember, in one of the odes.* In *Sympathy: An Ode* from *Historical Odes:* 'And the white clouds soar / Untraced in heaven from the horizon shore' (Quoted by Abbott, *LD*, p. 7).

111 Mount Street. The well-known Jesuit Church here was the centre of the Society's activities in England. Hopkins preached three sermons here during August.

so to me does Purcell's music. Cf. the prose introduction to the poem *Henry Purcell*, composed the following year: 'Whereas other musicians have given utterance to the moods of man's mind, he has, beyond that, uttered in notes the very make and species of man as created both in him and in all men generally' (*Poems*, p. 80).

As for 'proper hue'. According to Dixon (*LD*, p. 11), the painter Burne-Jones had been offended by the phrase in *Paradise Lost*, VIII. 618–19: 'The Angel, with a smile that glowed / Celestial rosy-red, Love's proper hue.' *NED* gives the meaning of 'proper' in heraldry as 'natural colouring'.

72   *Masson.* David Masson, Professor of English at Edinburgh, wrote a six-volume *Life of Milton*, 1859–80.

'*a French critic on Milton*'. Arnold's essay appeared in the *Quarterly Review*, Jan. 1877 (Edmond Scherer was a contemporary journalist and critic): '[Milton] is our great master in style, our one first-rate master in the grand style' (*Prose Works of Matthew Arnold*, ed. Super, viii, p. 183).

Newman should have fallen into the blunder. In *The Idea of a University* (4th edn., 1875), Newman compared the two passages referred to and asked: 'Does not Southey show to advantage here?' (p. 324).

Panathenaic frieze. The striking frieze which decorated the outside of the temple of the Parthenon. The British Museum had acquired parts of it in 1816.

teaboard. Tea-tray.

when I had to lecture on rhetoric. See p. 65 and note.

What I had written I burnt. See p. 65 and note on 'the Bremen stanza'.

the Falck Laws. Named after Bismarck's Minister of Worship, they penalized the clergy who refused to acknowledge state authority.

73 *in Campbell.* Both lines are from *The Battle of the Baltic:* cf. p. 65 and note. The second quotation is l.14.

in Shakspere. (A usual Hopkins spelling.) Cf. p. 65 and note.

cynghanedd. A form of Welsh verse in which internal rhyme and alliteration play an important part.

'Home to *his mother's house'.* This and the following line are from *Paradise Regained,* IV. 639 and I. 175.

74 *St. Giles.* The Jesuit church of St. Aloysius, which lies near the junction of the Woodstock Road and St. Giles, was opened in 1875. Hopkins worked here for nearly a year.

in one keeping. In harmony or congruity.

the Preface. Abbott suggests that this is the Preface which Bridges wrote for the edition of his poems published in 1880. In it Bridges explained that some of the poems were composed 'by the rules of a new prosody', invented by 'a friend, whose poems remain, he regrets to say, in manuscript' (*LB*, p. 310).

You so misunderstand my words. In his previous letter Hopkins had suggested that to compensate for his religious scepticism Bridges should 'Give alms . . . up to the point of sensible inconvenience'. Perhaps with a suspicion of how this would irritate Bridges, he added: 'I feel it is very bold, as it is uncalled for, of me to have written the above' (*LB*, pp. 60–1).

Pater. Hopkins's tutor at Oxford, Walter Pater, was known for his aesthetic interests rather than religious belief.

Even Walt Whitman nurses the sick. He did so during the American Civil War. Hopkins's ambivalent feelings about Whitman, of whose work he had read very little, are reflected in the remark a few years later: 'I always knew in my heart Walt Whitman's mind to be more like my own than any other man's living. As he is a very great scoundrel this is not a pleasant confession' (*LB*, p. 155).

75 *at the hospital.* For Bridges's work as a doctor, see the Biographical Appendix.

to 'derweesh' yourself. 'To throw yourself into a rage'. A *Letter from Egypt* in the *Academy,* 25 Jan. 1879, p. 76, describes 'Derweeshes', fanatic Muslims, performing a wild and violent ceremony.

Daniel advised Nabuchodonosor and Christ the Pharisees. Cf. Dan. 4:24 and Luke 11:41.

76 *the only person that I am in love with.* Christ. The first explicit confession of the spiritual aridity which culminated in the 'terrible sonnets' of the Dublin years.

77 *Thomas Vaughan.* A mistake for Henry Vaughan (1622–95), the mystical poet, of whom Thomas Vaughan was the less famous brother. A complete edition of Henry's works had been published in 1871. In the

preface to an early edition of his poems, he had apologized for the 'idle books' of his early life and praised 'the blessed man, Mr George Herbert, whose holy life and verse gained many pious converts (of whom I am the least)' (*Works*, ed. Martin, p. 391).

'*primrosed and hung with shade.*' Line 4 of *Regeneration* in *Silex Scintillans*. The other lines are 13–14 of *The Revival* in *Thalia Rediviva*.

'*chryselephantine*'. 'Of gold and ivory' (*NED*). Cf. the reference to Tennyson, p. 81

78 *keepings.* Period colour.

dedicated by permission to H.R.H. Tennyson dedicated the 1862 edition of *Idylls of the King* to Prince Albert who had died in 1861.

Lady Clare Vere de Vere. 'Clara', not 'Clare'.

downright haberdasher. (?) Cheap and common.

I owe him a grudge for Queen Mary. The play was written in 1875 and produced the following year. Coventry Patmore remarked: 'The moral is . . . simply the "No Popery" cry . . . Surely there is no passion which, when indulged, becomes so strong and so vile as the love of popularity' (quoted in Champneys, *Coventry Patmore*, I, 199). Abbott suggests that the 'other drama' is *Harold* (1876), but I have been unable to find the passage referred to. The quotation is, in any case, not Tennyson.

so high an opinion expressed of my poems. Dixon had written: 'They are among the most extraordinary I ever read and amazingly original . . . It seems to me that they ought to be published' (*LD*, pp. 26–7). He offered to mention them in an 'abrupt footnote' in the 2nd volume of his *History of the Church of England* (published 1881).

79 *Barnes' Dorset.* William Barnes (1801–86), Dorset rector and dialect poet, and one of Hopkins's favourite writers. Cf. the letter to Patmore, another admirer (p. 141 and note). An appreciative review by Edmund Gosse of Barnes's *Poems of Rural Life in the Dorset Dialect* appeared in the *Academy*, 26 July 1879, pp. 60–1. Comparing Barnes with Burns he wrote: 'In his hands the Dorset tongue becomes no mere philological curiosity, but a living language, producing living verse'.

their Westcountry '*instress*'. Cf. *Journal*, p. 250, 8 Aug. 1874 (Hopkins was on holiday in Devon): 'From a hilltop I looked into a lovely comb that gave me the instress of *Weeping Winifred*, which all the west country seems to me to have'.

I associate with airs. 'Weeping Winefred' is a Welsh song which has been arranged by Haydn. 'Pretty Polly Oliver' is printed in the Queen Anne–George II section of Chappell's *Ballad Literature and Popular Music of the Olden Times*, 1855–9, ii, p. 676 (1965 reprint).

80 *oxeyes.* Dog daisies.

Linden Ore. Presumably *Lindenore* and *In the Spring*, first published 1862.

the finest of your sonnets. No. 31 in the sonnet sequence, *The Growth of*

Love (1876). Hopkins comments in detail on this volume, *LB*, pp. 34 ff., including the line referred to here, which finally became, "'Tis joy to watch the folds fall as they do' (l.3).

in a nearly finished piece I have a very bold one. The reference is probably to *The Bugler's First Communion*, sent to Bridges in October (*LB*, p. 92): see stanza 10, l. 1.

St. Joseph's, Bedford Leigh. An industrial parish, some 12 miles west of Manchester, with which the Jesuits had long been associated.

Rochdale. Which Hopkins visited just before his reception into the Catholic church: see p. 24 and note.

a flat. 'The low ground through which a river flows' (*NED*).

81 *Marzials.* Theophile Marzials, minor poet and literary critic, and friend of Gosse.

he was acknowledging your book. Hopkins had begun a friendship between Bridges and Dixon by arranging for Bridges to send Dixon some of his verse.

no one can admire beauty of the body more than I do. The following distinction between physical, intellectual, and moral beauty is also made in the sermon preached a Bedford Leigh a few weeks later. See p. 84 for an extract.

the 'handsome heart'. The title of a poem which Hopkins had sent to Bridges earlier in the year on the theme of the pre-eminence of moral excellence (*Poems*, pp 81–2)

as we Aristotelian Catholics say. Like Aristotle, Aquinas emphasized the unity of soul and body; 'form' was the term used by both to describe this relationship. Cf. pp. 120–2.

82 *Tam o' Shanter.* Line 59.

St Paul. 2 Cor. 11:2: 'I am jealous of you with the jealousy of God'.

my work lay in St. Clement's, at the Barracks. The Chapel of St Ignatius in St. Clements was the original Catholic Church in Oxford. Newman heard his first public mass there after reception into the Church. The barracks – mentioned in *The Bugler's First Communion* – were at Cowley.

Fr Parkinson. Thomas Parkinson (1819–1904), a Cambridge graduate and former Anglican priest, joined the Jesuits in 1851. After being head-master of one of their schools, he was Superior at St. Aloysius 1875–87.

83 *Pray do not send the piece to the paper.* Earlier in the month Dixon had asked: 'Should you be angry that I sent your *Loss of the Eurydice*, or part of it, to one of the Carlisle Papers, giving your name, and a line or two of introduction from myself?' (*LD*, p. 29). Hopkins's opposition led to the request being withdrawn.

the Nineteenth Century. A well-known monthly founded in 1877.

You say truly that our Society fosters literary excellence. This remark does not occur in the collected correspondence up to this date, but cf. p. 103 and note. In the *History of the Church of England*, ii, 231, Dixon wrote: 'Literature owes far less to the [Jesuits] than to the later Benedictines'.

84 *Sermon at Bedford Leigh.* Hopkins's text was Rom. 13:11–14, and particularly 'Let us walk honestly, as in the day; not in rioting and drunkenness, not in chambering and impurities, not in contention and envy'.

Jesus Christ . . . is our hero. The idea was important to Hopkins. Cf. *The Loss of the Eurydice*, l.112, where Christ is the 'Hero' who 'savest', and p. 116 *post*, 'Christ's life and character are such as appeal to all the world's admiration'.

85 *Thou art beautiful*, etc. Ps. 44:3.

The account I have been quoting. The source is the apocryphal *Letter to Lentulus* of the 4th century, which was the inspiration of one tradition of the representation of Christ in art.

86 *the apostle says it.* Rom. 13:12.

87 *Now more than ever.* Cf. the 'red letter' to Bridges, pp. 54–5 and note. The drink question was one of the most publicized social problems of the day. The *Month*, Feb. 1879, discussed a series of articles on *The Alcohol Question* which had recently been appearing in the *Contemporary Review*. The writer remarked: 'With the public nuisance and the social damage sooner or later Parliament will have to deal. With the personal sinfulness of the miserable wretch preachers and confessors are deeply concerned' (p. 297).

88 *St. Francis Xavier's.* The principal Jesuit church in Liverpool, situated in Salisbury Street, and with a high reputation for its preaching. Hopkins worked there Jan. 1880–Aug. 1881.

The theme of the sermon, the mutual obligations of state and subjects, has a long history: 'As St. Paul and Plato and Hobbes and everybody says, the commonwealth or well ordered human society is like one man; a body with many members and each its function; some higher, some lower, but all honourable' (*LB*, p. 272). In Ireland a few years later Hopkins confessed that the essential tacit agreement between governors and governed was absent; Newman told him that it had never existed (*FL*, pp. 283 and 413–14).

89 *we share the common weal.* 'But . . . the curse of our times is that many do not share it' (*LB*, p. 273). The 'red letter' also reflects Hopkins's private misgivings on this point.

91 *handselled it on a poor consumptive girl.* Used it for the first time (the stole is worn in administering the sacraments).

I wrote to . . . Cardinal Newman. He was 79. Hopkins regularly sent him birthday congratulations from 1873 until Hopkins's death.

Lydiate. A place 5 miles south-west of Ormskirk with many Catholic associations. Thomas Lightbound JP lived at Rose Hill House, one mile from Ormskirk, which had a private chapel served by the Jesuits from St. Francis Xavier's. 'Mr Musgrove' is presumably Edgar Musgrove JP who lived at Aughton, near Ormskirk. (See Kelly's *Directory of Lancashire*, 1881.)

the Liverpool election. This by-election was held in February and aroused national interest because Liverpool was the largest constituency in the country and a general election was imminent. Lord Ramsay was defeated by the Conservative candidate, but in the General Election in April the Liberals were returned to power.

93 *Town Green station*. Two miles south of Ormskirk.

Grace. His youngest sister (1857–1945), who had strong musical interests. He was composing music for two of Bridges's poems and she was setting the accompaniments.

I do not remember quite what I said. 'Oxford was not to me a congenial field, fond as I am of it; I am far more at home with the Lancashire people' (*FL*, p. 243).

94 *Principium sive Fundamentum*. The *Principle and Foundation* is a brief general statement which prefaces the *Spiritual Exercises* proper. The first two sentences run: 'Man was created to praise, do reverence to and serve God our Lord, and thereby to save his soul. And the other things on the face of the earth were created for man's sake, and to help him in the following out of the end for which he was created' (Rickaby, p. 18).

the latter takes on the mind more hold. The idea of the individual self, rather than the external world, as a proof of God's existence is Scotist (see Devlin, *Sermons*, pp. 283 and 338 ff., on Hopkins's Scotism).

pitch. In the (Scotist) sense of 'individuality' or 'personality'. The concept is fully explained by Devlin.

95 *when I consider my selfbeing*. The Scotist influence is apparent in poems written about this time, *Henry Purcell* and *As kingfishers catch fire*. 'Each mortal thing', wrote Hopkins,

Selves – goes itself; *myself* it speaks and spells,
Crying *What I do is me: for that I came*.

(*Poems*, p. 90)

alum. A mineral salt, sweetish-sour in taste.

stress. i.e. experience, feeling of.

St. Agnes' Eve. 20 January. Hopkins refers to the first line of Keats's poem. There was severe weather throughout England for much of January, but a thaw reached Liverpool by the 27th. The *Liverpool Mercury* describes ice floating on the Mersey and seagulls being fed by ferry passengers.

96 *a snowwright or snowsmith*. In allusion to Bridge's poem, *London Snow*, which Hopkins greatly admired.

Majuba. A hill on the borders of Natal and the Transvaal where General
Colley was defeated by the Boers on 27 February 1881. It was a great
shock to public opinion. At the time the Gladstone government was
negotiating a settlement with the Boers over England's recent annexation
of the Transvaal, and the defeat intensified Conservative opposition. By
the terms of the Treaty of Pretoria signed in April, however, the Trans-
vaal was to be handed over to the Boers within six months. Hopkins was
deeply disturbed by the whole affair: see too pp. 97, 158, and notes.

a patriot and not a truckler to Russia. Gladstone; one of many contempt-
uous references to him which appear in Hopkins's later correspondence:
see p. 134 and note. The dislike was shared by Patmore. Gladstone was
sometimes accused of being pro-Russian because of his opposition to
Turkish policy in the Balkans.

Candahar. The town in Afghanistan recently occupied by British forces
in answer to Russian ambitions in that area. The Gladstone government
wished to withdraw and there was considerable public discussion on the
matter in the first months of 1881. It was returned to native rule in April.

Hallé's last concert. It was the last concert of the Hallé's 'cheap' winter
series in Liverpool. Seats for the *Faust* concert were three times as
expensive.

the procession. The first of May was the regular date for a procession of
horses through Liverpool.

97   *I admired the handsome horses.* As Gulliver admired the Houyhnhnms
and was repelled by the human race. Rider Haggard believed that the
physical deterioration of the urban Englishman was a reason for defeat
in the 2nd Boer War (*Rural England*, 1902, in P. Keating, ed., *Into
Unknown England*, pp. 216–22).

our troops funked and ran. Describing the British forces at Majuba, the
Times correspondent wrote, 3 March: 'In a moment our poor fellows
broke and rushed for the crest in the rear. I ran with them.'

Manresa House. Where Hopkins was for his tertianship, which is
explained in this letter.

a whole volume of Kingsley's essays. Perhaps *Literary and General
Lectures and Essays* (1880), which includes the remark: 'The time, we
think, for calling Popery all names is past; though to abstain is certainly
sometimes a sore restraint for English spirits' (p. 189).

with the repetition of 'My friend'. The phrase occurs twice in the first five
lines and once more near the end.

carried away with their dissimulation. Cf. Gal. 2: 13.

98   *The Ring and the Book.* First published in 4 volumes, 1868–9 (not 3, as
Hopkins states). A reviewer in the *Month*, Dec. 1869, complains that
Browning 'ought to know that there is a limit even to … openness of

statement; that modesty, even nature herself, teaches us to throw round some things the veil of silence' (pp. 623–4). The description of the market-place in Florence is in Book 1, ll. 38 ff.

99   *schola affectus.* 'School of the Love of God'.

Tu verba, etc. 'Thou hast the words of eternal life' (John 6:69).

semi-diameters or modules. Module: 'In the classic orders, the unit of length by which the proportions of the parts are expressed; usually the semidiameter of the column at the base of the shaft' (*NED*).

100   *Non ha l'ottimo*, etc. The first lines of a sonnet by Michelangelo (*Le Rime*, ed. Guasti, 1863, p. 173, no. xv). The second line should read, 'Ch'un marmo solo . . .' J. A. Symonds translates:

> The best of artists hath no thought to show
> Which the rough stone in its superfluous shell
> Doth not include.
>
> (*The Sonnets of Michael Angelo*, London, 1878, p. 46.)

Earth has not anything to shew more fair. The sonnet 'Composed Upon Westminster Bridge'.

good deal of this in Bridges' sonnets. Cf. p. 80.

Captain or colonel. Milton, 'When the Assault was intended to the City'.

Both them I serve. Milton, 'To the Nightingale', l.14.

τοὺς περὶ *Swinburne.* 'Swinburne and his followers'.

Gray's sonnet. Wordsworth quotes the whole sonnet in the Preface to the *Lyrical Ballads* and remarks that Gray 'was more than any other man curiously elaborate in the structure of his own poetic diction' (*Lyrical Ballads*, ed. Littledale, p. 234).

102   *Father Campion.* Edmund Campion (1540–81), Jesuit priest of many talents, now canonized, who was tortured and executed for his missionary work in England. Hopkins attempted an ode on the subject, but nothing survives. For Simpson's *Life* see below.

the first break or day of repose. In the course of the Long Retreat these were separated by approximately a week each.

103   *Our Society values*, etc. Dixon had written that he hoped that in writing verse Hopkins would be 'sanctioned and encouraged by the great Society to which you belong, which has given so many ornaments to literature' (*LD*, p. 90). But see p. 83 and note.

individual fame St. Ignatius looked on as the most dangerous. This is emphasized in both the *Exercises* ('Modes of Humility', p. 137) and the Jesuit *Constitutions:* 'Worldly men . . . love honours, celebrity and the reputation of greatness . . . but men who walk in the way of the spirit and are serious in their following of Christ our Lord love just the opposite things' ('The Spiritual Formation of Ours', Rule 11).

Fr Beschi. An Italian Jesuit (1680–?1746), who spent half his life in India, studied the Tamil tongue, and wrote one of its classics, *The Unfading Garland*, an epic poem in honour of St. Joseph.

Fr Southwell. Robert Southwell (1561?–95), probably, after Hopkins, the Society's most famous poet.

what a genius was Campion himself! His life had been written (1867) by Richard Simpson (1820–76), Catholic journalist and literary critic. Pages 30–41 of the biography cover Campion's career in Ireland where he wrote his *History* whilst eluding his pursuers. Simpson praised the 'vast dramatic power of the speeches' attributed to historical figures, and remarked: 'Some of his orations only want metre to be comparable with those of his great dramatic contemporaries' (p. 35). The work was published in *Holinshed* (1587) and used by Shakespeare in *Henry VIII*.

104 *I forget his name.* Daniel Seghers (1590–1661), 'the leading Flemish flower painter of the generation after Jan Brueghel' (*Oxford Companion to Art*). He became a Jesuit in 1614.

as Solomon says. 'All things have their season: and in their times all things pass under heaven' (Eccles. 3:1).

St. Stanislaus Kostka (1550–68), Polish Jesuit, who entered the Society at the age of 17 and died less than a year later. (See further in this letter.) A life was written in the year of his death by a Fr Warsevitz.

Bourdaloue (1632–1704), with Bossuet the most eminent French preacher of his time.

Suarez (1548–1617), Spanish Jesuit and eminent theologian. It was his views that Hopkins was taught while at St. Beuno's.

Molina, Luis de (1535–1600), Spanish Jesuit, with Suarez one of the Order's most renowned theologians. His *Concordia* (1588) began the bitter dispute, in which the Pope was forced to intervene, over the the problem of reconciling grace and free will.

St. Aloysius Gonzaga (1568–91), Italian Jesuit who entered the Society at the age of 17, and died while caring for the sick.

Blessed John Berchmans (1599–1621), canonized 1888, Belgian Jesuit, whose famous remark means that the simple, shared life of the religious community is the best way of attaining to God.

105 *Gregory XVI (I think).* It was Gregory XV.

the beauty of the king's daughter. 'All the glory of the king's daughter is within' (Ps. 44:14).

The 'hoity toity' passage. Dixon had apologized (*LD*, 90) for being 'too free, and what may be called hoity toity' in his remarks about the Jesuits in his *History*. Just before the passage about their disappointing contribution to literature (see note to p. 83), he had written:

'No art, no science was unwelcome here [in the Society] ... But it has been remarked with truth that the Jesuits, with all their culture, cannot boast the greatest names in any department. Their system consumed them.'

Bridges in his sickness. He was ill from pneumonia in the autumn of 1881.

Cobbett's Reformation. *A History of the Protestant 'Reformation' in England & Ireland* (1824–7) is a vigorous attack upon historical Protestant attitudes towards the Catholic Church. In Cobbett's view 'the present misery indescribable of the labouring classes in England and Ireland' is due to 'the event, called the "Reformation" ' (See Letters I and XVI, pp. 4 and 395–6 in Gasquet's modern edition).

I much wish some learned Catholic would reedit it. This was done (1898) by Francis Gasquet, a Benedictine historian.

Glasgow experience. In the interval between leaving Liverpool and starting his tertianship, he worked for two months, Aug.–Oct., at the parish of St. Joseph's in a slum area of northern Glasgow.

106 *Haynes Bailey.* Thomas Haynes Bailey (1797–1839), a popular writer of light songs.

domes, palaces, and temples. Hopkins is thinking of the sonnet *Composed Upon Westminster Bridge.*

107 *gaud.* 'Showy ornament' (*NED*).

On the Principle or Foundation. Cf. p. 94 and note. This was part of a commentary that Hopkins wrote on the *Exercises* while at Roehampton (to which he refers, p. 112).

108 *'The heavens declare the glory of God.'* Ps. 18:2.

I WAS MADE FOR THIS. For the Scotism here, cf. pp. 94–5 and notes and Gardner's note to 'As kingfishers catch fire', *Poems*, p. 281.

It is not only prayer that gives God glory but work. Devlin compares George Herbert's poem, *The Elixir*, for the same theme of work, however humble, giving God glory.

109 *Meditation on Hell.* Cf. *Spiritual Exercises*, ed. Rickaby, pp. 40–2. Hopkins uses St. Ignatius's words as a starting-point. James Joyce's virtuoso use of the same ideas in *Portrait of the Artist* is well known and some account of Jesuit precedents in the 'hell-fire' tradition is given in Morris and Nault, *Portraits of an Artist*, pp. 253 ff. The 'terrible sonnets' of Hopkins's Dublin years, especially 'I wake and feel the fell of dark', take up themes in the Meditation.

Christ speaks of the lost as being salted. 'For every one shall be salted with fire; and every victim shall be salted with salt' (Mark 9:49).

110 *a glassblower breathe on a flame.* Cf. *Poems*, p. 108, *To R.B.*, l.2.

Their worm, our Lord says. Isa. 66:24.

111 *To Bridges.* Bridges had visited Hopkins at Manresa on Corpus Christi,

8 June, and the first paragraph of this letter describes the confusion when Hopkins was seeing him off.

Flatman's 'serene and rapturous joys'. Thomas Flatman (1637–88) was the author of the poem *On the King's return to Whitehall* (1684), which was set to music by Purcell. The first line runs: 'From these serene and rapturous joys'.

the duels of archangels. In which no real damage can be done, as when Satan is 'wounded' by Michael, *Paradise Lost*, VI. 320 ff.

112 *Stonyhurst College.* The Jesuit boarding-school of nearly 300 boys, 8 miles north of Blackburn. See Introduction.

for the London B.A. degree. Catholics were forbidden by the Hierarchy from attending Oxford and Cambridge; a London degree, which was external, provided a convenient alternative.

the Provincial. Fr Edmund Purbrick (1830–1914), who had been appointed Provincial in 1880 after a ten-year term of office as Rector of Stonyhurst. He was responsible for the considerable rebuilding programme which Hopkins mentions in this letter.

one or other of the books I had named to him. Hopkins proposed a number of books and articles on a variety of learned subjects during the last seven years of his life, but none was completed.

I cannot get forward with my ode. The one on Edmund Campion. Cf. p. 102 and note.

a commentary on St. Ignatius's Spiritual Exercises. Cf. p. 107 and note.

113 *Supplices.* Both Sophocles and Aeschylus wrote a play by this name.

Worcester. Where there is a long established Jesuit parish. Close by the church was the site of the Worcestershire Exhibition, a display of artistic and industrial exhibits which attracted nearly a quarter of a million people from July to October 1882.

Yattenden. Bridges had recently gone with his mother to live at Yattendon on the Berkshire Downs.

a fine library. Cf. p. 50 and note.

two other dependent establishments. The nearer one was St. Mary's Hall where Hopkins had studied philosophy, and the other Hodder Place, the preparatory school to the College.

114 *philosophers and foppery.* The students whom Hopkins taught were allowed various privileges and liberties by comparison with the ordinary pupils of the College.

anemometer. Instrument for measuring the force of the wind.

icosihedron. A twenty-sided solid figure (more properly spelt 'icosahedron'). In this case a very elaborate form of sundial giving the time at twenty different cities all over the world (described in the *Stonyhurst Magazine*, Apr. 1925, p. 83).

ambulacrum. A large indoor games area.

Arundel chromos. A chromolithograph is a picture in colour reproduced from a drawing on stone. From 1849 the Arundel Society, with which Ruskin was connected, issued colour reproductions of Old Masters.

by either stealing or buying fruit. In an incident later remembered in Bridges's poem, *The Testament of Beauty*, Hopkins was unwilling for his friend to buy peaches from the Manresa garden when visiting him in the summer.

Prometheus. Bridge's poem was published in 1883.

could you not be a magistrate? He became one of the local board of guardians.

Swedenborg. Emanuel Swedenborg (1688–1772), Swedish philosopher and mystic, who influenced Blake and who seemed to the Catholic poet Coventry Patmore 99 per cent 'in perfect harmony with the Catholic faith' (B. Champneys, *Coventry Patmore*, II, 19). The incident to which Hopkins refers is described in the *Spiritual Diary*: 'In the middle of the day at dinner, an angel who was with me conversed, saying, that I should not indulge the belly too much at table. Whilst he was with me there clearly appeared to me, as it were, a vapour ... Seeing a fiery light in this vapour, and hearing a sound, I thought that thus all the worms which could be generated from an immoderate appetite were ejected from my body.' (Tr. Bush and Smithson, vol. I (1883), p. 130, para. 397.) The translator comments that this incident began 'an open intercourse with the world of spirits'.

Cagliostro, Count Alexander de (1743–95), famous confidence trickster written about by Carlyle (*Miscellanies*, 1867, vol. iii).

115 *the underthought.* A similar idea is understood in modern criticism. Cf. A. J. Waldock, *Paradise Lost and Its Critics*, chap. vi, 'Unconscious Meanings' in *Paradise Lost.*

116 *I could say much on the subject.* Newman had defined a gentleman, *Idea of a University*, Discourse VIII, section 10, in wider, less morally demanding terms than Hopkins, concluding that gentlemanly qualities 'are seen within the pale of the Church and without it, in holy men, and in profligate'.

such as appeal to all the world's admiration. Cf. p. 84 and note, the sermon on Christ as hero.

This mind he says, was in Christ Jesus. See Phil. 2:5 ff.

117 *Apelles.* Famous Greek painter of the 4th century BC.

'*the good that does itself not know scarce is*'. According to Abbot, a line from Patmore, but I have been unable to verify this.

118 *I shall be removed.* He was in fact reappointed.

The Holy Name. The Jesuit church, designed by Joseph Hansom and completed 1871, which stands opposite the present University of Manchester. Hopkins was acting as a temporary replacement.

119   *New Arabian Nights*. Published in 2 vols, Aug. 1882.

      I read a story by him. The Treasure of Franchard (not *Fourvières*, as
      Hopkins suggests below), published in *Longman's Magazine*, April–
      May 1883.

      a paper by him on Romance. A Gossip on Romance, also in *Longman's*,
      Nov. 1882. It is reprinted in *Memories and Portraits*.

120   *the little Indian boy*. Midsummer Night's Dream, II. i. 18 ff.

      Mano. Dixon's historical poem, dedicated to Bridges, which was pub-
      lished in June.

      I am dissatisfied with 'Beauty'. Here, and in following letters, Hopkins
      was commenting on a collected edition of Patmore's verse which the
      author had recently sent him. In this letter the references are to the
      volume called *Angel in the House*.

      is qui supplet idiotae. 'He who stands in the place of the common man'
      (?Quintilian).

121   *palmary*. Of supreme importance.

      p. 217 'The Koh-i-noor'. Actually p. 219 in the edition (1879) Hopkins
      was using. Patmore writes that what pleases him above all about the
      woman whom he loves,

                        Is, not that she is wise or good,
                        But just the thing which I desire.

      In the next passage quoted Patmore admires his wife for her obedience,
      which is 'by courtesy; / Not with her least consent of will'.

      Mommsen, Theodor (1817–1903), distinguished German scholar of
      Roman studies. He held that there were no absolute moral standards in
      politics and declared: 'When a government cannot govern, it ceases to
      be legitimate, and he who has the power to overthrow it has also the
      right' (quoted by Gooch, *History and Historians in the Nineteenth
      Century*, 2nd edn., p. 462).

      Dr Ward. William Ward (1812–82), Fellow of Balliol, who entered the
      Catholic Church the same year as Newman, and was well known as a
      controversialist. He was editor of the *Dublin Review*.

122   *Leonardo's famous picture*. A mistake for Titian's (so-called) 'Sacred and
      Profane Love', a picture which has been variously interpreted.

      'The low sun makes the colour'. Idylls of the King, Elaine, l. 134.

      'Let other bards', etc. Wordsworth, *To* – [His Wife], ll. 1–4.

123   *Honoria*. The heroine of *Angel in the House*.

      Mrs Graham. One of the main characters in *The Victories of Love*.

      1867 – 'Their Jew'. Patmore had written:
                        In the year of the great crime,
                        When the false English Nobles and their Jew,

By Gods demented, slew
The Trust they stood twice pledged to keep from wrong.

           (*1867*, in Book I of *The Unknown Eros*.)

1867 was the year of Disraeli's electoral Reform Bill, which had upset extreme Conservatives like Patmore, who accused him of failing to represent those principles for which he had been elected. Cf. note on 'Mr Disraeli', p. 35, and Patmore's essay, *Courage in Politics*, p. 14 in the volume of that name.

'*look for another*'. Matt. 11:3.

Disraeli in 1871 overreached and jewed his constituents. '1871' must be a mistake for 1867 (Disraeli was out of office in 1871). 'Constituents' means the electorate as a whole. (Lord Blake, privately.)

124 *primrose worship.* Primroses began to be associated with the name of Disraeli (and the Conservative party) in 1868 when the Queen first sent them to him. April 19, the anniversary of his death, was observed as Primrose Day in 1882, and the Primrose League was established the following year.

A letter to 'Nature'. Nature was a weekly established in 1869 for the purpose of publicizing scientific discoveries and developments. Hopkin's letter was part of a correspondence about the unusual skies observed in all parts of the world in the latter months of 1883. (The cause was later established as the Krakatoa eruption in August.)

Mr Piazzi Smyth. The Astronomer-Royal for Scotland.

126 *Derbyshire alabaster.* A mineral, often reddish in colour, quarried in Derbyshire.

one of the observatory staff. Cf. p. 49 and note. Fr Stephen Perry, Director of the Stonyhurst Observatory, had an international reputation as an astronomer.

gadroons. Sets of convex curves or arcs joined together to form a pattern.

celadon. Pale green.

brindled. Having streaks of different colour.

mallow. Reddish.

127 *University College.* For Hopkins at University College, see Introduction.

128 *for purposes of study very nearly naked.* Most of the books were withdrawn when the Irish bishops handed over control to the Jesuits: 'The dismantling of the library was really a pitiful sight ... [The books] are now at Clonliffe – available for the ecclesiastical students there, who do not want them; and beyond the reach of the lay students in St. Stephen's Green, who do want them' (*Dublin Review*, Oct. 1887, p. 356.)

Furbough House. Seven miles west of Galway, a 'prettily-situated residence, affording pleasant contrast to the sterile rocks and highlands inland' (Murray's *Handbook for Ireland*, 1912, p. 260). It was the property of John Archer Daly, *né* Blake, High Sheriff and Deputy Lieutenant of the county. The Blakes were an old Galway family, going back to the 14th century.

your best man. In September, Bridges was to marry Monica Waterhouse, daughter of the architect Alfred Waterhouse.

the cliffs of Moher. Black's *Guide to Galway, Connemara* (Edinburgh, 1870) describes the 'well known Cliffs of Moher, which extend for two or three miles in length, and rise at one part to a height of 668 feet above the sea as an absolutely vertical wall' (pp. 237–8). Cf. the sonnet, *No worst, there is none*, written within the next twelve months:

> O the mind, mind has mountains; cliffs of fall
> Frightful, sheer, no-man-fathomed.

129   *Our society.* The Jesuits.

The editor and sub-editor of our Month. Cf. p. 64 and note on Fr Coleridge. Although not officially sub-editor at the time, it has been suggested (see Fr A. Thomas, *Rejection of the Deutschland*, in *English Studies*, Dec. 1968, and *Journal*, p. 382) that Fr Sidney Venn Smith (1843–1922) had a hand in the *Month's* policy over Hopkins's poetry. He was writing for the journal well before the date of the *Deutschland*, and a 20th-century editor of the *Month* described him as a man who 'often confessed his inability to appreciate poetry, and, during his period of editorship [1897–1901], saved himself the worry of estimating the value of what was sent to him by excluding verse-contributions altogether' (*Letters and Notices*, xxxvii, 403).

Fr Cyprian Splaine (1843–92) taught at Stonyhurst 1869–74 and was in charge of the Rhetoric (6th form) pupils 1881–7. He was known for his 'scholarly and classical tastes' (ibid. xxi, 515).

Fr Francis Bacon (1839–1922) entered the novitiate in 1867 and studied at St. Beuno's 1873–5. The Journal mentions walks with him. He later taught in Glasgow.

130   *Mr O'Brien MP.* William O'Brien (1852–1928), Parnellite MP and editor of the Nationalist journal *United Ireland*, had been suspended from the House of Commons on 24 February as the result of an interjection during a debate. *The Times*, 2 Mar., reported: 'A public meeting, convened by the National League, was held today [1 Mar.] in the Phoenix Park to protest against the action of the speaker in regard to the expulsion of Mr William O'Brien MP, on Tuesday night last. There was a gathering of about seven or eight thousand persons. Some dozen bands, with flags, banners, etc, attended.'

Fr Mallac. Fr Mallac came from the French Province to teach philosophy at University College, Dublin, 1884–9. Hopkins gives a fuller account of this vivid personality, *FL*, p. 167.

131   *Mr Curtis.* Robert Curtis S.J. had been appointed Professor of Mathematics at UCD at the same time as Hopkins. The son of a Dublin barrister, he had been the first Catholic Scholar at Trinity in 1871, and had entered the Jesuit noviceship in 1875. He taught at Clongowes 1877–82,

but was never ordained because of epilepsy. He died suddenly in 1893 at 'about forty years of age' (*Memorials of the Irish Province S.J.*, i, no. iv, June 1901, pp. 224–5).

our German count. Count Max Walburg – his name is variously spelt – was a son of the ex-King of Württemberg who came to University College at the end of January to improve his education. Hopkins gives an amusing account of the preparations for the royal visitor, *FL*, p. 166. He does not seem to have stayed longer than a few months. (I am indebted to Dr Norman Wright of the National University for access to his research on this quaint episode.)

132   *poor Geldart.* Edmund Martin Geldart (1844–85), Balliol 1863–7 (where Hopkins gives a grotesque pen-portrait of him, *FL*, p. 70), had been a Unitarian minister but resigned in 1885 because his socialist opinions displeased his congregation. In a state of depression he set out on the evening of Friday 10 April for a continental holiday, but disappeared on the Newhaven–Dieppe boat (see *Pall Mall*, 20 Apr. p. 10). His satirical *A Son of Belial*, Autobiographical Sketches by Nitram Tradleg, London, 1882, gives an account of life at Oxford in which Hopkins figures as Gerontius Manley, 'my ritualistic friend', and Jowett as Professor Jewell.

Nash. Thomas Nash (1845–85), Balliol 1863–7, was a barrister.

have thus drowned themselves. Hopkins might perhaps too have remembered the 19-year-old Digby Dolben who was drowned, apparently accidentally, in the River Welland in 1867. They had met only once, through Bridges, but Hopkins was deeply impressed by his character and the religious conflict he was passing through. Suicide as well as madness were in Hopkins's thoughts during the Dublin years, cf. p. 161 and note.

Coles. Vincent Coles (1845–1929), at Balliol with Hopkins and a friend of Liddon, became an Anglican priest in 1870, and had great spiritual influence at Oxford and elsewhere.

Jeune. Francis Jeune (1843–1905), double First at Balliol 1865, later became a QC and judge.

MacInnon. Not identified.

Hannah and MacFarlane. John Hannah (b. 1844), Balliol 1862–6, whose elevation as Vicar of Brighton is discussed in rather patronizing terms in a letter to Baillie, May 1888 (*FL*, p. 290). Macfarlane, see p. 27 and note.

133   *'Yes, you are a fool'.* Hopkins 'proved' this statement in a fantastic syllogism in a letter to Baillie, 10 July 1863 (*FL*, p. 199).

'Busy curious thirsting fly'. 'Busy, curious, thirsty fly', the first line of a famous Anacreontic by William Oldys (*Oxford Book of Eighteenth Century Verse*, p. 236).

the Dying Christian to his Soul. The lines beginning 'Animula, vagula, blandula', attributed to the Emperor Hadrian on his death-bed and put into English verse by Pope.

134   *Mr Gladstone.* Prime Minister at the time, but shortly to be defeated in the General Election in the summer, following on setbacks to policy in

Africa and Ireland during his period of office. A few weeks before this letter Hopkins had privately reprimanded himself: 'Let him that is without sin [cast the first stone] – Pray to keep to this spirit and as far as possible rule in speaking of Mr Gladstone for instance. (*Sermons*, p. 260.)

every man by forty is his own physician. A proverb going back to classical times listed in various forms in *The Oxford Dictionary of English Proverbs*, p. 215.

I saw that Ulysses *was a fine play.* Full title, *The Return of Ulysses*, described by a critic sympathetic to its author as, 'Perhaps the least dramatic play [by Bridges], where all are undramatic' (Edward Thompson, *Robert Bridges*, p. 39).

135   *Prometheus.* Privately printed 1883, *Prometheus the Firegiver.*

      Barnes' poems. Cf. p. 79 and note.

136   *qui occidere nolunt.* Qui nolunt occidere quemquam, / Posse volunt (Juvenal, *Sat*. x. 96–7). Even they who lack the will to kill, would fain enjoy the power (*Satires*, ed. Mayor, 3rd edn., 1881). The satire that inspired Johnson's *Vanity of Human Wishes* is particularly appropriate to Hopkins's misgivings about fame.

      I have had a holiday. He had spent part of August with his family in the South of England and with the Patmores at Hastings.

137   *Everard Hopkins* (1860–1928), the youngest member of the Hopkins family, studied at the Slade School of Art and became a professional artist and illustrator, working for many well-known magazines.

      Clongowes Wood College. A Jesuit boarding-school of about 150 pupils, 20 miles west of Dublin, near the market town of Naas. Hopkins also visited the school on other occasions and there is a photograph of him with the community. The Rector, Fr John Conmee, is immortalized in the work of James Joyce, a pupil there 1888–91.

      you cd. make any one understand my poem by reciting it well. Hopkins is here referring specifically to *The Loss of the Eurydice,* but cf. his remarks about *The Wreck of the Deutschland*, pp. 65–6 and 69–70.

138   *The phonograph.* Invented 1877 by Edison, who was originally concerned with recording speech, rather than music.

      Wordsworth's Margaret. Hopkins quotes the first line of *The Affliction of Margaret*, a poem which also moved Coleridge (*Biographia Literaria*.) Everyman edn., p. 235).

139   *the beautiful new edition of your works. Poems*, 2 vols, 1886.

      Your poems are a good deed done for the Catholic Church. Cf. the letter to Bridges a few months later, p. 143. The question of England's imperial responsibilities, especially in India, was frequently discussed in the Catholic weekly, the *Tablet*. It warned Englishmen not to rule India as Ireland had been ruled (13 Dec. 1884, pp. 922–3) and regretted the abandonment of the Catholic theory that 'Government had duties to the souls as well as to the bodies of its subjects. St. Thomas Aquinas, in a well-known passage of the De Regimine, lays it down that the end which the ruler ought first and chiefly ... to keep in view is his and their beatitude' (12 Jan. 1884, p. 42).

140 *it is not hard, as Socrates said.* 'Had the orator [over the Athenian dead] to praise Athenians among Peleponnesians, or Peleponnesians among Athenians, he must be a good rhetorician who could succeed and gain credit. But there is no difficulty in a man's winning applause when he is contending for fame among the persons who are being praised' (Plato, *Menexenus* 235, tr. Jowett).

Tremadoc is said to take its name. 'Tremadoc' means 'Madog's town'; Madog is a common Welsh name.

141 *I made a drawing (its ruins enclosed).* Abbott remarks, *LB*, p. 227, that the drawing 'in its present state' is too unsatisfactory to be reproduced.

the papers from the St. James's. In June Patmore had promised to send a series of these articles which had been reprinted in book form called *How I managed and improved my Estate.*

Barnes. Barnes died on 7 October. On the 9th an essay on him by Patmore appeared in the *St. James's* (reprinted in *Courage in Politics*, pp. 118–21), echoing some of Hopkins's sentiments.

off his orthodoxy. ? Unable to appreciate the sort of poetry Barnes writes.

142 not *an individuum genericum or* specificum. 'Not a member of a species or genus'. The terminology is scholastic: Hopkins is claiming the uniqueness of every individual poet.

manmuse. Hopkins's coinage.

cynghanedd. Cf. p. 73 and note.

Paladore and Polly dear. These words occur as 'cynghanedd' in the 7th line of several verses of Barnes's *Shaftesbury Feair* (*Poems of Rural Life in the Dorset Dialect*, 3rd collection). A modern editor comments: 'Barnes's worst attempts at cynghanedd' (*Poems of Barnes*, ed. Jones, I, xx).

Mrs Patmore and the Miss Patmores. Patmore's third wife and two daughters by his first marriage.

143 *though in itself one of the most dangerous things.* Cf. p. 103 and note.

We must then try to be known. 'To seek [fame] is even a solemn duty for men endowed with more than ordinary powers of mind' (Coleridge, quoted by Patmore, *Courage in Politics*, p. 97).

τῇ ποιήσει ἐνεργεῖν. 'To engage in poetry'.

Let your light shine. Mat. 5:16.

144 *of that hand within the mind the imagination.* ? The phrase seems unintelligible.

live the Major in Pendennis. See chap. 1 of Thackeray's novel. A writer in the *Month* also comments disapprovingly on the worldliness of this character (June 1869, p. 526).

145   *Ulysses.* Cf. p. 134 and note.

Wordsworth's ode. Dixon had written of Wordsworth's *Ode, Intimations of Immortality:* 'I do not see that it is particularly good (for Wordsworth, or as Wordsworth), much less great.' The critic Mark Pattison, however, had said it was 'the second poem in the language, Lycidas being the first' (*LD*, p. 145).

146   *You know what happened to crazy Blake.* Crabb Robinson records that when he read to Blake lines 51–7 of the *Ode*, 'It was this very stanza which threw him almost into an hysterical rapture' (Gilchrist, *Life of Blake,* i, 386–7, in the 1973 reprint of the 1880 edn.).

'*O joy that in our embers*'. Line 130 of the *Ode*.

'*The moon doth with delight*'. Line 12.

'*When grace of God is gone and spent*'. 'When house and land are gone and spent, then learning is most excellent' (*Oxford Dictionary of English Proverbs,* p. 308).

goes to make the greatness of a nation. Cf. the letter to Patmore, 4/6 June 1886, pp. 139–40.

147   *vae unum,* etc. Alas, one goes and another comes.

my return from Cadwalader. The visit to Wales. Cadwalader was a 7th century king of Gwynedd.

he took it with his usual sweetness. 'After what you say I feel certain I must be mistaken about it' (Dixon, *LD,* p. 149).

the article on him which followed the news of his death. Cf. p. 141 and note A very sympathetic account of Barnes's life and work appeared in the *Saturday Review,* 16 Oct., where the writer quoted from Barnes's poetry to illustrate his use of the Dorset scene; Hopkins may be referring to the first stanza of *Went Hwome.*

Treasure Island. First published in book form in 1883.

consecutive fifths. i.e. narrative improbabilities, 'poetic licence'. Consecutive fifths are theoretically unacceptable in music, although the greatest composers have used them.

King Solomon's Mines. Published Sept. 1886.

ἀγροικία. 'Lack of fine feeling, insensitivity'.

like a bellglass or glass frame over cucumbers. For a time while at St Stephen's Green Hopkins had 'a kind of charge of a greenhouse' (*FL,* p. 165).

148   *a writer in a late* Academy. H. C. Beeching's review of J. A. Symonds's *Ben Jonson* in the number for 16 Oct. 1886, pp. 251–2. He quotes

Symonds's criticism of the episode referred to (in Act III) as 'the heaviest blot upon Jonson's construction'.

Jekyll and Hyde. Published Jan. 1886.

Utterson frowning. ' "This is a very strange tale, Poole; this is rather a wild tale, my man," said Mr Utterson, biting his finger' (Swanston edn., v, p. 266).

Dr Lanyon. ' "Well, life has been pleasant; I liked it; yes, sir, I used to like it. I sometimes think if we knew all we should be more 'glad to get away' " ' (ibid. 257).

Pavilion on the Links. First published in book form in *New Arabian Nights,* 1882.

gift and genius which goes into novels. Cf. Patmore's essay, *Hardy's Novels* in the *St. James's Gazette,* 2 Apr. 1887: 'The wealth of this century in prose fiction is scarcely yet appreciated' (*Courage in Politics,* p. 132).

Blackmore. But Hopkins was disappointed by his next book, *Springhaven* (1887), and wrote, 'Hardy is a finer man' (*FL,* p. 390).

Evans—Eliot—Lewis—Cross woman. After George Lewes's death, George Eliot married John Cross, dying six months later.

149 *Miss Tynan.* Katherine Tynan (1861–1931), the Irish writer, well known in Dublin literary circles, whom Hopkins first met towards the end of 1886, 'a good creature and very graceful writer' (*LD,* pp. 150–1). Her autobiography contains reminiscences of Hopkins.

there is such a subject. The often referred to work on Greek metre which never materialized.

Wives and Daughters. Her last, unfinished novel (1866).

the course of late Homeric criticism. Hopkins discusses this at greater length with Baillie, 20 Feb. 1887, where he also explains the 'small but ... important point', which concerns Homeric scansion (*FL,* pp. 276–7).

150 *Feast of Bacchus.* 'A comedy in the Latin manner' partly translated from Terence, published 1889.

not pleased, Mr Patmore by a late letter. Hopkins had suggested that an article written by Patmore for the *St. James's* might not be understood by the general reader; Patmore was not upset by the criticism (*FL,* pp. 376–7).

Mrs Patmore. Cf. p. 142 and note.

Yesterday Archbishop Walsh had a letter in the Freeman. William Walsh, Archbishop of Dublin, and Thomas Croke, Archbishop of Cashel, were both prominent supporters of the Nationalist cause. The Parnellite MP John Dillon was one of the organizers of the Plan of Campaign which encouraged tenants not to pay unjust rents to their landlords. The trial of Dillon 'and his fellow-traversers' attracted great publicity December–February 1886–7. The well known Nationalist paper, the *Freeman's*

Journal, printed (17 Feb.) a letter from Walsh enclosing £10 for the accused's 'Defence Fund' and complaining that 'a fair trial is no longer a matter of possibility', and that the jury 'has been most unfairly packed'. The following day, a letter from Croke complained of Irish tax-payers's money being used to Ireland's disadvantage and supported '*on principle*' the idea of not paying taxes. Both letters were the subject of approving editorials.

what happened in the last century. A period of intense Nationalist activity in the latter part of the century culminated in the abortive rising of 1798.

151 *Douglas Jerrold's joke*. Jerrold (1803–57) was a well-known wit, but as Abbott points out the same remark was made by Charles Lamb: 'Wordsworth, the great poet, is coming to town ... He says he does not see much difficulty in writing like Shakespeare, if he had a mind to try it. It is clear, then, nothing is wanting but the mind' (*Letters*, ed. Lucas, ii, 51).

Grand Old Mischief-maker. G.O.M., 'Grand Old Man', was a favourite title for Gladstone by his supporters.

152 *the Paper you sent*. This was *Thoughts on Knowledge, Opinion, and Inequality*, an attack on the idea of democracy, which appeared in the *Fortnightly Review*, 1 Aug. 1887, later reprinted in the collection of Patmore's essays, *Principle in Art &c*, 1889.

the contentio. Tension, concentration of effort.

He seems to be thinking 'Gibbon is the last great master'. In *The Idea of a University*, 3rd edn., 1873, Newman remarks: 'I seem to trace [Gibbon's] vigorous condensation and peculiar rhythm at every turn in the literature of the present day' (p. 323), but states elsewhere: 'You must not suppose I am going to recommend his style for imitation' (p. 285).

153 *the parable of the carcase*. Patmore compares a sheep's carcase alive with grubs with the state of democratic England: 'Democracy is only a continually shifting aristocracy of money, impudence, animal energy, and cunning, in which the best grub gets the best of the carrion' (*Principle in Art &c*, pp. 216–17).

a review by you of Colvin's book on Keats. Sidney Colvin's book was published in the 'English Men of Letters' series, 1887, and Patmore's review appeared on 28 June.

his Otho. *Otho the Great*, a tragedy, written 1819. *The Cap and Bells* was Keats's unfinished last poem.

154 *keepings*. Images, ideas.

County Paris as a book. *Romeo and Juliet*, i. iii. 80–95.

Matthew Arnold has written. In his introduction to the selection from Keats in Ward's *English Poets* (1880), vol. iv, where, discussing the sensuous strain' in his character, he concludes: 'Keats had flint and iron in him ... he had character' (p. 433). (Reprinted *Essays in Criticism*, 2nd Series.)

jelly-process. A method of reproducing copies by which an impression is made on a sheet of jelly from which copies are then taken.

Grace. Cf. p. 93 and note.

155 *the Coda.* A coda consists of a trimeter and two pentameters linked by rhyme with each other and with the rest of the poem. Hopkins used two codas to conclude the sonnet *Tom's Garland* written the previous September. Milton used the form in *On the New Forcers of Conscience under the Long Parliament.*

Harry Ploughman. This 'extended' sonnet was sent to Bridges in October. 'Dividing a compound word by a clause' presumably refers to ll.14–15.

short prose arguments. He had done something like this with *Henry Purcell.* The account of *Tom's Garland* (*LB*, pp. 272–4) would certainly be an example of an 'argument' 'even longer than the piece'.

156 *you not admiring Dryden.* In his *Dryden on Milton,* first published 1903, Bridges wrote: '[Dryden] sinks to dulness of metre, dulness of rhythm, dullness of rhyme ... dulness of matter ... If all poetry had been like Dryden's, I should never have felt any inclination towards it' (*Collected Essays,* 1932, pp. 274 and 279).

157 *The Pope has just dealt us a stunning blow.* Hopkins ironically adopts the Irish viewpoint on the Papal condemnation of the more extreme forms of Nationalist activity. In July 1887 the Vatican sent to Ireland an emissary, Ignatious Persico, to investigate the clergy's association with the Nationalist movement, and in April 1888, before he had completed his report, a Papal letter was issued concerning both the Plan of Campaign and Boycotting. The Irish hierarchy was deeply embarrassed, and press and politicans critical of what they suspected was the result of English intrigue.

the Holy Office of the Inquisition. The document to the Irish bishops was entitled: *A Letter from the Supreme Congregation of the Holy Roman and Universal Inquisition.*

What I most dislike in towns. With this paragraph cf. the two Liverpool letters of 2 March and 1 May 1881, pp. 96–7 and notes. Gladstone had been in opposition for two years in 1888, but was still vigorously pursuing the cause of Home Rule.

158 *Milltown Park.* In south Dublin, the house of Philosophy for the Irish Province of the Society of Jesus.

the force of your criticism. Cf. p. 153.

'*O for a life of impressions*'. 'O for a life of sensations rather than of thoughts!' (Letter to Bailey, 22 Nov. 1817). Arnold – see p. 154, note – also quotes (correctly) this line.

160 *the vision is introduced in* Isabella. Stanza xxxv.

I can not of course say it is wholly useless. With the pessimism of this paragraph, cf. the Retreat Notes, pp. 163–5.

161 *Judge O'Hagan's at Howth.* John O'Hagan (1822–90) had been a judge since 1881, although known for his nationalism in his younger days. He was the author of some patriotic songs and articles on literary topics. His wife was the daughter of Ireland's first Catholic Lord Chancellor. The house still stands and now belongs to the Irish Sisters of Charity to whom it was given by Mrs O'Hagan.

from Fort William. Where Hopkins spent a fortnight's holiday in August.

discursive. 'Dealing with a wide range of subjects' (*NED*).

a shocking thing that has just happened. The case is reported in the *Freeman's Journal*, 5 Sept. 1888; the details in Hopkins's account are the same. The person concerned was 'James E. Gannon, medical student, aged 26', who had already shown signs of insanity in a previous incident and was on bail in the care of his brothers.

162 *a patriotic song for soldiers.* The poem, in four verses, 'What shall I do for the land that bred me' (*Poems*, p. 195), printed in Rockstro's setting, *Journal*, p. 491.

Doughty. Charles Doughty (1843–1926), author of *Travels in Arabia Deserta*, 2 vols., which received conflicting reviews. The *Saturday Review*, 31 Mar. 1888, despite criticisms, conceded that 'the merits of the book are extraordinary' (p. 391).

''tis gone, 'tis gone, 'tis gone'. ? An adaptation of *Hamlet*, IV. v. 196.

163 *the Nation.* A well-known Nationalist weekly.

Addis. See p. 15, note. Addis did in fact marry, and after ten years as a Nonconformist minister eventually returned to the Anglican Church.

Retreat Notes. An eight-day retreat is a regular annual event in the life of a Jesuit priest. Hopkins dated the Notes 1888, but this is evidently a mistake: the retreat is referred to as about to take place in a letter written at the end of December 1888 (*FL*, p. 190). St. Stanislaus College, near Tullamore in Central Ireland, was a Jesuit boarding-school until 1886, when it moved to and amalgamated with Clongowes. The building became the novitiate for the Irish province. On the text for the retreat cf. pp. 94–5, 107–8, and notes.

164 *as Pope says.* 'His [mode of faith] can't be wrong whose life is in the right' (*Essay on Man*, iii, 306).

our College in that. In fact the Jesuits of University College tended to be identified with the English cause, and this was especially the case with the Rector, Fr Delany.

can much wish to prosper. Cf. *Carrion Comfort*, ll.3–4.

Justus es, Domine, etc. 'Thou art just, O Lord: and thy judgment is right' (Ps. 118: 137). With these notes, cf. the poem, 'Thou art indeed just, Lord', written the following March.

the Three Sins. The sin of the angels, of Adam and Eve, and of the individual human being. The first week of the Exercises opens with this meditation.

166 *St. Ignatius speaks of the angel* discharging his mission. In the Meditation on the Incarnation, the second week of the Exercises.

exiit sermo a Caesare Augusto. 'A decree went out from Caesar Augustus', Luke 2:1. The Vulgate reads *edictum,* not *sermo.*

167 *The Italian tour.* Bridges, his wife, and his niece Mary Plow, toured S. France and Italy, January 1889 (Abbott).

in the language of St. Thomas. The phrase 'quod est inconveniens' is occasionally used by Aquinas in arguing a point.

Brunswick Road. Which runs near St. Francis Xavier's Church.

the Irwell. A river running through the industrial areas of S. Lancashire. Cf. Ruskin's description of polluted Surrey streams in *The Crown of Wild Olive,* 1.

Carl Rosa (1842–89), founder (1875) of the famous company which performed English versions of foreign operas.

168 *grand old traitor.* Gladstone (see note to p. 151), who was on holiday in Italy, Dec. – Feb. 1888–9.

the Commission. The Special Commission established July 1888 to investigate *The Times's* charges against Parnell and his followers of advocating political violence. The hearings dragged on well into 1889, but reached a dramatic climax in the last days of February when Richard Pigott, an Irish journalist of dubious repute, was almost certainly proved to have forged letters used by *The Times* against Parnell. Pigott fled and shot himself in Madrid on 1 March.

such anxiety about me. This is the last letter in Hopkins's hand. He had first written to his father of his illness on 3 May and died of typhoid fever on 8 June in the presence of both his parents.

Dr Redmond. There were three Redmonds practising in Dublin at this time. This one may have been Joseph Redmond of Clare Street, who was also physician to the Mater Misericordiae Hospital.

169 *Mary.* ? A family servant.

Lionel. See p. 64, note. He appears to have come on leave to England some time in the spring / summer of 1888.

my Paper. He wrote to Lionel on 1 March (*FL,* p. 193) that he was preparing a paper on the Argei, a Roman ceremony which consisted in throwing bundles of rushes once a year into the Tiber. Nothing of the paper has survived.

WORKS REGULARLY CONSULTED

The Holy Bible, Douay Version, London, 1956.

Dictionary of National Biography, ed. Leslie Stephen *et al.*, 1885–1971.

Tom Dunne, *Gerard Manley Hopkins, A Comprehensive Bibliography*, OUP, 1976.

Basil Champneys, *Memoirs and Correspondence of Coventry Patmore*, 2 vols, London, 1901.

Derek Patmore, *The Life and Times of Coventry Patmore*, London, 1949.

W. H. Gardner, *Gerard Manley Hopkins, a Study of Poetic Idiosyncrasy in Relation to Poetic Tradition*, 2 vols, London, 1944–9.

St. Ignatius Loyola, *The Spiritual Exercises*, tr. and ed. Joseph Rickaby, S.J., London, 1915.

Alfred Thomas S.J., *Hopkins the Jesuit, the Years of Training*, OUP, 1969.

Meriol Trevor, *Newman, the Pillar of the Cloud* and *Newman, Light in Winter*, London, 1962.

Edward Thompson, *Robert Bridges*, OUP, 1944.

Norman Weyand S.J., ed, *Immortal Diamond, Studies in Gerard Manley Hopkins*, London, 1949.

Hopkins Quarterly, 1974–.

Hopkins Research Bulletin, 1970–6.

Month, 1864–.

Tablet, 1840–.

Letters and Notices, 1863–. [Regular internal publication of the English Province, S.J.]

INDEX

For correspondents, the reader should consult the list of contents

Paperbacks from Oxford

*

THE POEMS OF
GERARD MANLEY HOPKINS

*Edited by W. H. Gardner and
N. H. MacKenzie*

This Fourth Edition of Hopkins's poems brings together all the known poems and fragments, including the early verse first published in the poet's *Journals and Papers* (1959), and the remainder of his Latin verse, with translations into English of all the Latin poems which are fully original compositions. The edition retains the most important features of the First Edition of 1918, as edited by Robert Bridges, but a number of more authentic readings have been established by checking the poems against the MS. sources, and the poems have been arranged in a more strictly chronological order. The Notes include a selection, from the MSS., of the marks used by the poet as guides to rhythm and expression.

'The indispensable Fourth Edition of Hopkins's poems is not only the one complete and accurate text, but for the first time it puts him in his true chronological order of development.' *The Guardian*

EDMUND CAMPION
SCHOLAR, PRIEST, HERO, AND MARTYR

Evelyn Waugh

Campion came from relatively humble origins, but his brilliant scholarship assured him the highest offices at Oxford, where adoring undergraduates called him 'a second Cicero'. But though he was able, at the beginning of his career, to swear allegiance to Elizabeth I, his conscience finally led him to Douai, and to the Society of Jesus. In 1580 he returned, on a Jesuit mission, to England, where his brilliant personality and vital interpretation of his faith made him a threat to Elizabeth's Church that her government could not ignore. Campion was captured whilst secretly preaching to Catholics, and racked in the Tower. He would not recant, and was executed in 1581.

Waugh's biography of his fellow-Catholic was written in the 1930s, almost forty years before Campion's canonization. It is a model for hagiographers: historically sound, extremely readable, matching Campion's own prose, it has established itself as a classic.

A Literary Pilgrim in
England

Edward Thomas

Edward Thomas here roams England in search of the homes of some of our most famous writers. He visits Blake, Shelley, Tennyson, Coleridge, Hardy, Cobbett, Borrow, Swinburne, Wordsworth, and many others. He quotes extensively from their works, illustrating how the landscapes and cities of their youth and maturity developed their idiosyncrasies and influenced their art.

As one would expect, no revealing detail of humour or character escapes Edward Thomas's observation, so the book is at once a series of exact biographies and a feast of evocative prose.

THE JOURNALS OF DOROTHY WORDSWORTH

Edited by Mary Moorman

Wordsworth's 'exquisite sister', as Coleridge described her, was not only the cherished companion of two great poets, but was herself a poet in prose. The journals she kept at Alfoxden in 1798, when her brother and Coleridge were composing the *Lyrical Ballads*, and at Grasmere from 1800 to 1803, when she and Wordsworth were living at Dove Cottage, are more than a valuable record of their daily life. Dorothy combined an intense and minute observation with a genuine poetic imagination, whose influence can be seen in many of Wordsworth's poems of this period (printed at the end of this book).

THE HILLS AND THE VALE

Richard Jefferies

With an introduction by Edward Thomas

This collection of Jefferies's essays, spanning the 1870s
and 1880s, was brought together by Edward Thomas and
published in 1909. Amongst them are examples from
nearly every kind and period of Jefferies's work: he writes
as reporter, archaeologist, sportsman, politician, natural-
ist, and philosopher. The book ends with some of the
finest and most powerful of his nature writings, in which
he grasps 'a meaning waiting in the grass and water' of a
'wider existence yet to be enjoyed on the earth'.

Carrington
Letters and Extracts from her Diaries

Edited by David Garnett

Gifted painter, intimate companion of Lytton Strachey, friend of Virginia Woolf, Augustus John, Ottoline Morrell, and E. M. Forster, Dora Carrington led a fascinating life. At the age of 22 she met Lytton Strachey, a homosexual and an intellectual. Carrington detested her own femininity and had been haphazardly educated. Nevertheless, she and Strachey formed a deeply affectionate relationship which lasted until his death. Three months later Carrington shot herself. Despite her suicide, she was not made for tragedy. Her letters and diaries, punctuated by enchanting drawings, testify to a child-like exuberance of spirit which retains its power to capitvate. This book constitutes one of the most candid, entertaining, and moving autobiographies ever written.